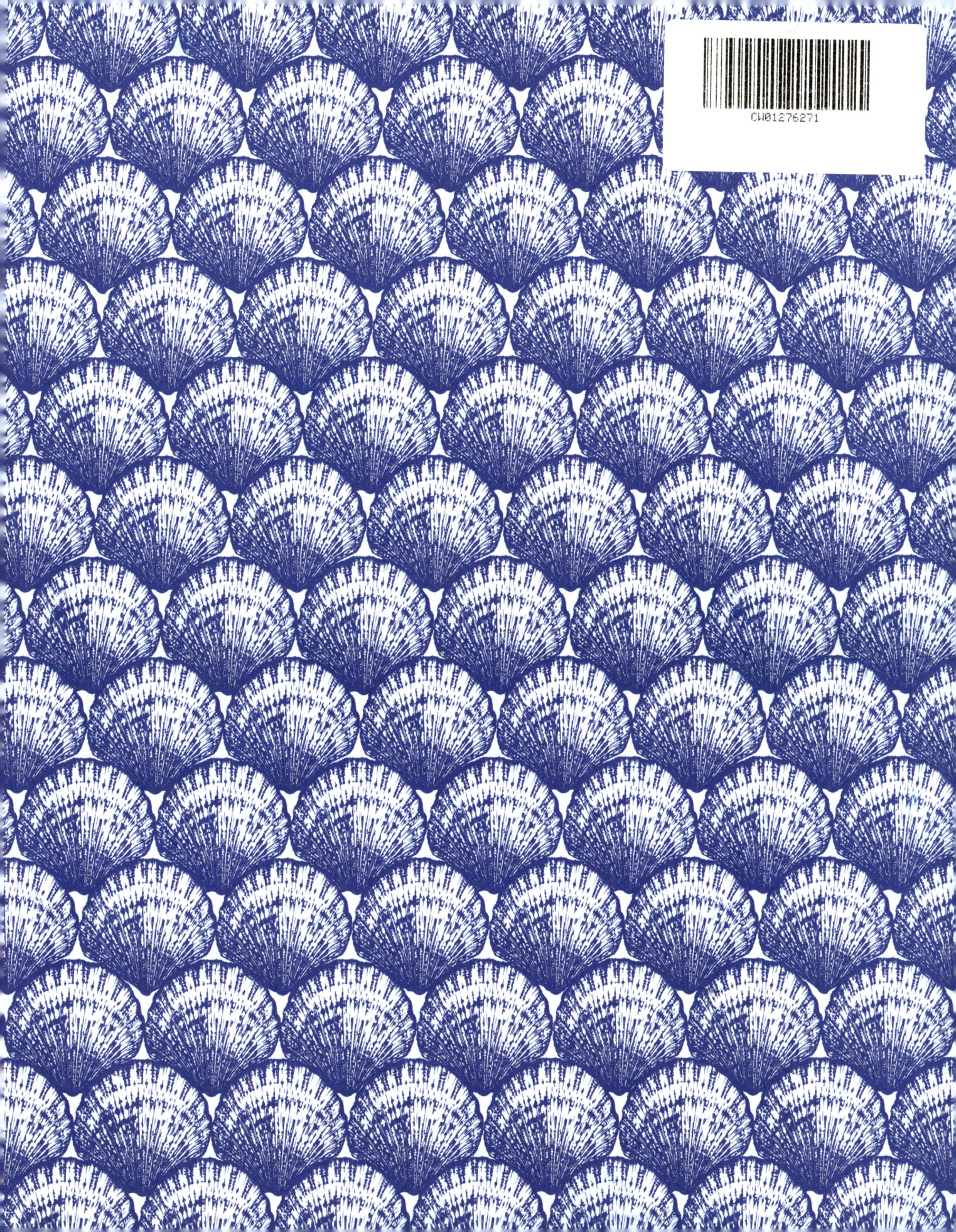

THE SEAFOOD RESTAURANT COOKBOOK

For all of our team members who have worked at The Seafood Restaurant over its 50-year history, those who are currently working with us and all those who will join the team in the future. We also could not have achieved this milestone without the wonderful farmers, growers and fishermen who provide us with such quality produce.

THE SEAFOOD RESTAURANT COOKBOOK

Recipes & Stories

Rick Stein   Jill Stein

in association with The Seafood Restaurant Ltd

CONTENTS

Foreword *by Nathan Outlaw*	6
The Seafood Story	8
The Seafood Signature Recipes	102
1975–1984	104
1985–1994	140
1995–2004	174
2005–2014	204
2015–2025	240
Stocks, Sauces & Salads	270
Memories	272
General Index	280
Cookery Index	282
Credits & Acknowledgements	284
Visit Us & Key Suppliers	286

Foreword

How on Earth could you possibly know when you opened a restaurant in 1975, half a century ago, you would have such an immense effect on the hospitality industry and so many people's lives? I can only imagine that you couldn't.

Jill and Rick have achieved something that, as far as I'm aware, nobody else ever has. A family-owned and run seafood restaurant that has lasted for fifty years and is still going strong. The Seafood Restaurant is not any normal seafood restaurant. It is a pioneering, trail-blazing seafood restaurant that has been a catalyst for so many others. "Legend" is a word that is so over-used, but with what Jill and Rick have achieved, and continue to achieve, that word isn't enough. "Iconic" is probably more fitting, due to the distinctive excellence they have maintained and how widely known they both are for what they have done for the hospitality industry.

Rick's repertoire of dishes is quite simply the most exciting and delicious I've ever been tasked to cook, and it was an honour to have been able to do that. I worked at The Seafood Restaurant for just under two years of those fifty – the restaurant had already been going for 23 years, so it was already a Titan.

When you get to work in a kitchen like the one Rick has created, you grow at a rate that is unparalleled anywhere else. Rick's food is a collection of the finest recipes that he has witnessed being cooked around the world, but he's had the foresight and incredible ability to translate them into "Cornish" back in the kitchen in Padstow. The sheer spectrum of recipes, cultures and ingredients you are witness to in his kitchen grows your own knowledge massively and at pace – and that, I think, is the lasting inspiration I took from working there; well that and the need for "more salt", one of Rick's favourite sayings.

The day-to-day service ran with a sturdy confidence and buzz. In fact, "buzz" is a very good word to describe what I witnessed while working there. Everyone and everything buzzed. It was like orchestrated chaos, but in an exciting way. The dining room buzzed with customers laughing, eating and drinking. The waiters walked briskly with a skip in their step, carrying the iconic, towering fruits de mer, gigantic lobsters and plates and plates of the finest fish seen anywhere. Pouring, clearing, crumbing and juggling, service went at electrifying pace at times.

When it did calm down, the sense of achievement and pride was like no other place I'd worked. It was an exciting time to have been part of, at a place that was thriving as a consequence of Rick's travels and TV popularity. Everyone who was anyone wanted to eat there.

At The Seafood Restaurant, Jill has created, designed and evolved one of the most beautiful and unique dining rooms that you can have the pleasure to sit in. The space itself has morphed a number of times, with structural change, style change and logistical change, over the years – an evolution that is no easy task. You need to live and breathe a space to know how to do this, and Jill, in my opinion, is the master of design and style.

So, what of beyond fifty years and the future of The Seafood Restaurant? Well, it's in great hands. Ed, Jack and Charlie (Jill and Rick's three sons) all grew up in the hospitality industry and each of them has his individual skills and personality – just what The Seafood Restaurant needs to continue with the dream of what Jill and Rick set out to do all those years ago.

Nathan Outlaw / Sous Chef, The Seafood Restaurant (1998–99) / two Michelin-starred chef and author

THE SEAFOOD STORY

The Great Western Nightclub on Padstow's harbourside in 1974.

Beginnings

In 1974, with the three-day week putting paid to Rick Stein's ambitions to become a journalist, he and his girlfriend, Jill Newstead, cobbled together enough money to buy a third share in an ailing members' club in the sleepy fishing village of Padstow, Cornwall. There, with their business partner and friend Johnny Walter, and his wife, Jill's best friend, Teri, and dreams of "bright young things" dancing the nights away, they established their first foray into brick-built hospitality. "Brick built" because it was, in fact, an evolution of Rick's mobile DJ years in his van "The Purple Tiger".

Things didn't, as the story is now well known, turn out quite the way those dreams intended. Bringing a little London glitz and glamour to Padstow's harbourside was not really what the place was looking for. Its fishermen, and so the club's customers, were a plucky bunch – working hard all week, trawling the waters for their catch and hauling them ashore among rusty fishing boats and heavy, clanking chains. This was hard work for hard men. At the end of a shift at sea, those men needed to unwind hard too, spending nights drinking in Padstow's pubs and then rolling into the club, by then called The Great Western, ready for a fight. And fights there were – skirmishes that even though he actively tried to stay out of them, resulted in several trips to A&E for twenty-something Rick. The local landlords were fed up (their best customers would disappear to the club after closing rather staying for a lock-in) and the neighbours were fed up too – no street brawls in their backyard, please. Eventually, the police were on high alert, and the club's days were numbered. Having sent officers to pose as customers to catch out the lawlessness of the operation, the police had everything they needed. Terms of the license meant that every entry had to be checked for membership (no one bothered) and food had to be available for every customer (it was scarce or non-existent). Rick and Johnny had their day in court and the license was withdrawn.

Almost. In fact, by a stroke of luck (or perhaps pity – Rick was to find out years later that the police had felt sorry for The Great Western and how impossible it was to control those fishermen), Rick and Johnny retained the license to serve food and drink in the two floors above the club. And that is where this story – this celebration – begins.

Above: An early poster advertising The Great Western Disco. Rick now has this poster framed in his cottage in Padstow – a reminder of where it all began.
Opposite: From left to right, Johnny, Jill, Teri and Rick (pictured in the early 1980s) – the original four business partners for The Great Western Nightclub.

The Seafood Story

The Seafood Restaurant's very first menu, handwritten by Rick, in 1975.

MENU

Prawn Cocktail (45)
Crab Cocktail (45)
Smoked Mackerel (38)
Mackerel Pâté (32)
Baked Crab cooked with Butter and Cheese (50)

Avocado Pear with Prawns (60)
Vinaigrette (35)
Corn on the Cob (35)
Chilled Melon (30)

Baked Mackerel with Garlic Butter and Fresh Herbs (70)

Lobster Thermidor (2.50)

Crab Salad (1.15)

Cold Lobster with Mayonnaise and Salad (2.00 – 2.90)

Lobster Grilled with Butter (1.90 – 2.80)

Seafood Salad [Crab, Camel, Salmon whole and peeled prawns with Mixed Salad] (2.00)

Dover Sole (2.20)
Lemon Sole (1.50)
Plaice (1.30)

VEGETABLES
New Potatoes (12)
French Fried Potatoes (15)
Green Beans (12)
Peas (12)
Fresh Courgettes (25)
Asparagus (30)

Mixed Salad (25)
Green Salad (15)

Treacle Tart with Cream (35)
Apple Pie with Cream (35)
Meringues with Cream (40)
Mela Menthe (50)
Chocolate Mint Ice (30) with Liqueur (50)
Orange or Lemon Surprise (60)
Chocolate Ice Thunder and Lightning (45)
Coffee (15)

First service

These days, restaurants tend to open on a single day, often after many months of planning, test runs, soft launches and then, finally, first service. The Seafood Restaurant's story is a far more evolutionary tale. An iteration of the club – although a far less raucous one – continued to operate under an employee's license on the ground floor of the building, while above there were two further floors that Rick, Jill, Johnny and Teri needed to put to good use. So, as the mid-70s approached, Rick had an idea for opening a small restaurant serving simple, fresh fish dishes on the top floor. Close by, The Blue Lobster had been doing very well at just that – although Rick wanted it simpler, an ethos that survives today. He and Jill scoured local house sales and second-hand furniture stores to gather a few tables and chairs, and bits and bobs for decoration. Rick tidied up the walls by papering over the rough plaster with chip paper, and they employed a young, local chef, Sally Prosser, to make something of the fish that came in fresh from the sea.

That left the middle floor, which (after a failed attempt at using it as a family restaurant serving roasts and homely puddings) became Padstow's first burger joint, bearing in mind that this was a time when burger joints were a new craze that had only recently hit the streets of London. Several hours from England's metropolis, in a small Cornwall fishing village, the burger joint lasted a year before the combination of smoking fat and lack of significant interest made it unviable.

Nonetheless, ticking away upstairs was that small, simple fish restaurant, and this is where Rick realised he had a future – if he took it on himself. While Jill ran their home as a guesthouse and continued to manage the mobile disco in order to make sure they had regular money coming in, Rick started to cook. It was a direction that he hadn't expected, but one from which he would never turn back. He and Johnny, still business partners, agreed that Teri and Johnny would take over the top two floors of the building (which they turned into holiday flats) and Rick, Jill and the fish restaurant would move downstairs into the space of the now-closed club. More DIY, more house-sale shopping, and lots of time spent mulling over what to call the reinvented fish restaurant gave rise, finally, to The Seafood Restaurant, its doors opening on to a view of the harbour, with the day's catch informing the menu and Rick and Jill working all hours to keep themselves afloat.

Jill and Rick outside The Seafood Restaurant in 1986. The photo was used in an advert for Miele appliances (see page 277).

Looking back, everyone agrees that however much hard graft it took, moving downstairs was the first of several positive turning points in the life of The Seafood Restaurant. In the first year, takings more than doubled, giving Rick and Jill all the confidence they needed to know that they were on to something special. What's more, over the following years, the fishermen, who had once been the cause of so much trouble as they rolled in to and out of the club, became crucial allies, landing fish and delivering it to the back door as fresh as any fish can be. Mackerel, salmon, crayfish, crab, scallops... all came in abundance.

Having decided after the first winter that closing from the end of September to around Easter the following year was the most economical way to run the restaurant, Rick and Jill made the winter months their time for refurbishment, making sure their profits went back into the restaurant to expand it both in terms of covers and giving Rick a "proper" kitchen to work in. Rick even eventually installed lobster tanks, where the local fisherman would deposit their catch, take their fee and leave Rick to turn the sea's spoils into something delicious.

16   The Seafood Story

The Seafood Restaurant before the conservatory went up.

Rick's first book, *English Seafood Cookery*, was illustrated with drawings by Katinka Kew, including one of this iconic view of The Seafood Restaurant across the harbour.

If a job's worth doing...

Rick notes that in those early years of the restaurant there was "no wastage", but not just in terms of the food that came through the door. There was also no wastage in time and effort. If something needed doing, Rick and Jill did it. If someone needed to step up, the two of them worked harder. At the start, there was no one else to call upon, and anyway there wouldn't have been enough surplus profit to pay them if there had. That went for the marketing too – the pair would leaflet around Padstow, popping flyers under windscreen wipers to drum up the evening's business; Rick even took a megaphone to the local caravan parks, literally calling for custom.

Eventually, though, practical help did come. Penny Rabey, one of Rick's early assistant cooks, who worked in the restaurant for about five years from around 1977, remembers, "When we were really busy, pans flying around and us dripping with sweat, Rick and I would look out of the back door and comment how lovely Rock looked, with the sea and the boats and the ferry; people enjoying themselves while we worked hard." Shaaron Nicholas, who came in to the restaurant in the early 1980s, also remembers that time fondly – working at maximum effort over service, then sitting down when the doors were closed and catching up about the evening's experiences over a drink or two. The restaurant was small, the team was small, but the sense of belonging and the sense of potential were huge.

Jill in the late 1980s, before the first restaurant refit.

"In the old days, I did all the cheese ordering from Patrick Rance, the famous cheesemonger who wrote The Great British Cheese Book. *He knew all about the up-and-coming cheeses and taught me all about Irish cheese. And we ordered oysters from Loch Fyne. They would come down on the train from Scotland, and then either the bus driver would pick them up, or we'd collect them from the station."*

Jill Stein

Front of house

If Rick's hard work made the kitchen his kingdom, he was matched only by Jill, who took on Front of House. Her easy charm and warm manner – with a keen dose of northern grit and graft thrown in – made her a natural for pulling in and caring for the customers. While Rick honed his craft behind the scenes, Jill was responsible for hosting their guests, organising the staff's wages, distributing the tips, selecting the décor (a portent of the future, of course), and, when the occasion demanded, dealing with tricky customers. As the customers came in and were seated, she made sure their experience was happy enough to entice them into coming back. It's the stuff of legend that, so mortified that a group of diners left because their food took too long to come, she tracked them down the following day and begged them to return, which they did.

The result was to build a fierce loyalty among their early customers, some of whom still return year after year (often several times a year). Lady Susan Wolfson, for example, who spent her Easter and summer holidays in Padstow from about 1976, would eat in The Seafood every Friday night. She still does when she's in Cornwall, fifty years later.

Winter Escapes & Culinary Adventures

The summer seasons at The Seafood Restaurant were punishing for Rick and Jill – juggling the restaurant and family life and making sure there were enough customers to keep them going. Winters, though, provided the opportunity for a bit of downtime – and adventure. As it would turn out, the first few of those adventures had a profound impact on what Rick was going to serve up back at home.

In 1986, as Rick was turning forty, he, Jill, Johnny, Teri and the three (very) young Stein boys set off for Australia. Two years later, they made the trip again. Both journeys made a lasting impact on The Seafood. Jill tells the story in her own words...

A little Jack Stein, in Singapore, enjoying noodles.

"During the first years of the restaurant, we opened only during the summer, closing at around October half term and not reopening until the following Easter. In a sense I suppose we were very lucky. It was only Rick and me and one or two others who were working in the restaurant at the time. We worked incredibly hard during our open season, but when the footfall fell away, we were able to take an extended break. The winter months gave us the opportunity to do some pretty amazing travelling.

Opposite, left: Jack (left) and Ed (right) on Bilgola Beach, Sydney, Australia in 1986. *Opposite, right:* Ed (front) and Jack (behind) in Singapore in 1986.

"In 1986, with Charlie as a toddler, and Jack and Ed about five and seven, respectively, I suggested to Rick that we visit Australia – which felt pretty ambitious with three small children in tow. Our stopover for that inaugural trip was Singapore and it was the first time I had been anywhere so different from home. The humidity and the incredible, unfamiliar smells as we stepped off the plane are etched in my memory – it was like nothing I'd ever experienced before. We stayed in the original Raffles hotel, which was far less glitzy and glamorous than it is now. Nearby, the streets bustled with Malay, Chinese and Indian restaurants, serving wonderful and (it seemed to us) exotic food. One night, we sat down to dinner at the Banana Leaf Apolo restaurant. The restaurant served its delicious southern Indian cuisine on banana leaves. The whole experience was magical – imagine three little boys (and their parents) wide-eyed at the notion of eating from a leaf. It's where Rick got the idea for chilli crab, and it was quite a first adventure.

"A few years later, we headed to Australia again, this time stopping in Thailand. I'll never forget the tom yum soup – so incredibly spicy and utterly delicious. And then there was Goa. There, at the Ronil Hotel at Baga Beach, we met Rui, the hotel manager, who inspired in us a love of southern Indian cooking.

"Absorbing all that culture and all those cuisines had a subliminal effect on the menu at The Seafood. Rick and I had opened our eyes to completely new flavours and, whether we were conscious of it or not, their influence found their way into dishes we were serving in Padstow. Vindaloo is a particular classic of Goa, and I've no doubt that our monkfish vindaloo very much has Rui to thank."

Monkfish Vindaloo & Other Eye-openers

When The Seafood Restaurant first opened, two flights up the stairs, Rick was serving simply poached or grilled fish with homemade mayonnaise and new potatoes and other vegetables from local suppliers, or even from the garden at his family home. Lobster Thermidor (see page 112) was an early attempt at something a little more sophisticated. As Rick's confidence and influences grew, though, so did the menus. In the first decade, he concentrated mainly on serving dishes with French influence, born of journeys to the Continent in the early winters (Brittany, Normandy, Loire and Provence). The Bourride (see page 154) is a particular result of this time. However, it was those first trips to the Far East, as the Steins made their way to Australia, that really saw innovation come to Cornwall.

Rick, holding a dish of classic fruits de mer, with Jill from a photoshoot in the late 1970s.

The Seafood Story

Eastern flavours

In Singapore, Rick discovered Chilli Crab (see page 147), something that has appeared on The Seafood Restaurant's menu consistently since that trip. In Singapore, the crabs were easier to break apart than those caught in Cornish waters, but the principle was to serve up the crab with shells cracked open, stir-fried in a spicy sauce. It was not only new to The Seafood Restaurant in the late 1980s, but pretty new to English dining altogether. Rick remembers, "When we had the crabs in Singapore, we had bibs – but that sort of takes the fun out of it. Here, we served them with linen napkins – and we still do."

In Goa, though, friendships, chefs and even equipment rippled their effects across the oceans to Padstow. Rui, the hotel manager at the resort Rick, Jill and their boys stayed in for several years in a row, proved a huge influence on the menu at The Seafood. Watching Rui's chefs prepare their meals, Rick realised that the great difference between the curries that were just beginning to find their way on to English menus at home and those in Goa was the fact that in their rightful home all the spices were freshly ground, the masalas freshly made and so the results full of flavour and clean, spicy heat. While there, Rick took it upon himself to track down an electric spice grinder (small by hotel standards, but still significantly bigger than anything we might find in a kitchen at home), shipping it back in his luggage to Cornwall, where he set about experimenting with Eastern flavours on his own menus. Rui even sent him off with jars of authentic vindaloo sauce so that he could try to recreate it perfectly. Rick believes his dish comes close, but even now it's still not as perfect as the original dish he ate in Goa itself. Nonetheless, the Monkfish Vindaloo (see page 210) has rarely left the menu.

And then there was the Mackerel Recheado (see page 160), fresh mackerel fillets, with a masala paste sandwiched between them and tied together. The masala was beautiful – and once it was on the menu at The Seafood, it was rarely absent.

Simple and enduring

Throughout, though, Rick has never lost his philosophy of serving simple food beautifully – a principle that has endured now for fifty years, on a menu that gently reinvents its classics, and seamlessly introduces dishes from all over the world, from the Far East to America, to, of course, Australia, where Rick now also owns and runs restaurants with his second wife, Sarah (Sas) Stein. Sas, too, knows how much The Seafood means: "I love The Seafood Restaurant. It's so special. Rick and I have had so many happy times there over the last twenty years. Congratulations to everyone." The philosophy of simple and enduring is one that Jack and his brothers, as they take up the mantle, intend to hold firmly on to. Jack remembers a time when his dad's notion of simple food was spurned a little among other chefs, but before long the wheel turned and the importance of simple, interesting food made brilliantly was recognised for the genius it is. Ed believes that the trust the fishermen and the customers have in The Seafood Restaurant – in Rick – are what makes that work. In a sense, it didn't matter how much Rick encouraged new flavours or cuisines on the menu, as long as the fish was fresh from the sea, the customers would trust it, and would keep coming back for more.

Rick in the kitchen with The Seafood chefs (2009). From left to right: Stephane Delourme, Luke Taylor, Rick, Paul Harwood, Miles Corbett, Mark Puckey and David Sharland.

The Extended Seafood Family

The Seafood Restaurant is a family business but it's much more than that. When talking to both the Steins and those who have worked for and dined regularly with them, it's almost as if The Seafood has a life of its own. Like any much-loved institution, it's greater than the sum of its parts.

Rick and Jill started out working sixteen-hour days, living and breathing their restaurant and making sure that if something needed doing it was one of them who did it. That commitment, of course, was born out of necessity – to turn a profit there was no spare cash for any more members of staff than were essential. Rick recalls, "There were only a few of us initially. There was Penny, who helped me in the kitchen, and Marie, who helped Jill front of house. They both came over from The Blue Lobster [the restaurant above The Shipwrights pub in Padstow, which had closed] and gave us a lot of help because they knew how to work in a successful restaurant."

First staff

By the time the restaurant had made it through its first decade, though, Rick and Jill could afford to take on some more help. In 1989, Paul Sellars, an experienced chef, turned up at the door of The Seafood, having eaten there the night before, and asked for a job. His experience had taken him from the kitchens of the House of Commons to a restaurant in Surrey, and now all he wanted was to live by the sea, to cook and to surf. Interestingly, Rick talks openly about his anxiety at working alongside a fully trained chef, even describing feeling overpowered by Paul's talent. As far as Paul was concerned, though, things worked the other way: "I was a chef with a decade of experience by the time I arrived at The Seafood and I thought I knew everything. But then I worked with Rick and that was when I really learned to cook. Rick's passion, and his philosophy for food (keep it simple; let the ingredients speak for themselves) is a lasting legacy." Paul's skills meant that the menu could begin to include more complex dishes – Rick coming up with ideas that Paul could execute with ease, even on the days when Rick would arrive in the kitchen and change the menu with mere hours – sometimes minutes – to go before service. The two worked well together and Rick describes Paul even to this day as a big influence on him.

The team of chefs in the kitchen grew – with Paul and Rick were another four, meaning that the restaurant could cope with up to ninety covers in a service. Still Rick held on to his ethos of wasting nothing – stocks, sauces, soups all used up every last of everything the fishermen were bringing to the door (a practice that, like so much else, survives today).

Celebrated chef James Knappett (far right, with Nick Street Brown, John Walton and Martin Tyrrell) worked in The Seafood Restaurant between 1999 and 2001.

Famous names

Paul now lives in New Zealand, and while he may have been the first trained chef to work alongside Rick, there are many others who either trained at The Seafood, or refined their skills there before setting out on their own. Among those familiar names are Roy Brett, now chef-proprietor at award-winning seafood restaurant Ondine, in Edinburgh; James Knappett, owner of two Michelin-starred Kitchen Table, in London; and Nathan Outlaw, who has his own acclaimed Michelin-starred seafood restaurants, up the coast in Port Isaac. There have been some formidable chef-guests, too: Jean-Christophe Novelli, who worked for Keith Floyd and went on to own a host of restaurants, earning him several Michelin stars, among them.

38 The Seafood Story

Opposite, top: Jill (centre, seated) with members of both kitchen and front-of-house staff in 1994. Jill's sister, Roni, is in the second row, fourth from left. *Opposite, bottom:* Chefs on the harbourside, with Fiona Haley, the only female chef in the kitchen at the time, second from left.

The years between the early and mid-1990s seem to hold memories that feature particularly strongly in the minds of the chefs and others who worked in Rick's kitchen. Matthew Owsley-Brown, who was there between 1992 and 1994, remembers vividly how stressful it was keeping the lobsters alive: "I lost sleep over the lobsters. The larder section housed the live lobster tanks – about three or four, one above the other. We were always so busy that the tanks were often crammed full and I was constantly checking the temperature, salinity and clarity of the seawater, unclogging the filters and changing the seawater altogether. If the temperature rose too much, there wouldn't be enough oxygen in the tanks and the lobsters would start to die. The responsibility used to keep me awake at night." Dave Miney, chef between 1989 and 1994, calls The Seafood Restaurant simply the best place to learn about seafood cookery. For David Wong (Chef, 1992–94), the treat was that Rick would still come to "work the stoves" every day. Fiona Haley remembers being "a young girl from Cornwall launched into a kitchen filled with male chefs" but is so grateful for her time there, especially working in the pastry section, learning her craft and eventually taking over the section herself. In her words, "the best time with the best people". For former waitress Pauline Tune, "Working was like being a performer. It was hard work, but I loved my job."

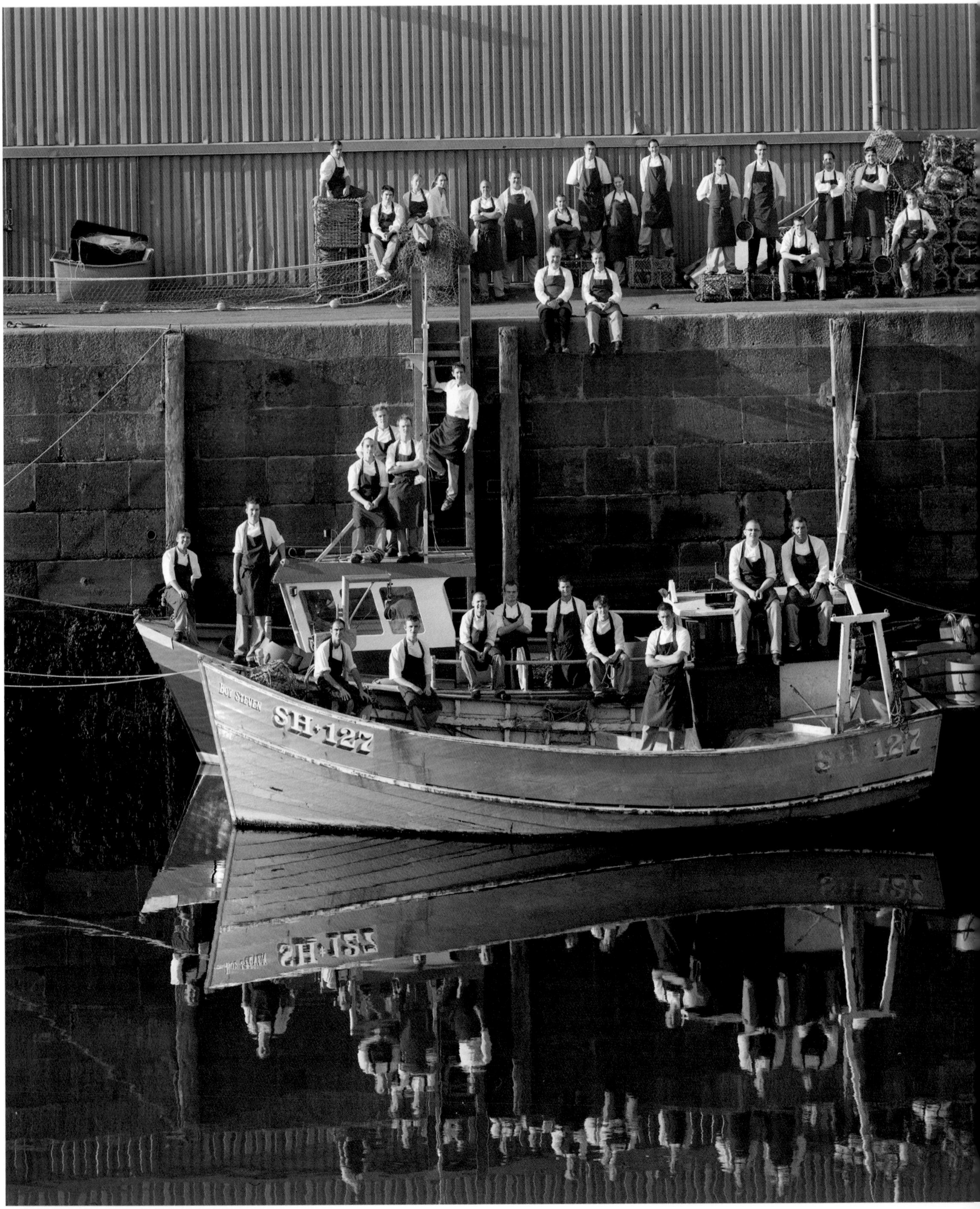
BOY STEVEN
SH-127
SH 127

"Even in the early days, you could clearly feel that Rick, Jill and the team were slowly and quietly making a huge impact in Padstow and surrounding areas. I was so impressed by Rick's discreet, consistent and efficient everyday hard work, matched by Jill, who used to bring the Cornish glamour and a defined touch of elegance and control to the service."

Jean-Christophe Novelli

Opposite, top: Rick, Jack, and Stephane Delourme, who cheffed at The Seafood for 25 years. *Opposite, bottom:* Roni, Jill's sister, has been working at The Seafood as sommelier since the late 1980s, and works there to this day.

Service gongs

There are two members of staff who particularly stand out for length of service. Stephane Delourme joined the restaurant in November 1998, staying for 25 years to work his way up from Chef to Head Chef, and finally Group Chef for the last four years of his service. Talking to him about his time at The Seafood Restaurant, he reveals an acute sense of belonging to that extended family, and feels intrinsically part of the restaurant's culture and growth over those significant years: "I think of myself as having been so lucky to have been part of this great story. It was a fantastic opportunity and a great privilege for me to work with Rick and Jill, watching Ed, Jack and Charlie grow with the business, and seeing the whole family's passion and drive. I have made fabulous memories that I will hold in my heart for ever."

Then, there is Roni Arnold, whose place in the family business is as much about genuine family as it is about that Seafood DNA. Roni, Jill's sister, arrived in Padstow, from Manchester, in 1988 with a passion for food and a fascination for the theatre of a restaurant kitchen. That winter, when Rick, Jill and the boys made their second trip to Australia (see page 27), they asked Roni to work her way through the wine cellar, tasting, making notes and learning the craft that would become her job for life. At a time when wine was a man's world, it felt a risk. But, Roni spent that winter making her notes, working hard to prove herself and metamorphose from a self-professed "whisky girl" to an expert sommelier. Throughout Roni's early years, Bill Baker, who would later inspire Charlie Stein into the wine world (see page 96), was her mentor, advising her when she needed help and building her confidence when she hit an obstacle (often in the form a difficult, male customer, suspicious of a female sommelier, no matter how impeccable her knowledge). So loved and respected is she within The Seafood, the chefs took to banging saucepan lids in delight when, a few years ago, she changed her mind about retiring and decided to stay on. "I feel so privileged," she says, "to have worked for thirty-six years in a place with so much heart."

The Seafood Story 43

In his seventies, Jill and Roni's dad, Jack (not to be confused with his grandson), played piano in the restaurant. He quite happily played on a ship's piano, which has only five octaves, to save space. So many customers from that time remember him and how wonderful it was that he would play requests. Mary Vernon, a guest, remembers asking him to play "As Time Goes By" from one of her favourite films, *Casablanca*. He willingly obliged, asking her to stay by the piano so that he could play it specially for her. Grandson Jack also remembers that time with his granddad fondly. Jack (senior) had been a musician all his life, playing with bands in Lancashire and Yorkshire to support his young family.

No foray into the extended Stein family would be complete without mentioning Chalky. "Chalky was part of the whole thing," remembers long-term guest Lady Wolfson. "One of the family." Certainly, Chalky seems an ever-present four-legged friend in the memories of so many of The Seafood's customers and staff. And, of course, Chalky's fame was secured when he appeared on television with Rick, in every series Rick made from the very start of that TV career, until the beloved family Jack Russell died, in 2007. In their pet's memory, Ed had the idea that, with Sharp's Brewery, they should develop a new beer – Chalky's Bite.

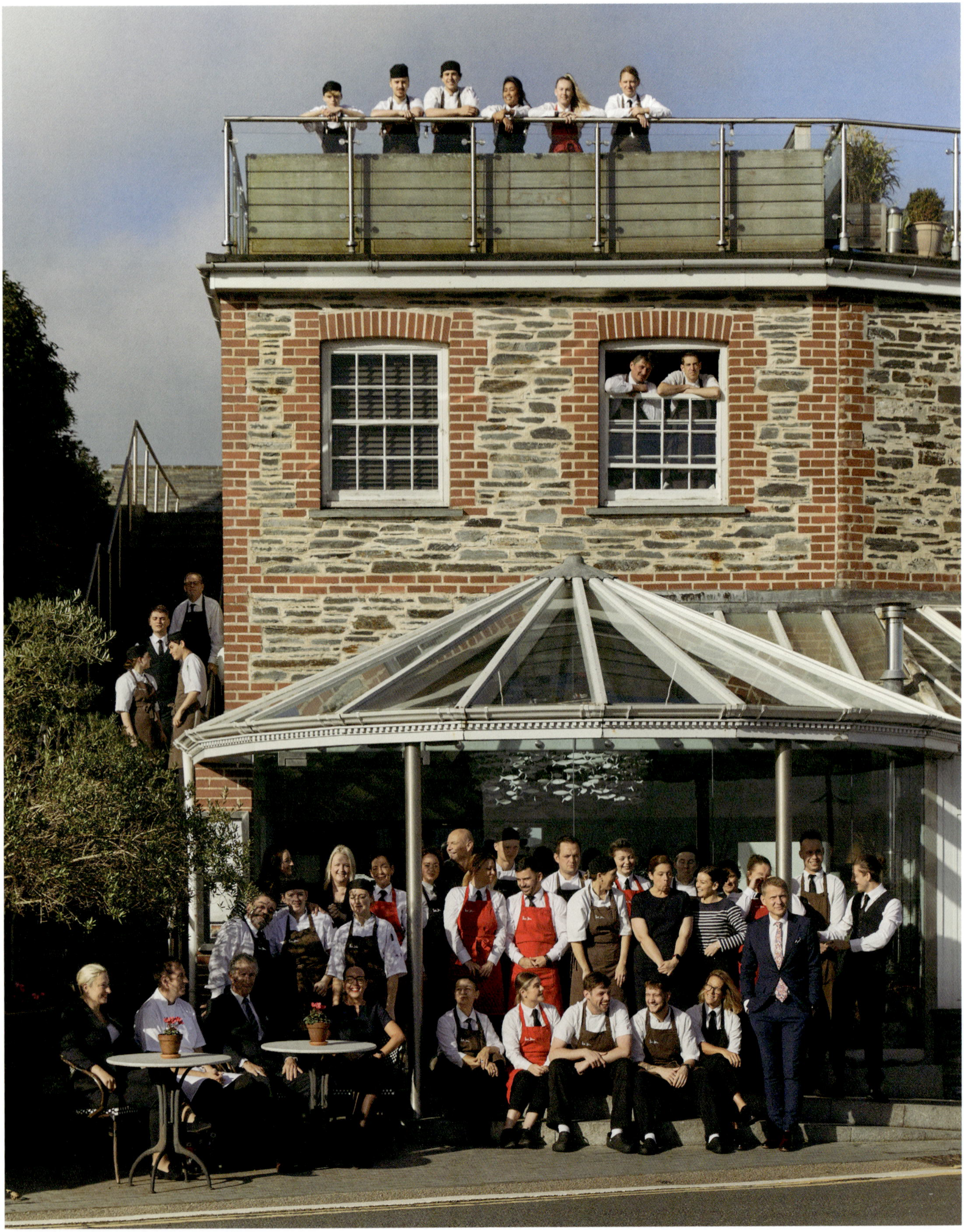

Modern times

The closeness of the extended family (which is now around 600 staff across the whole business) is obvious when you look at some of the photographs that come up of the early years – staff parties on the beach (and stories of shooing away uninvited passersby, who took a fancy to what was cooking on Rick's barbecue), antics in the kitchen, and camaraderie on the harbourside. There is clearly a sense that those who worked hard for Rick and Jill wanted to – and knew they were helping to – make The Seafood a success. Part of that success must surely be down to how Rick and Jill led by example – working hard themselves in the kitchen and front of house, and in the care of their teams, whose dedication has enabled The Seafood to thrive.

48 The Seafood Story

Phil Kelly's painting of The Seafood Restaurant in full service (oil on canvas, 1991).

The Seafood Story 49

50   The Seafood Story

This photo, which appeared in the BBC TV series *Memoirs of a Seafood Chef* (2009), shows Rick hanging from a harbour ladder in Padstow – a testament to how fresh the food at The Seafood can be.

Books, TV & the Power of the Media

Although by the mid-1980s The Seafood Restaurant was doing very well, Padstow was still a far-flung fishing village on the westernmost coast of England, where tourists came during the summer months, but mostly stayed away during winter. That was fine for a while, but Rick and Jill were finding it increasingly hard to find staff who were interested in a job just for the summer – there are only so many chefs like Paul Sellars, who are happy to be surf dudes for half of the year too. This meant they had to look at opening throughout the year, and that needed footfall. As it would turn out, the power of the media was the key.

Finding Floyd

When the restaurant won its first award in 1984 (see page 71), Rick had already begun regularly writing recipes to appear in *Woman's Realm*, a weekly women's magazine that had been running since the late 1950s. He used his platform, on the advice of its editor, Richard Barber, to send what we might now call a media release to all the local newspapers and television channels in the hope of getting some publicity and drumming up some business for the restaurant. The plan worked, and Sue King, a journalist working for BBC Southwest, visited the restaurant and loved what she saw. So much so that when, in 1985, Keith Floyd was making a TV programme called *Floyd on Fish* and needed a venue to visit in the southwest, she recommended that his producer, David Pritchard, visit the Steins. The clips of Rick and Keith floating on a boat, eating and drinking wine, down the Camel Estuary are now the stuff of TV gold.

Rick with Keith Floyd in a still from the BBC's *Floyd on Fish* – the first time Rick appeared on national television.

The Seafood Story

Below: The cover of Rick's first book, published in 1988. *Opposite:* The book was illustrated with specially commissioned drawings by artist Katinka Kew.

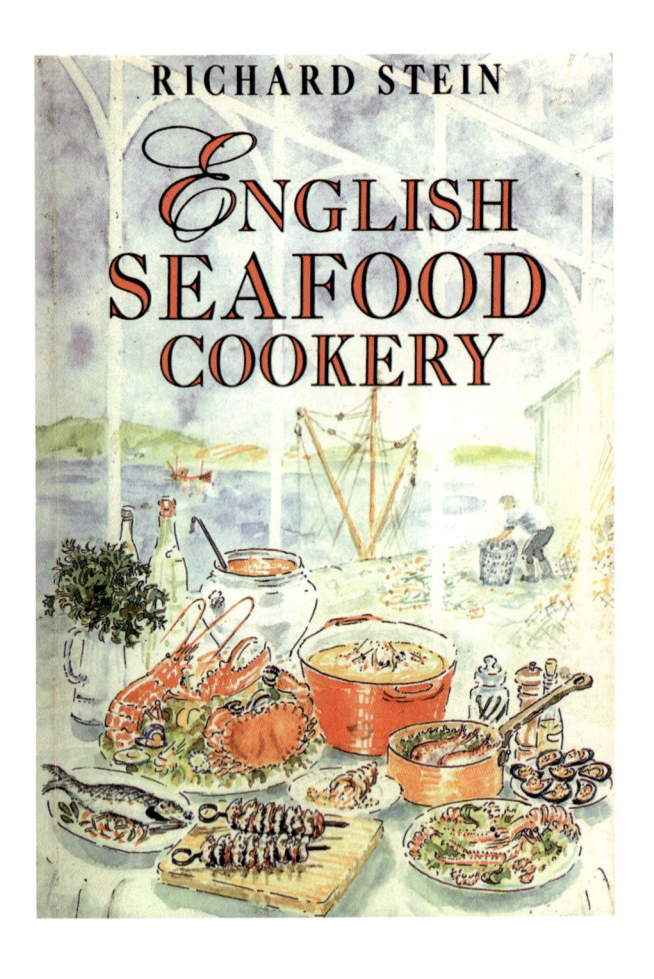

Rick's first book

At the TV launch party of *Floyd on Fish* in 1985, Rick was introduced to Jon Croft, Keith's publisher who, with his own imprint, Absolute Press, was co-publishing Keith's TV tie-in book with BBC Books. Rick mentioned he was planning on writing a seafood cookery book. Jon, then fully engaged with managing the high-maintenance demands of the soon-to-be-famous Keith Floyd, suggested that perhaps Rick should approach Penguin. The idea was briefly put on hold, but a few years later, Rick met with Penguin, via an introduction made by Richard Barber. They signed a book deal and Rick delivered the manuscript for his first book, *English Seafood Cookery*, which was published just before the family headed out to Australia in 1988. The book was very much born from the restaurant. It wasn't Rick's style to write anything other than recipes that he took from the commercial kitchen and adapted for making at home. He used the platform to teach people how to prepare and cook fish just as he was doing at The Seafood. The book wasn't illustrated with luscious photographs of the recipes as you might find in any of Rick's books now, but rather gorgeous black-and-white illustrations by artist Katinka Kew that brought into view (for those who didn't know) the charm of Padstow, its harbour, its fishermen, and The Seafood Restaurant itself. There is even an illustration of Jill, Johnny and Teri – The Great Western founders – eating around a table.

The Seafood Story

The Seafood Story 55

Becoming a destination

Arriving on the television, first with Keith Floyd, and then in his own programmes from 1995, and having his first book published, projected Rick into homes around the country: "In those days, mainstream TV was far more influential than it is now," says Rick. The first television series with Rick front and centre, *Taste of the Sea*, was the one where things really started to show in the bookings at the restaurant. Suddenly, Rick was something of a household name; people knew about The Seafood Restaurant and they wanted to eat the food they were watching on television and reading about at home. The effects were almost instant – Jill describes the telephone ringing off the hook, and Rick remembers how taking on more staff became an overnight necessity. The restaurant had very much become a destination.

Fame and fortune are what they are, but the wonderful thing was that the huge increase in covers – and so turnover – meant that there was profit to really grow the business. Rick and Jill ploughed money back into the restaurant, updating equipment, crockery and glassware and both expanding The Seafood Restaurant's rooms and buying up property elsewhere in Padstow. It's this turning point that demonstrates just how much that decision to open a seafood restaurant on the harbourside in Padstow becomes the roots from which all other Stein ventures grow, and the reason why when anyone in the family talks about The Seafood Restaurant, it's with a mind to protect it above all else.

Rick's success on television had its effects on the menu at the restaurant too. Once he was travelling all over the world for his series, he had the perfect excuse to broaden the dishes the restaurant was offering; in a sense to indulge that passion he'd had since visiting Singapore, Thailand and Goa during those family winters, for adding exotic flavours and dishes to the menu. Doing so didn't come without nerves, however – Rick worried that restaurant critics, and in particular *The Good Food Guide*, would look unfavourably on a truly international menu. He was concerned that, as a result, the restaurant would come under pressure. His worries were unfounded, and for the restaurant that first gave Cornwall a seafood vindaloo and chilli crab, challenging palates and inviting guests to take a culinary adventure from the safety of a beautiful table looking out on to Padstow harbour, was met with only delight and praise.

Jill chose this painting, by British artist David Inshaw, from the artist's studio, to hang in The Seafood. It is a self-portrait of Inshaw with his then-girlfriend dining in the restaurant.

The Seafood Story

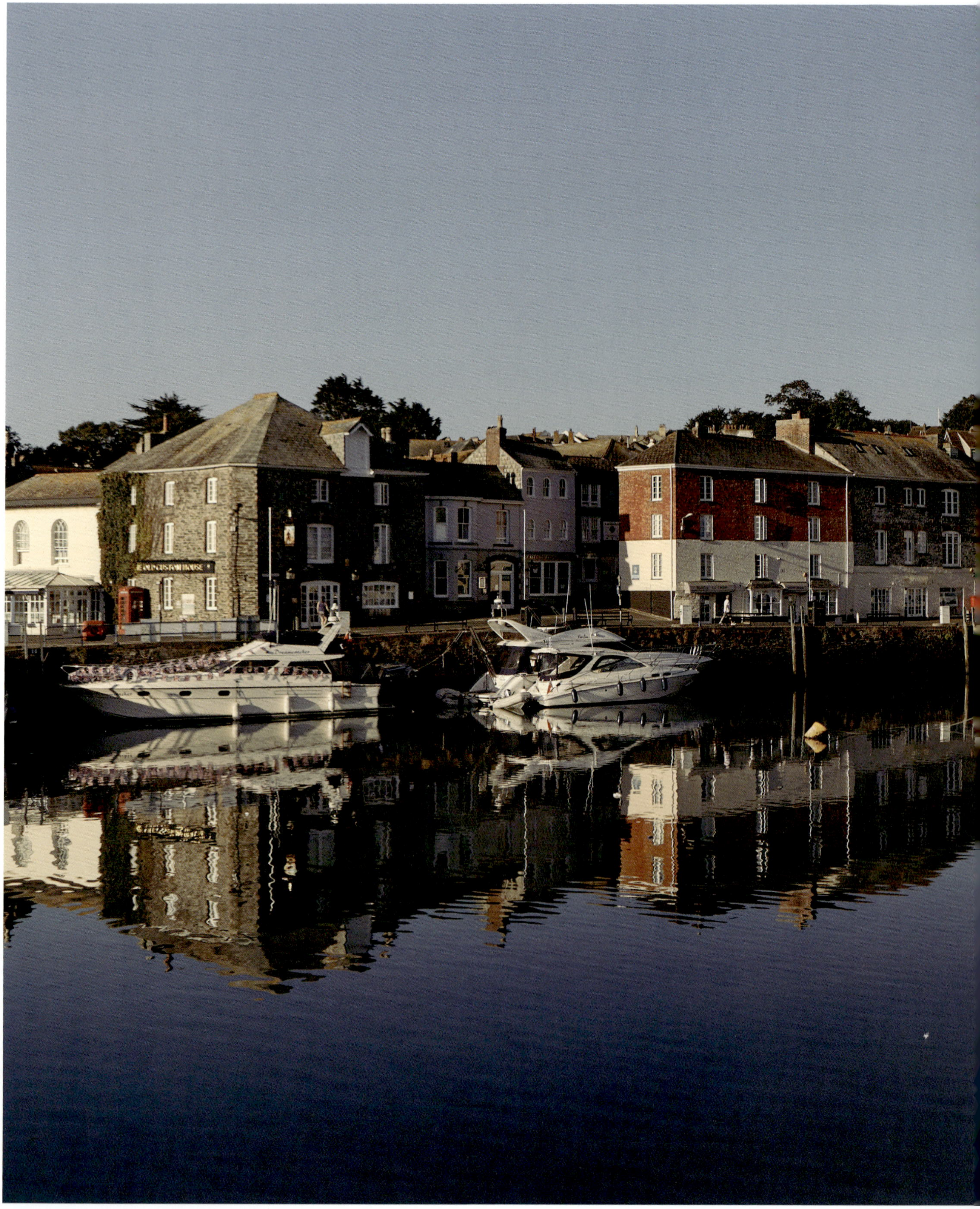

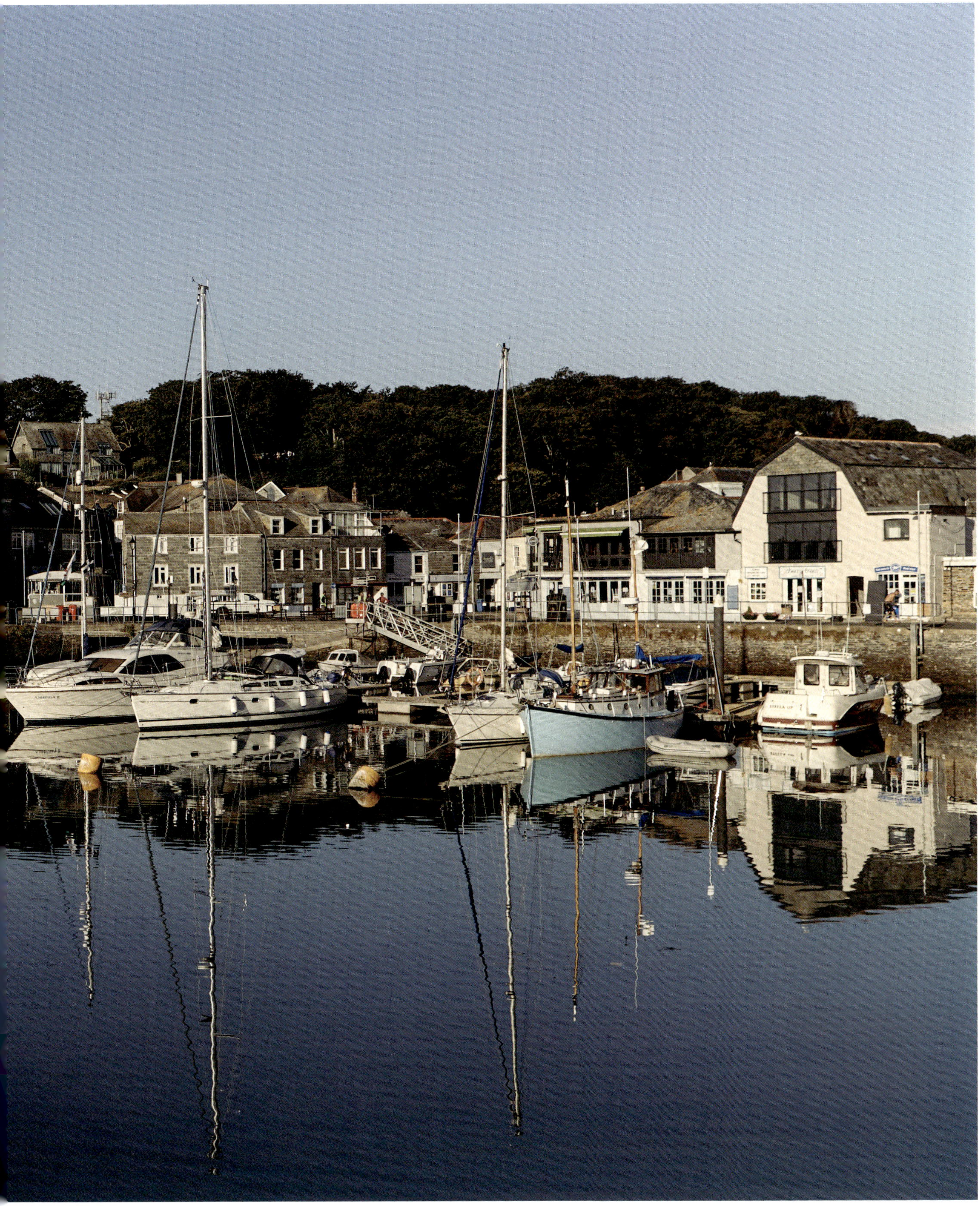

Rooms & Refurbs

With The Seafood Restaurant a success, it was time for Rick and Jill to take on the flats that their business partners – and great friends – Johnny and Teri had been running since they first rearranged the business back in 1977. So, in the mid-1980s, The Seafood Restaurant became the proud owner of the flats upstairs too.

The Seafood Story 61

Rick and Jill turned those flats into their first eight rooms. With the same ethos of thrifty enterprise with which they had started their restaurant, they set about sourcing beds and furnishings from hotel sales, and did much of the hard graft themselves. They installed an ensuite in each room and hand-picked the décor. When called upon to do so, Rick even fixed the blocked drains.

The approach was inspired by the restaurant-with-rooms concept – different from a hotel because the emphasis was on the food rather than the comfort of the sleeping space. They were much influenced by trips to France, where rooms were quite often very spare but the pleasure of not having to travel anywhere after a good dinner was real. Rick and Jill soon realised that the profit from the rooms was higher and more secure than the restaurant, which was subject to fluctuating prices of fresh seafood and the costs of preparing, cooking and serving. Better profits meant more funds to plough back into improving everything.

In 1996, Rick and Jill bought the house and garden behind The Seafood. When they had first moved the restaurant from the top floor down to the old club on the ground floor, Rick had set up a simple kitchen consisting of a six-burner stove, a deep-fryer and a grill in what was the old bar of the nightclub. He built a partition wall in front of the bar to divide it from the restaurant. There were no thoughts of chefs cooking on immaculate equipment seen by all the diners in those days. Over the next twenty years, the kitchen improved substantially, but in the end it was just too small and hot. By digging out the garden of the house and moving the kitchen into the space created, they were able to expand the kitchen and restaurant and increase dining capacity. They reinstated the garden above the new kitchen. Rick said it was a bit like the Home under the Ground where the Lost Boys lived in Neverland.

Those who have been regulars since the earliest days also comment on the addition of the conservatory. When Rick, Jill, Johnny and Teri first bought the building, there was just a simple front with a door on the corner of the street. In 1982, however, Rick and Jill added the conservatory, giving the restaurant a space in front where diners could enjoy a drink with an uninterrupted view of the harbour before they were shown to their table. It's interesting that so many reviews of the restaurant over the decades comment on that pre-dinner ritual as part of the whole experience.

Seafood style

Of course, the building changes are one thing, but the last fifty years have seen a significant shift in the way those buildings have been styled too. From that 1975 restaurant pulled together with second-hand tables and chairs, ferns hanging from the ceiling, fishing nets on the walls, and cobbled-together crockery, The Seafood is now the epitome of elegance – white tablecloths, low lighting and decoration that is beautiful, unique and welcoming, with a pervading sense of calm. That, as well as the décor of the rooms, is thanks to Jill, whose love for interior design began in the antiques stores in Wadebridge – although she is quick to clarify that the original restaurant interior fell to her because "no one else wanted to do it". Now, though, styling those spaces is both a career and a passion.

Wicker chairs and white tablecloths were very much the thing in the 1980s. Jill's eye for evolving fashion has made sure that The Seafood's décor has always kept up with the latest trends.

In the 1980s, as Jill updated and added to the look of the early restaurant, came of-the-time basket chairs and cushions in Sanderson fabrics. During the early 2000s, she honed her skills working on projects not just in Cornwall, but all over the world. For The Seafood, her ethos is that the interior of the restaurant has to be as inviting as the food that comes out of the kitchen. One hugely significant move towards exactly that came in the form of the major refurb in 2008, with the addition of the magnificent central bar, where diners can sit and watch cocktails be shaken, and revel in the artistry that comes with creating plates of oysters and the like. The idea came from a visit of Rick's to Zuma in Knightsbridge, London. At The Seafood, the bar provides the ultimate relaxing and fun place to eat, emerging as a favourite spot for dinner for two for those who want to be right at the heart of The Seafood buzz. (Other favourites are the circular table in front of the large windows for groups of six or more, while the table in the corner at the back is definitely the preferred choice for a quieter, more intimate meal.)

In 2009, Jill established Jill Stein Interiors, and now, with her daughter-in-law Kate (pictured together, right), designs all the rooms and restaurants, at The Seafood and beyond.

The Seafood Story 67

The Scabetti light sculpture, "Shoal", which sits in the entrance to The Seafood, has become as iconic as the restaurant itself. Celebrated shoe designer Jimmy Choo once remarked to Jill, "Ah, it is feng shui. So important – it gives you a feeling of calm." Jill first saw the sculpture during a visit to The Design Show, in London: "I was immediately taken by the Scabetti, and thought I had to have it for the newly refurbished Seafood. I spoke to Frances Bromley, the artist, and she was thrilled. Then, I consulted Rick, and he agreed. However, soon after it became clear that we were going to go over-budget on the refurb. Rick said to me that we could have either the sculpture or new windows. Obviously, we had to have the windows. So, I went back to Frances, apologised, and told her that we couldn't have the sculpture after all. But she insisted – she offered that the design studio would cover the installation and that we could pay for the sculpture in instalments. And so it was that, with a huge thank you to Frances and to Scabetti, we got the sculpture after all. I love that it's the first thing you see as you come in to the restaurant – as Jimmy Choo said, it's feng shui."

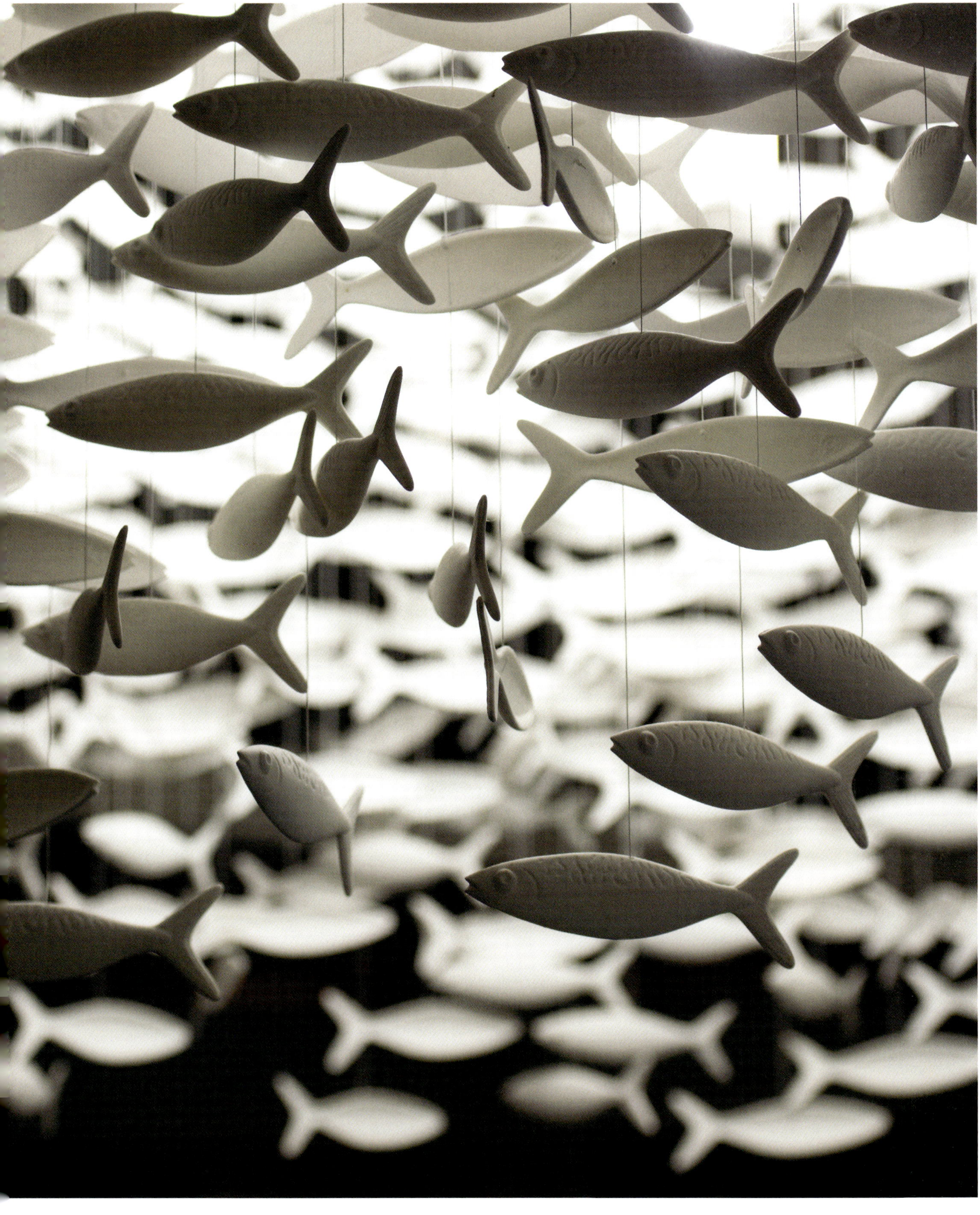

Egon Ronay presents Rick and Jill with their first award: RAC/*Sunday Times* Taste of Britain – Best Restaurant.

Awards & Honours

In 1984, The Seafood Restaurant won its first restaurant award – The RAC/*Sunday Times* Taste of Britain Best Restaurant. Very impressive for an eatery in Cornwall established less than ten years earlier by two people who, to this day, describe themselves as "enthusiastic amateurs".

Presenting the award was Egon Ronay, whose restaurant reviews, along with *The Good Food Guide*, pioneered a drive to raise standards in British dining. The Seafood wouldn't have been unknown to him – by 1984 it had already made its first appearance in the *Egon Ronay Guide*, and given that Ronay was famed for personally visiting each and every establishment that appeared, he had definitely taken a seat in Padstow. His own commentary in the 1984 edition reads, "*A bright, airy quayside restaurant, well situated to take advantage of all that's best from the day's catch. Cream of mussel soup with saffron is a popular (and quite delicious) starter, and you could go on to lemon sole with hot buttered prawns, salmon trough in puff pastry or grilled Padstow lobster. A couple of meat dishes too, and some very nice sweets.*" He also notes the superior wine list.

Opposite: One of the Phil Kelly paintings that was commissioned specifically for The Seafood Restaurant.

In 1996, The Seafood Restaurant went one better than an entry in the guide and won *Egon Ronay*'s Restaurant of the Year. By then, the conservatory was in place and the restaurant had just been expanded to add more covers and a much bigger, revamped kitchen (see pages 62–3). The review makes mention of arriving to a drink and olives with a view of the harbour, before sitting down to "exquisite" food. It also makes a point to mention that the "The" in The Seafood Restaurant is justly deserved – a delightful (and presumably unknowing) nod to semantics that weren't entirely lost on Rick when he, Jill, Johnny and Teri named the restaurant twenty years earlier.

In the years between *The Sunday Times* and the *Egon Ronay Guide* accolades, The Seafood Restaurant would gather several more Best Restaurant awards too. Notable gongs include that from *Decanter* magazine in 1989, and the César Award for the country's best restaurant with rooms ("in a class of its own") from *The Good Hotel Guide* in 1995 – whose accompanying write-up cited seafood dishes that are "as good as seafood at any restaurant in the country", even "the best".

The Seafood Story 73

These early accolades began something of a rich and illustrious string of both commercial and personal honours for Rick and Jill. Among them, in 2002 the restaurant received the *AA Food Guide* Restaurant of the Year; and in 2004 took bronze, behind Heston Blumenthal's Fat Duck in Bray and Terre á Terre in Brighton in the Waitrose Best Restaurant (over £20 per head) awards, with the announcement in *Observer Food Monthly* calling the restaurant the "standard bearer for British fish cookery". Then, 2003 brought personal honour for Rick, when he received an OBE in the New Year's Honours List for services to Cornwall. In 2013, Jill received her own recognition in the Honours List, this time an OBE for services to hospitality, which she received accompanied by Ed, Jack and Charlie at Buckingham Palace.

That year also brought the restaurant the *Food & Travel* Timeless Classic Award.

Anyone could be forgiven for thinking that, after decades of hospitality service, The Seafood's time on the red carpet might be eclipsed by new kids on the restaurant block, but it's a testament to the ethos with which Rick and Jill have continued to strive for excellence that the awards just keep coming, each one as appreciated and humbling as the one before. In fact, recent years have been pretty phenomenal. In 2018, Rick received a CBE in the New Year's Honours List for services to the economy. In both 2020 and 2022, The Stein Group as a whole was named among the top 100 best large companies to work for, and in 2023 there was a fitting passing of the baton when Jack received *Food Magazine*'s Best Chef of the Year reader award, just ahead of his dad receiving the Fortnum & Mason Special Award for lifetime achievement.

And it's not over yet. With three AA rosettes to its name, and plans for its fiftieth birthday in full swing, The Seafood Restaurant was, in 2024, given the incredible honour of winning the AA's Food Service Award – an amazing achievement by an entire and remarkable staff. The sky continues to be the limit.

Jill collecting her OBE at Buckingham Palace in 2013, with (left to right, either side of her) Charlie, Ed and Jack.

In Safe Hands

Jill Stein often says that if you'd told her when she was mopping up the debris of another night in The Great Western Club on Padstow harbourside that a little over fifty years later she would still be in residence, but now with one of the country's most successful, enduring, loved and honoured restaurants to her name, along with a host of other businesses (both hospitality and interior design), she wouldn't have believed you. Ed, Jack and Charlie have also said that neither Jill nor Rick has ever put pressure on any of their sons to take over the business. Which makes it all the more delightful and reassuring, somehow, that – organically – as they celebrate the fiftieth anniversary of The Seafood Restaurant, each son has, over time, been drawn back by their own choice.

The sons all sit on the Board and each now has his own role in the businesses. When there is a decision to be made, all of them are consulted, just as, over the last five decades, Rick and Jill have always consulted each other when the need dictated. Equally, though, the sons retain some autonomy within their own expertise – and, remarkably for siblings, they rarely (if ever) argue. What becomes very clear in conversation is that they are united not just as brothers, but also in their commitment to The Seafood Restaurant and everything it represents.

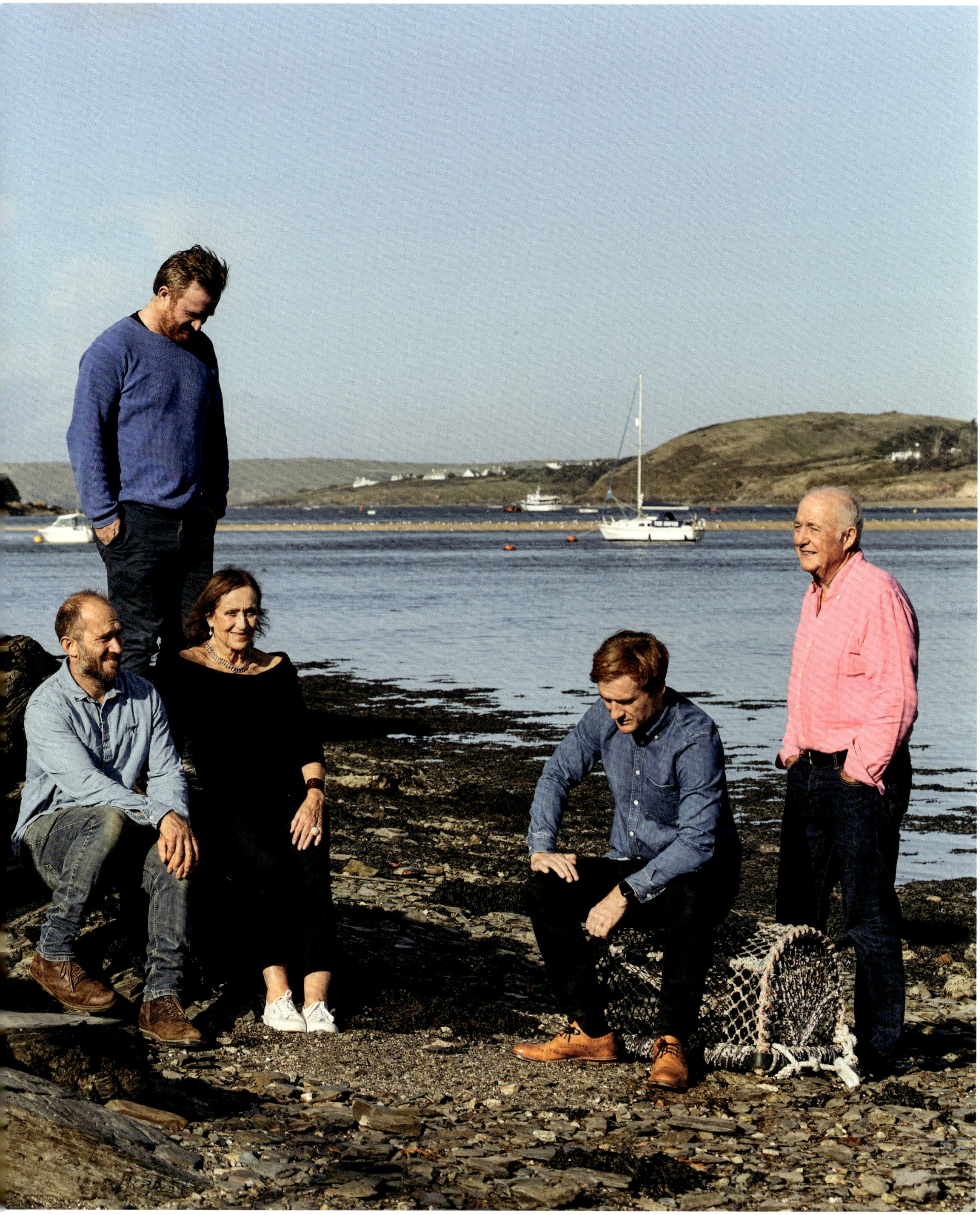

78 The Seafood Story

Ed's story

Born in January 1979, Ed was the babe in arms as Jill was taking bookings and running front of house at The Seafood, while Rick perfected his skills as a chef. Among Ed's earliest memories are what a treat it was to be taken down to the restaurant, and allowed to meet all the chefs and front-of-house staff who were working there.

He began working for Rick, in the restaurant, at around fifteen years old, earning money in the kitchen during his school holidays. Over the years, he worked in every aspect of the business – knowledge that stands him in good stead today. After university, and marrying his wife Kate, Ed came back to the restaurant for a time, working as a chef around the same time as Nathan Outlaw (see page 37). Ed notes that Nathan so clearly knew that he wanted to be in a kitchen cooking amazing food. It brought into focus somehow that Ed himself had never felt like that. For him, cooking wasn't the passion that he saw in his dad and Nathan, and he felt acutely that the split shifts were at odds with family life. So, he moved to other parts of the business – the shop, and the bakery, using his chef skills to make some of the takeaway food that was served there.

However, Ed's inherent artistic nature needed an outlet, and he became increasingly convinced that he wasn't going to find it in the catering side of hospitality. He began labouring for a local builder, enjoying the more nine-to-five aspect of the job and that's when he decided that he needed to retrain. By now in his thirties, he took up a place at a London art school where he learned to become a sculptor. Then came a six-month stay in Italy, honing his craft with marble in Carrara on the Tuscan coast.

When Ed arrived back in England, he and Kate moved to Hampshire, where Ed used his skills as a freelance stonemason, carving headstones – among other things.

At the same time, in Cornwall, the Stein businesses were expanding, including into holiday cottages. Jill was overseeing the building and interiors' projects but the scale of everything they were doing meant that there was one venture that she felt needed a dedicated project manager. She asked Ed if he would consider taking on the organisation of the build at The Cornish Arms, a family-friendly pub in the village of St Merryn just outside Padstow (a pub that Charlie remembers as a place they visited as a young Stein family and hoped one day they might run). He did. Ed hired the whole team locally, beginning a new phase of his involvement with Stein businesses.

Rick and Ed photographed for a feature in *Delicious* magazine while Ed was working as a chef in the Steins' production unit.

The Seafood Story

"We want to maintain The Seafood as an institution. There are many dishes that haven't changed over the years, but we also want to keep it relevant, in tune with a new generation, but with the same values that my mum and dad have always had. In the end, people love The Seafood just as it is."

Ed Stein

Over the following years, Ed project managed all the refurbishments and new openings, not just in Padstow, but in Winchester, Barnes (London), Sandbanks, Fistral and Marlborough too. In every place, his attention to detail and sensitivity towards the buildings and locations have ensured that the fundamental principles of simple, authentic and beautiful, which characterised everything about The Seafood Restaurant even from its earliest days, hold true. Now, with a team of local, trusted tradesman to call upon, Ed is able to consult on the building projects and refurbishments, still overseeing the annual updates in the ensuites and other spaces, while at the same time running his own, successful renovation business. His passion is the spaces, but, having worked in every part of the business, he has knowledge and understanding of it all.

Kate Stein, Ed's wife, has carved her own niche too. A designer and artist, she works closely with Jill on the interiors of all the Stein properties, as well as designing beautiful soft furnishings that are used to decorate the rooms and houses, and which are for sale in the shops. She and Jill have a shared creative vision – "complementary and similar tastes", says Jill – for how the interiors should look, so the relationship works really well, and in turn ensures that Jill herself has someone on hand to continue her vision long into the future.

Jack's story

Jack was born 18 months after his older brother, Ed, in October 1980. Among his earliest memories are how mysterious his parents' job felt. There was no lunch service at the restaurant during those years, so Jill was always at home to make the boys a meal during the day. Then, at around teatime, Mum and Dad would disappear up the hill from the house to go to work, leaving the two brothers with nannies or family members, before Jill would come back to put them to bed (and then head back to the restaurant, of course). After a while, the pattern would shift and in the long, winter breaks they would have several, largely uninterrupted months together. Any sense of mystery probably wasn't helped by the fact that, when he was old enough, Ed would tease his younger brother that Mum and Dad were off every night to far-flung or exotic places… Japan, Paris… only to return by the time the boys woke up.

Jack was aware that his parents worked very hard. There was a home from home among the legs of the tables in the restaurant (what better place to make a den?), and an extended family in the kitchen and front of house. The chefs remember the two of them (and Charlie, once he was old enough) running in and out of the kitchen,

The Seafood Story

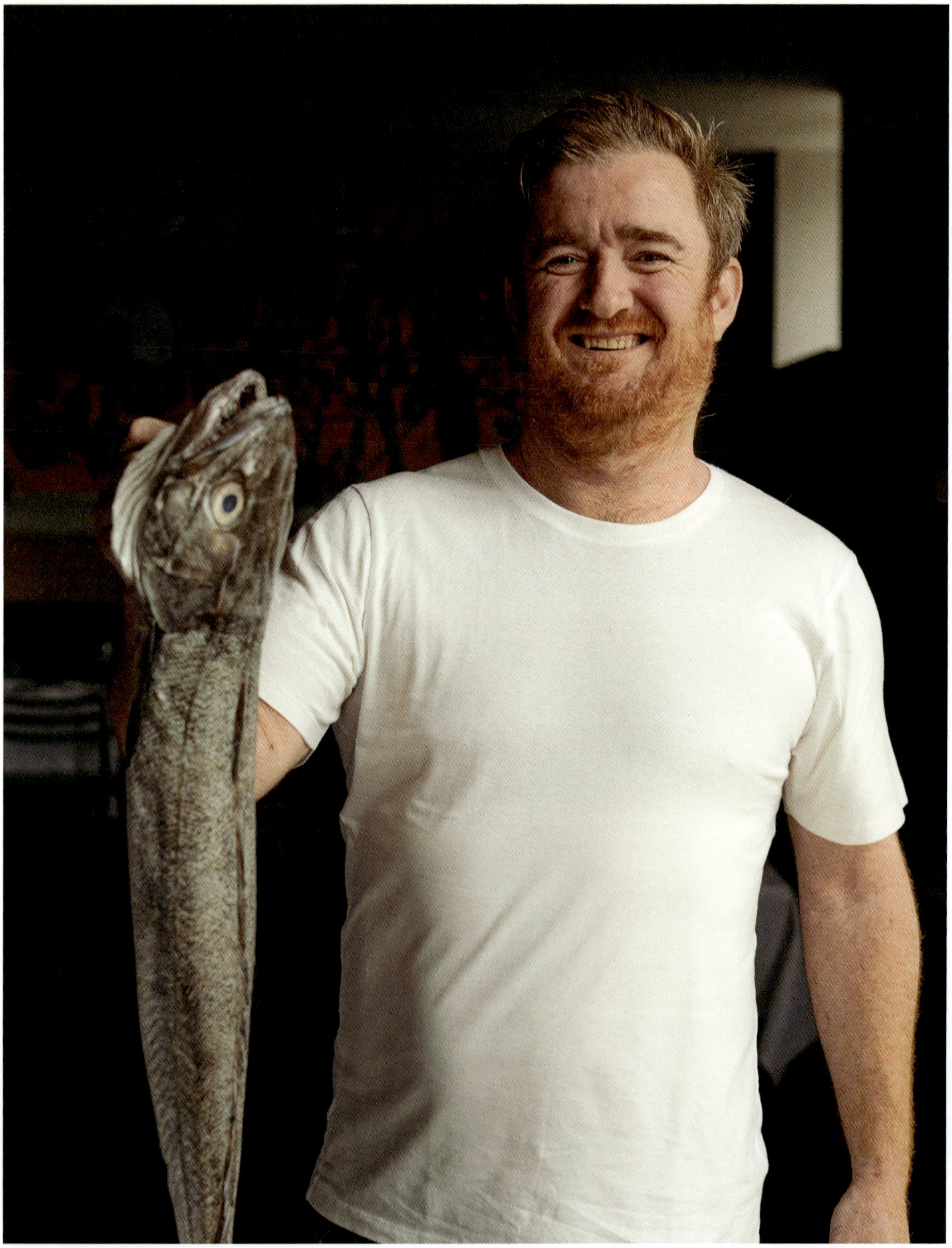

with the odd appearance from Chalky (see page 45), the family Jack Russell too. The early winters of Jack's childhood, between 1980 and 1986, were often spent with time in France – Brittany, Normandy, Loire – when Rick and Jill would seek out restaurants serving delicious French seafood, gathering ideas for dishes they could serve at home (after all, as Rick notes, the northern French coast was not so different from the coast around Cornwall). Jack feels that a lot of the early ideas, like the fish soups, were inspired during that period. He was five when they went to Australia in 1986, stopping off in Singapore and Bangkok for a first experience of Asian food.

By the time Jack was seven or eight years old, he remembers The Seafood as a place that had become a fully fledged part of his life, and by twelve he had begun working there as a kitchen porter three nights a week. Jack calls it a culturally "different time", when dissent in the kitchen almost certainly ended with a firing. He loved it, but it was hard work. And, of course, the influences from the kitchen weren't always good ones. One of the chefs taught Jack all about the Beastie Boys, including the craze they incited of removing the logo badges from parked VW cars and wearing them as necklaces…

At around fifteen, Jack moved front of house. He notes that for many chefs that transition is hard, but it came easily to him. By then, Rick had been on television and the restaurant was thriving. Jack loved the interaction, being part of the buzz of people enjoying themselves. Even now, he seeks out that energy whenever he can.

With school finished, Jack took a gap year in Australia, inevitably, perhaps, working in restaurants to pay his way and learn more about what it takes to run a hospitality business. He came back to the UK to study Psychology at Cardiff University, and then, degree accomplished, decided to go back into the kitchen at The Seafood. On Jack's first day, in October 2001, Stephane Delourme, head chef at the time, paired him up with a Swiss chef called Dominic, who for two weeks put him through his paces ("He beasted me," remembers Jack), teaching him techniques and processes that Jack still uses today. There were no favours – although perhaps there might have been had Dominic realised who Jack's father was: "I'd been working with Dominic for about two or three weeks and one day Dad came in and asked what time I finished and if I wanted to go for a beer. Dominic couldn't believe it; he asked how I knew Rick. 'He's my dad,' I said. He was horrified that I hadn't told him. The next day, though, I had a chocolate cake on my section as we set up."

At the turn of the millennium, Jack was working in The Seafood full time, and was learning both actively and by osmosis how the whole Stein group operated. By the mid-2000s, he was dividing his time between The Seafood and the Café as Sous Chef, but, as in any career, there is benefit in leaving and working somewhere else in order to learn more. A brief stint in other restaurants, including Heston Blumenthal's The Fat Duck in Berkshire, meant that Jack had really cut his teeth as a chef, learning not just more ways to cook, but more ways to develop recipes for consistency. In 2009, after the big refit of the restaurant (see page 66), Jack came back.

The Stein sons were invited to join the Board as shareholders in 2008, but before Ed came back to Padstow and while Charlie was still at university and then carving his own path, it was Jack who represented everyone while Rick was so often away filming and setting up his restaurants with Sas in Australia, and Jill was busy building up her own interior-design business. Jack needed to answer questions on behalf of the family, and he was the person the family expected to explain to them what was going on. He acted as Chef Tournant, doing the rounds in the kitchens of all the businesses to make sure there was consistency throughout (six kitchens at the time), and he was Sous Chef at The Seafood for two years. It was busy.

Now, Jack is Chef Director, responsible (among much else) for the development of new dishes, which he says they always try out in The Seafood Restaurant first – "If The Seafood can do it, everybody can do it." And he loves the fact that in all the years he's now been a chef and all the kitchens he's seen, he is still in awe of how the fish arrives at the door. "To this day, I don't know many restaurants that get fish through the back doors like we do. When we get sea bass in, for example, the fisherman will come in, take the sea bass upstairs and scale them. I once arrived at the restaurant to find three sea bass sloshing around in the sink – the fishermen catch them in the harbour and they are still alive and kicking by the time they are with us. It's amazing. I think it's really important for our chefs to have those interactions with the fishermen; I think it is really unique to The Seafood."

Perhaps the thing that is really striking about Jack is that he has followed in his father's footsteps not just into the kitchen, but also on to television and into publishing. His book, *World on a Plate*, was published in 2018 and he regularly appears on television as a guest chef, and most recently as Chef Mentor in *Cooking with the Stars*. He and Charlie have had their own series: *Wine, Dine and Stein*. But, no matter where the other parts of his career take him, his life is still in Padstow, and The Seafood lies, once again, at the heart of everything he does: "I think The Seafood is the tree that has a lot of branches, all of them symbiotic in the way they rely on one another."

"Having a famous father was just life. When I was learning to be a chef, I got to go to Japan (to Tokyo) and so many other places and all of that was because of the opportunities my parents afforded me."

Jack Stein

Charlie's story

Five years after Jack was born, in 1985 came Charles – Charlie. Like his brothers, he is conscious that during his childhood (and throughout his life), his parents worked hard, but he too, remembers the long winters together and the amazing trips that exposed them all to the inseparable weaving of food and place. In those days without the internet, visiting was the only way to learn properly about worlds other than your own. He was too little to remember the first trips to Australia, where the family stopped off in Singapore and Bangkok, so his earliest travel memories are the trips to Goa, India. He remembers the vivid sights and smells, his parents' awe at the shift in culture, and he and his brothers running around the food markets and shops (as children do). Travel, now, is very much in his bones – and he is lucky. The path he has chosen to take within the business brings the opportunity for travel at every turn.

The Seafood Story

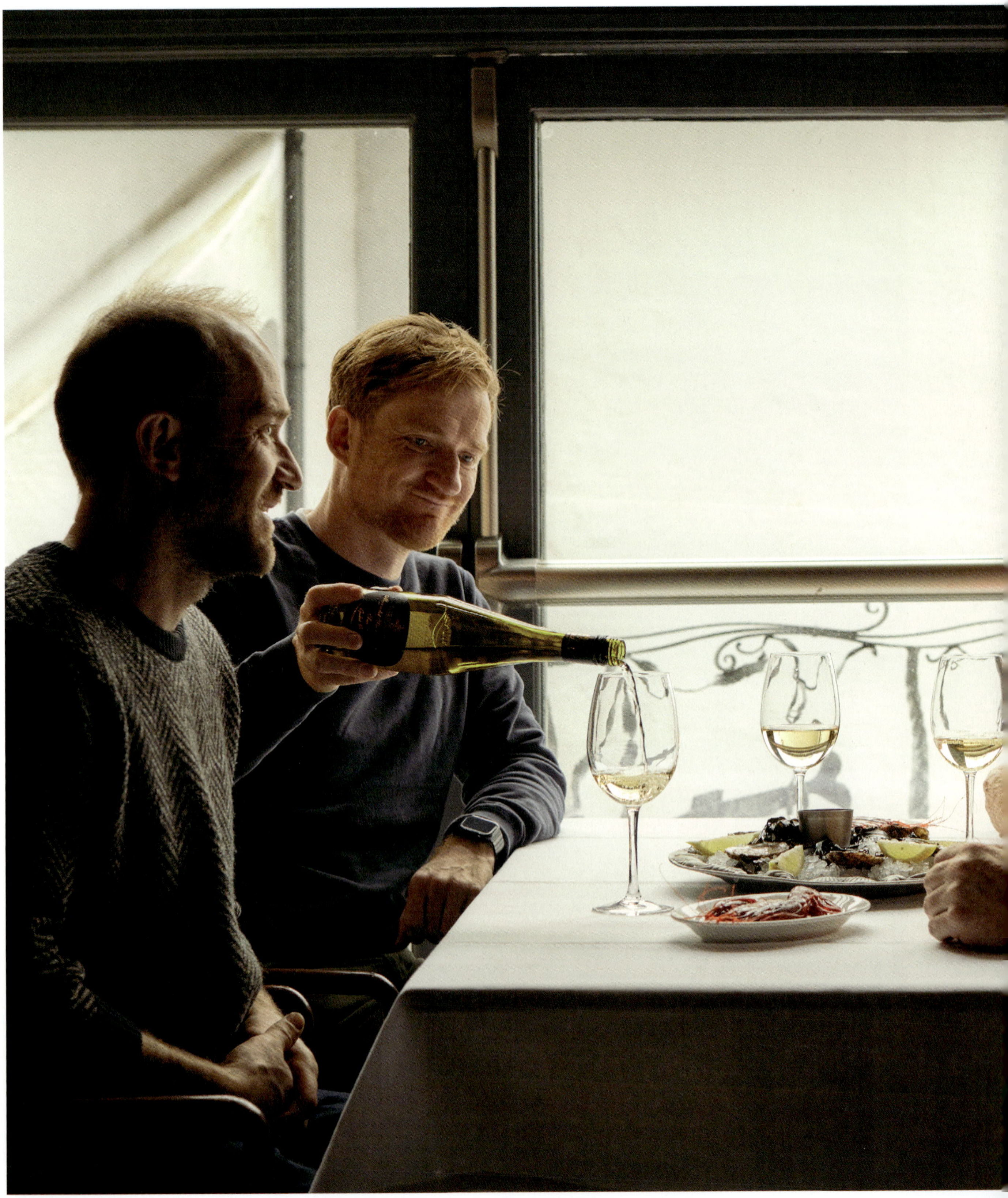

"The Restaurant is so emotionally connected to us – we spent our whole childhood growing up there, it's a home to us. We would spend our evenings and our days in the kitchen and the office upstairs. It means so much."

Charlie Stein

Charlie was still only about five years old when Rick began regularly appearing on television, but even at that age, he was aware that overnight things seemed to change. The restaurant, suddenly, became a lot busier. By the time he was around ten, Rick was filming a lot, including with Bill Baker, a larger-than-life and well-known wine merchant, who advised Rick on the wine list for The Seafood. Bill became a great friend – Charlie has vivid memories of the parties his parents hosted at their home in Trevone, at which Bill was a frequent attendee. But it was during the filming of an episode for Rick's television series that Charlie first realised what a powerhouse of knowledge Bill was, and how inspirational. Watching the filming, he was with Rick and Bill as they paired a Chablis with some oysters. It's this moment, he says, that made him realise that becoming a wine expert was a thing and that it was fascinating (and fun). That experience was compounded in his mid-teens during visits to Australia, when the family would stay with Rick's friends who owned a vineyard. With his whole history bound up in food and drink, and hospitality, it was clear early on that Charlie, like Jack and Ed, would, naturally, find his niche within the family business.

Of course, school, then university came first, along with a stint in The Seafood Restaurant, working in the kitchen and front of house in his late teens. He also, of course, had his aunt, Roni (see page 42), to teach him how to taste wine – just like all the other waiting staff, he was involved in the training that enabled them all to advise their customers as they sat down to order. It's interesting to hear him talk about the rightness of things too – for Charlie, there is no excuse not to bring guests their drinks before taking their food order, a detail of good hosting that, among many others, make dining at The Seafood Restaurant such a special experience.

After university, Charlie moved to London to work for Tom Gilbey at the wine merchant The Vintner, first in the marketing department, then in sales, and then as a buyer. He took his Level 3 WSET exams and decided that, rather than do his Diploma (the next step), visiting and talking to producers and tasting the wines made for a far better way to become an expert. He was with The Vintner for eight years, during which time he made frequent trips to Burgundy and Bordeaux, exploring wineries and building up relationships with the growers.

Eventually, though, the draw of Cornwall and The Seafood Restaurant took hold. When Charlie came back, he did so with buying in mind: "The wine buying at The Seafood has been through so many different eras. People like Bill made the restaurant what it is. He was such a character. And Roni as well – so many of the guests were suspicious of a female sommelier in the early days, but she is so great." There are about 150 wines available at The Seafood, some stored on site and others stored at a site just outside Padstow. Wines come both from merchants in the UK and directly from producers. And while some of the original wine lists at the restaurant included wines that were several thousands of pounds a bottle, the list now is curated for interest as well as budget (magnificent or modest). For example, Charlie is keen to make sure that anyone ordering the sashimi (see page 224) from the menu has the opportunity to try a sake – a sweet or a sparkling – with it.

Charlie divides his time between London and Cornwall, and feels blessed that he is able to do so. He also still gets to travel a lot – on buying trips and staff trips, especially to Bordeaux, making sure everyone knows where the wines come from and how to recommend them. And then there are the cocktails – Charlie has noticed a shift in the buying patterns for cocktails, with significantly more guests ordering a cocktail now than his parents say would have been likely in the '70s. Like wine, cocktails are fashion. He's especially proud that as The Seafood goes into its fiftieth year, it has an expert mixologist, Norbert, behind the bar: "The Seafood is the best place to get a cocktail," he says.

Asked how important The Seafood is to the family, Charlie refers to a time when their emotional attachment to it came into sharp focus. When the Covid-19 pandemic forced the hospitality industry into nationwide closure, there was, of course, an immediate panic about what that might do to the Stein Group as a whole, but it was The Seafood Restaurant that they knew they had to protect at all costs: "That building and that restaurant and that history are so important. We were worried about everything else – but The Seafood was different; it has a personality, it's the fourth child in our family. The idea of losing that was surreal."

The Seafood Story

Beyond Fifty

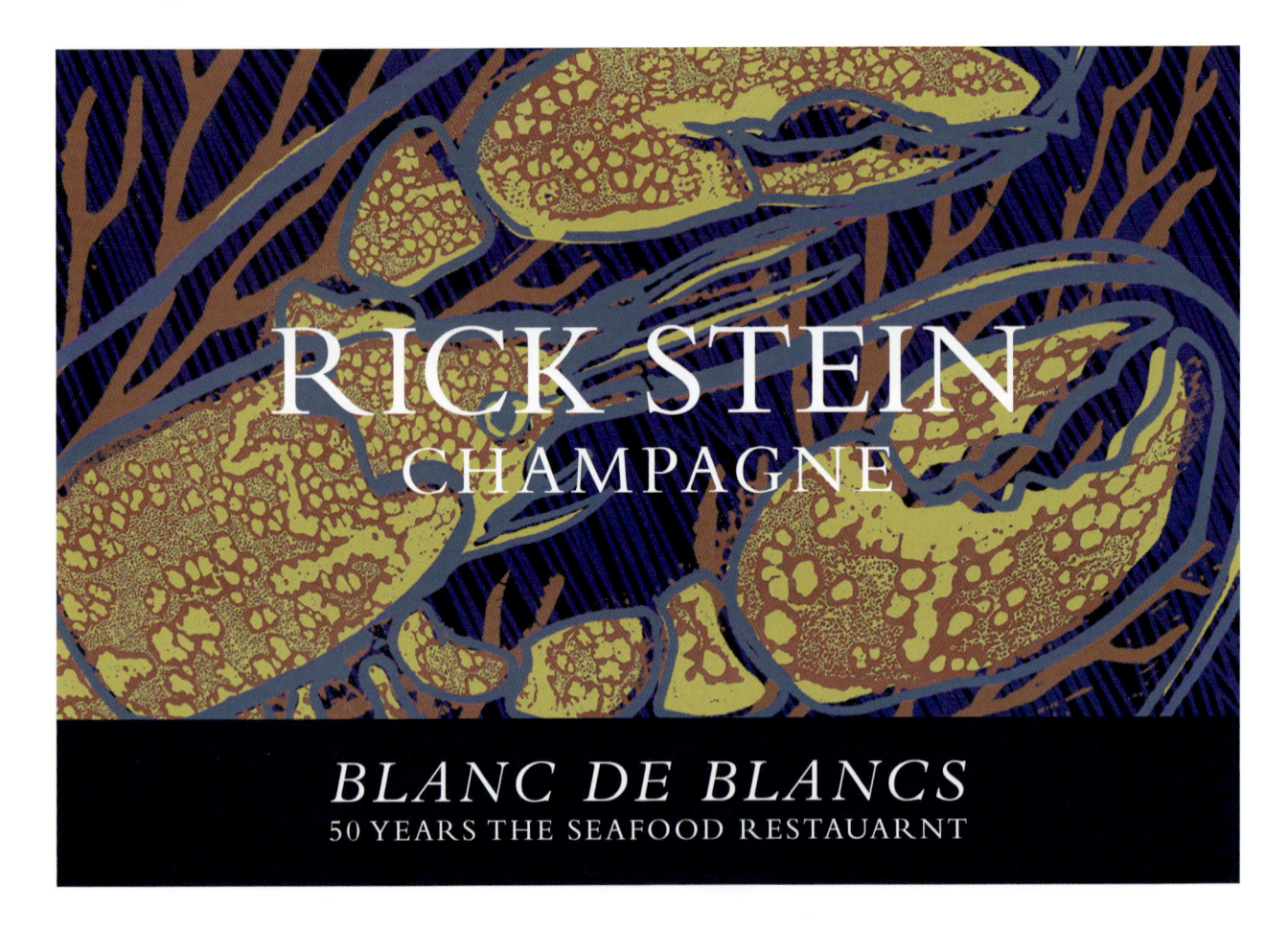

RICK STEIN
CHAMPAGNE

BLANC DE BLANCS
50 YEARS THE SEAFOOD RESTAUARNT

The anniversary label for Rick Stein Champagne. René Beaudouin, whose Champagne house lies east of Reims, France, and whose wines have appeared on The Seafood wine list since the early 1990s, has worked on a Prestige Cuvée Blanc de Blanc specifically to celebrate the restaurant's fiftieth birthday. The label design is by Kate Stein.

Rick Stein's love of Padstow began in childhood, when he and his family would holiday there, long before anyone considered it a particular destination. Rick's dad bought a boat – *The Boscastle Belle* – with fisherman Johnnie Murt, whose grandson, Johnny, supplies The Seafood with catch to this day. There are legacies in the kitchen of the restaurant that are precious not just for the Stein family, but for families throughout the Padstow community, and beyond. Celebrating those legacies as we cast the restaurant's net into the future is exactly what this book is about.

The Seafood Restaurant has, as Jill has pointed out, survived two recessions and a pandemic. And the common theme among the stories of the Stein brothers is that they understand that their succession into the business comes with enormous responsibility – both to honour the legacies and to make sure that The Seafood Restaurant continues to evolve in ways that protect it for the next generation of Steins, should they choose, to take up the mantle.

As Charlie said, "The future is keeping the ethos. The history is my whole life. All of my great memories are at The Seafood. All my birthdays and anniversaries. And I try to eat there every time I'm in Cornwall, to talk to the team and the customers. I work with the management team really closely and I want to build on our core of good, strong values and positive culture. In our birthday year, we're taking a group of our longest-serving staff members to San Sebastian, Spain, for a few nights to celebrate their loyalty – they've all been with us for thirty years or more, so they absolutely deserve it."

For Ed, there's a need to make sure that the menu continues to honour the legacy of fishermen who have been delivering to the back door of the restaurant for its whole life, and to make sure The Seafood does justice to that catch on the menu, making use of fish stocks that are often under-represented in restaurant meals: "Something like weaver fish is great, tasty and abundant." Although he also points out that fish is seasonal and availability isn't always consistent, which will keep them all on their toes. "It's about staying relevant," he says.

Of course, as the brothers unite in the business of running the restaurant, the dishes themselves will fall to Jack, who is aware of the importance of keeping the menu and everything else they are doing in line with the times. That includes resting fish when stocks dictate and finding ways to remain true to the defining simplicity of The Seafood menu while evolving it to reflect modern cooking and, of course, ethics: "When dad first put the vindaloo on the menu, we could use shark – now, of course, we would never do that."

All that said, Rick and Jill are unlikely to disappear completely as The Seafood's clock turns to fifty. As Jack points out, "Dad isn't ready to retire and Mum is fiercely protective of everything she has worked so hard to achieve. I don't think either of them is going to be going off to put their feet up." So, while the day-to-day running and decision-making will now fall to Ed, Jack and Charlie, Rick and Jill – those "enthusiastic amateurs" – are a wealth of knowledge that will continue to provide counsel, no doubt long into the next fifty years.

THE SEAFOOD SIGNATURE RECIPES

1974–1985

1974 THE GREAT WESTERN NIGHTCLUB

Rick and his friend Johnny Walter buy the Padstow harbourside building known as The Whitehouse Club, which will become The Seafood Restaurant. Rick's ambition at the time is to run it as a permanent home for The Purple Tiger, his previously mobile DJ business. He and Johnny open as The Great Western nightclub with Jill, and Johnny's wife, Teri.

1976 PURPLE TIGER'S KITCHEN SOUNDTRACK

Abba's *Greatest Hits*, released in April 1976, turns out to be the decade's best-selling UK album. Although Michael Jackson's *Thriller* (released six years later, in 1982) takes the crown as the best-selling original album (closely followed by *Bat Out of Hell* by Meatloaf, and *Rumours* by Fleetwood Mac, both in 1977).

1977 THE SEAFOOD RESTAURANT

Jill and Rick move the fish bistro downstairs to the ground floor of the building, and name it The Seafood Restaurant. Their business partners, Johnny and Teri, remodel the top two floors of the building as holiday flats.

1975 A SEAFOOD BISTRO

The Great Western runs into licensing difficulties. The Club closes. Rick and Johnny open the first version of The Seafood Restaurant on the top floor of the building.

FIRST TEAM

As the 1970s became the 1980s, Jill and Rick start to employ a small, dedicated team of help in the kitchen and front of house.

1981 THE GOOD FOOD GUIDE

The Seafood Restaurant makes its first appearance in *The Good Food Guide* (see page 138).

1982 THE DELI

Rick and Jill buy a closed-down wool shop on Middle Street and re-open it as a deli, selling condiments and other food items, many of which Rick makes himself. They also buy the house behind to function as staff accommodation – later the ground floor of that house would become the pâtisserie.

THE CONSERVATORY

Rick and Jill move the front of the restaurant to add the conservatory, giving guests a place to enjoy a drink and a bowl of olives before their meal.

AT THE CINEMA

E.T. The Extra-Terrestrial is released and becomes the UK's highest-grossing movie during these years, knocking out *Jaws* (1975) and *Star Wars* (1977).

1984 TASTE OF BRITAIN

The Seafood Restaurant wins the RAC/*The Sunday Times* Taste of Britain Best Restaurant Award.

1985 FIRST ROOMS

The success of The Seafood Restaurant means that Rick and Jill are able to buy the holiday flats above the restaurant from Johnny and Teri, their business partners since the beginning, and reinvent them as eight ensuite rooms (opening in June 1986).

1975–1984

Ray wings with black butter

This dish felt like a permanent fixture on our menu during the late '70s and early '80s. I probably first had it in Paris, during one of our early trips, which would have been around 1978 or '79. Although Jill and I were on holiday, we always made a point of testing things out and picking up recipes and ideas for the kind of restaurant we should aspire to be. When fish conservationists began discouraging people from fishing for skate, we realised that ray was okay – so this dish was born.

Serves 4

4 skinned ray wings, of 225g each
15g nonpareilles capers in brine, drained and rinsed

FOR THE COURT-BOUILLON
300ml dry white wine
85ml white wine vinegar
2 bay leaves
12 black peppercorns
1 onion, roughly chopped
2 carrots, roughly chopped
2 celery sticks, roughly chopped
1 teaspoon salt

FOR THE BLACK BUTTER
175g butter
50ml red wine vinegar
1 tablespoon chopped flat-leaf parsley

First, make the court-bouillon. Put all the ingredients into a large pan with 1.2 litres of water. Bring to the boil and simmer for 20 minutes. Set aside to cool, which will allow the flavour to improve before using.

Put the ray wings into a large pan. Pour over the court-bouillon, bring to the boil and simmer the wings very gently for 15 minutes until they are cooked through.

Carefully lift the ray wings out of the pan, leave the excess liquid to drain off and then place the wings on to 4 warmed plates. Sprinkle with the capers and keep warm.

For the black butter, melt the butter in a frying pan. As soon as it starts to foam, turn quite brown and smell very nutty, add the vinegar, then the parsley. Let it boil down for a minute or so, until slightly reduced. Pour the butter over the ray and serve.

Charlie's Wine Notes

Nutty brown butter and delicate ray wing bring lots of flavours to balance in this dish. For that reason, I would tend to go for a medium-bodied white – a dry Pinot Blanc from Alsace hits the mark.

Jack's Chef Notes

This is such a classic French dish. As a chef, it's really satisfying to get the colour and consistency of the black butter just right.

The Seafood Signature Recipes 109

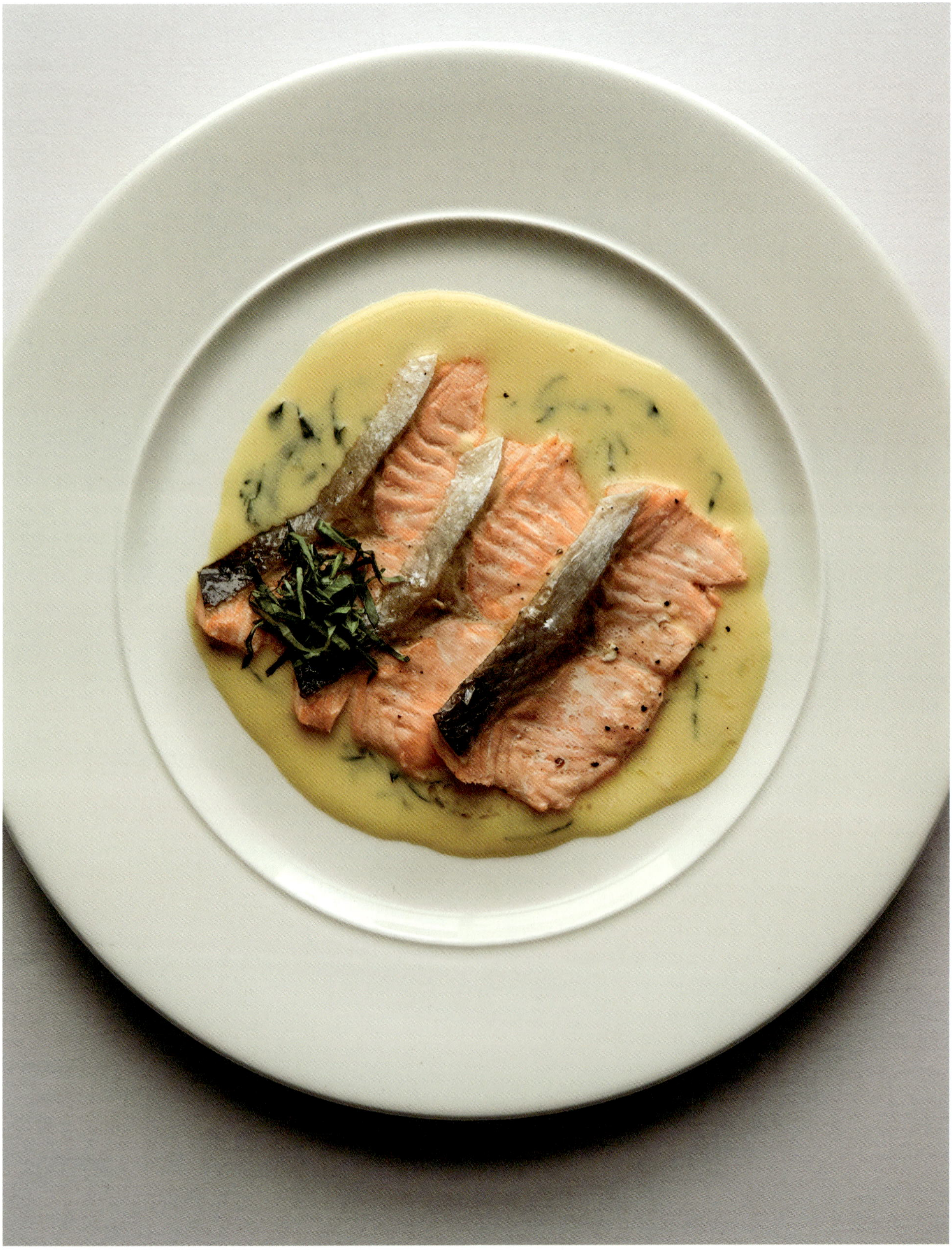

Escalopes of salmon with a sorrel sauce

Sorrel was one of those herbs that I started growing in our garden at Trevose Head, so I could gather it to use in the restaurant. In this dish, the sorrel really lifts the results. The best thing about this recipe, though, is that the salmon is sliced into escalopes and only just cooked, so it is very slightly underdone in the middle. I love it that way. This was one of The Seafood's most popular dishes.

Serves 4

750g salmon fillet, skin on
2 tablespoons sunflower oil
600ml Fish Stock (page 270)
175ml double cream
50ml white vermouth
25g sorrel leaves
75g unsalted butter
2–3 teaspoons lemon juice
salt

Remove any bones from the salmon fillet with tweezers. Then, with a sharp filleting knife, cut the salmon on a slant of about 45° into 12 wide slices, known as escalopes. Lay them on a lightly oiled baking sheet, brush with a little more oil and season with some salt.

Pre-heat the grill to high. Put the fish stock, half the cream and all the vermouth into a medium pan and boil rapidly until reduced by three-quarters. Meanwhile, wash the sorrel leaves, remove the stalks and finely shred the leaves.

When the stock-and-cream mixture has reduced to the required amount, add the rest of the cream, and all the butter and lemon juice. Reduce a little more, then stir in all but a few pinches of the shredded sorrel.

Grill the salmon escalopes for 1 minute. To serve, pour the sauce equally over 4 warmed plates, then place the escalopes on top. Sprinkle with the remaining chopped sorrel.

Charlie's Wine Notes

What a classic. I'm looking for a young Chenin Blanc from the Loire, which will give enough weight to take on the sauce, but also lots of earthy, cool citrus to match the sorrel.

Jack's Chef Notes

This is The Seafood's take on a famous recipe by Pierre Troisgros, the late French chef and restaurateur. Dad couldn't buy sorrel in Cornwall in the 1980s, which is why he started growing it at home.

Seafood thermidor

I think Seafood Thermidor is probably the most popular dish we had in our first decade of The Seafood Restaurant – it's the dish that made me realise we were really on to something. We had it on the menu from day one, inspired by The Blue Lobster, which had been just across the quay from us. Our version had lobster, but also crab and North Atlantic prawns, and, importantly, monkfish, which no one else was really using, except to make scampi. I added the breadcrumbs and cheddar cheese, and the cayenne on the top to give it a bit of heat and colour.

Serves 4

60g unsalted butter, plus extra, melted, for brushing
1 onion, finely chopped
90ml dry white wine
300ml Fish Stock (page 270)
90g button mushrooms, thinly sliced
120ml double cream
180g skinless lemon sole fillet
180g skinless monkfish fillet
meat from 4 large scallops
120g peeled raw North Atlantic prawns, cooked
1 tablespoon Colman's English mustard powder, made up with a little water, plus extra to taste if needed
juice of ¼ lemon, plus extra to taste if needed
90g mature cheddar, grated
30g panko breadcrumbs
pinch of cayenne pepper
salt and freshly ground black pepper

First, make the velouté (ingredients overleaf). Place the stock and milk in a pan over a medium heat and bring to the boil, leaving it to reduce and thicken a little. Meanwhile, melt the butter in a separate, heavy-based pan and add the flour. Cook the flour mixture for about 2 minutes, stirring constantly, without letting it colour too much. When it starts to smell nutty, remove from the heat and cool slightly.

Off the heat, gradually add the hot stock mixture, stirring all the time, until the sauce is smooth. Once you have incorporated almost all the stock, return the pan to a medium heat. Add the remaining stock, stir and turn the heat right down. Simmer for 40 minutes. Pass the sauce through a conical strainer into a bowl, cover the surface of the sauce with a piece of greaseproof paper to prevent a skin from forming, then leave the sauce to cool. If you're not using the velouté immediately, transfer it to an airtight container and keep it in the fridge. It will store indefinitely if you re-boil it every three or four days. Flour-based sauces don't freeze well.

To make the thermidor, turn on your grill to high.

Melt the butter in a small saucepan over a medium heat. Add the onion and fry for 3–4 minutes until softened. Pour in the white wine. Leave to reduce a little, then add the fish stock and 30g of the mushrooms. Simmer the mushrooms for 10 minutes, then increase the heat and boil rapidly to reduce the volume by two thirds.

...ingredients and method continued overleaf

The Seafood Signature Recipes 113

FOR THE VELOUTÉ
  (MAKES 600ML)
600ml Fish Stock (page 270)
300ml whole milk
50g unsalted butter
40g plain flour

In a medium saucepan, heat the velouté carefully. Stir in the cream and leave it simmering on a very low heat while you prepare the fish.

Cut the sole and monkfish into 1cm pieces. Slice each scallop into three. Put all these fish pieces into a large, shallow gratin dish (or use individual gratin dishes, if you prefer – just divide the mixture and other elements equally). Scatter the rest of the mushrooms on top and brush with melted butter. Season with salt and place under the grill for 2–3 minutes until the fish has turned white but is still a little underdone (it will cook more when you finish by gratinating the dish under the grill). Add the prawns to the rest of the fish in the dish.

Add the mustard and lemon juice to the simmering sauce and taste; it should be slightly hot with mustard but not overpoweringly so – add more mustard or lemon juice, as necessary. Pour the sauce over the fish and mushrooms.

In a bowl, mix the grated cheese with the breadcrumbs, the cayenne pepper and a couple of twists of a black pepper mill. Sprinkle this mixture evenly over the sauce. Gratinate under the grill to a nice golden brown – about 2–3 minutes.

Jack's Chef Notes

One of our original recipes, Seafood Thermidor is great way to make a good-value main course. This had a renaissance when we started to do our charity lunches in the late '90s and it's a really good dish for a dinner party.

Charlie's Wine Notes

It's safe to say this is a gloriously rich dish, so we need an equally decadent and rich white wine to match. I'm not looking anywhere else but my favourite wine region of Burgundy, and the wines of St Veran, in particular.

The Seafood Signature Recipes 115

1975–1984

Fish and shellfish soup with rouille and croûtons

This recipe was inspired by our early visits to bistros in Provence, and elsewhere, in France, and is probably the longest-lasting dish on our menu. I always loved the fish soups I tasted on those trips – they seemed to bring together the flavours of the Mediterranean and gave me everything I needed to know about how to create a really tasty result. Although the soup has changed over the years (originally it was a straightforward fish soup, but now it's fish and shellfish), it's still on the menu today. Filleting our own fish means that we are able to minimise our waste – all those delicious trimmings that don't fit the bill for grilling or poaching, say, find their way here.

Serves 4

90ml olive oil
75g each onion, celery, leek and fennel, roughly chopped
3 garlic cloves, sliced
juice of ½ orange, plus 2 strips of orange zest
200g canned chopped tomatoes
1 red pepper, seeded and sliced
1 bay leaf
1 thyme sprig
a pinch of saffron strands
½ teaspoon chilli flakes
100g unpeeled prawns
1kg mixed skinless fish fillets, such as cod, hake and ling
salt and freshly ground black pepper

First, make the rouille. Cover the slice of bread with the stock or water and leave it to soften. Squeeze out the excess liquid and put the bread into a food processor with the harissa, garlic, egg yolk and salt. Blend until smooth. With the machine still running, gradually add the oil through the feed tube until you have a smooth, thick, mayonnaise-like mixture. The rouille will keep in the fridge for up to three weeks.

To make the soup, heat the olive oil in a large pan. Add the onion and garlic and cook gently for 20 minutes until the onion is soft but not coloured. Add the pared orange zest, tomatoes, red pepper, bay leaf, thyme, saffron, chilli flakes and prawns, and the fish fillets. Cook briskly for 2–3 minutes, then add 1.2 litres of water and the orange juice. Bring to the boil and simmer for 40 minutes.

Meanwhile, for the croûtons, thinly slice the baguette on the diagonal. Heat the olive oil in a frying pan over a medium–high heat and fry the slices (in batches if necessary), turning until crisp and golden on both sides. Drain on kitchen paper and rub one side of each slice with the garlic clove. Set aside.

The Seafood Signature Recipes

FOR THE ROUILLE
  (MAKES 300ML)
a 25g slice of day-old crustless white bread
a little Fish Stock (page 270) or water
2 tablespoons Harissa (page 270)
3 fat garlic cloves, peeled
1 egg yolk
¼ teaspoon salt
250ml olive oil

FOR THE CROÛTONS
1 small baguette
olive oil, for frying
1 garlic clove, peeled

TO SERVE
½ quantity rouille (see above)
25g Parmesan, finely grated

Pour the soup into a blender or liquidiser and blitz. Pass the liquidised soup through a sieve into a clean pan, pressing out as much liquid as possible with the back of a ladle. Return the soup to the heat and season with salt and pepper to taste.

To serve, ladle the soup into 4 warmed bowls. Serve the rouille and croûtons on the side, leaving each person to spread the croûtons to their liking and float them on their soup, then finally sprinkle them with Parmesan.

Jack's Chef Notes

This fish-soup recipe has been on the menu as far back as I can remember – and before. The fish has changed quite a lot over the years, as we've responded to availability and sustainability. We used to use things like conger eel to thicken the soup but now we look to fish like ling and cod.

118   The Seafood Signature Recipes

Charlie's Wine Notes

The key here is to choose a wine with enough oomph to withstand the Fish and Shellfish Soup's strong flavour, but not too much body as to be out of balance with its consistency. I'd go for a well-chilled Provençal rosé.

The Seafood Signature Recipes   119

Baked hake with lemon, bay leaf, onion and garlic

Around this time, we really looked up to Sonia Stevenson, who ran The Horn of Plenty and was the first woman in the country to be awarded a Michelin star. Her restaurant, sitting on the banks of the Tamar, had such a great location and she was such a fantastic cook – in particular, she was a great fish cook and she was absolutely the inspiration for this dish. It appeared on our early menus and we still regularly serve it to this day. A true testament to how good it is.

Serves 4

100g unsalted butter
1 onion, chopped
4 garlic cloves, chopped
85ml white wine
juice of ½ lemon
½ teaspoon salt, plus extra to season
rind of 1 lemon, cut into long, paper-thin slices
2 bay leaves, very thinly sliced; or 2 dried bay leaves, crushed
300ml Fish Stock (page 270)
4 hake steaks, of 225g each
freshly ground black pepper

Melt half the butter in a pan over a medium heat and add the onions and garlic. Gently fry for 5–6 minutes until they are soft. Add the white wine, lemon juice, salt, half the lemon rind and half the bay leaves. Cover and leave to cook gently for 40 minutes until the onions are very tender. You can prepare this garlic and onion confit some time in advance.

Pre-heat the oven to 230°C/210°C fan.

Take a flameproof casserole dish large enough to hold the fish in a single layer. Place the onion confit with half the fish stock in the bottom. Place the hake steaks on top.

Sprinkle the fish with salt and pepper, and the rest of the bay leaves and lemon rind. Cover with foil and bake for 13 minutes. Remove the foil and bake for a further 4 minutes until cooked through and lightly coloured.

Remove the fish from the dish and transfer one steak to each of 4 warmed plates. Sprinkle again with salt and black pepper. Add the rest of the fish stock to the casserole dish, place it on the hob and bring it to the boil. Add the rest of the butter and reduce to a thick sauce. Pour the sauce around each portion of the fish and serve.

Charlie's Wine Notes

I'm a big fan of a peachy, refreshing Spanish Albariño with hake dishes. I'd go for a *sobre lias* (on the lees), which gives the wine more weight and texture to match the sauce, and lots of citrus notes to complement the lemon.

Jack's Chef Notes

When this recipe first appeared on The Seafood menu, hake would have been a fairly unpopular fish to serve – and cutting it across the bone was also unusual. But, it's a great dish. The sauce is the kind of sauce that chefs would eat with some bread after a busy service.

The Seafood Signature Recipes

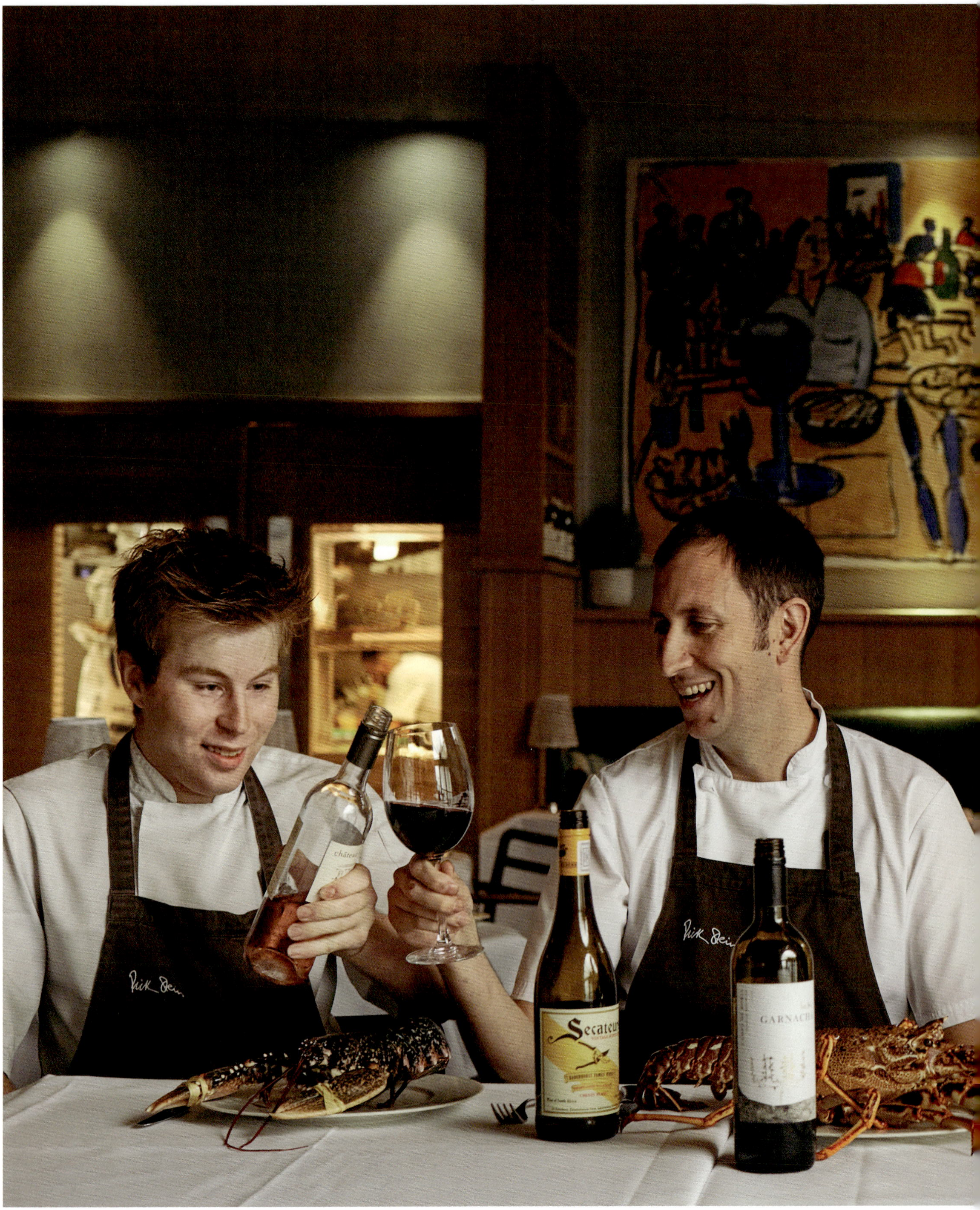
Secateur
GARNACH

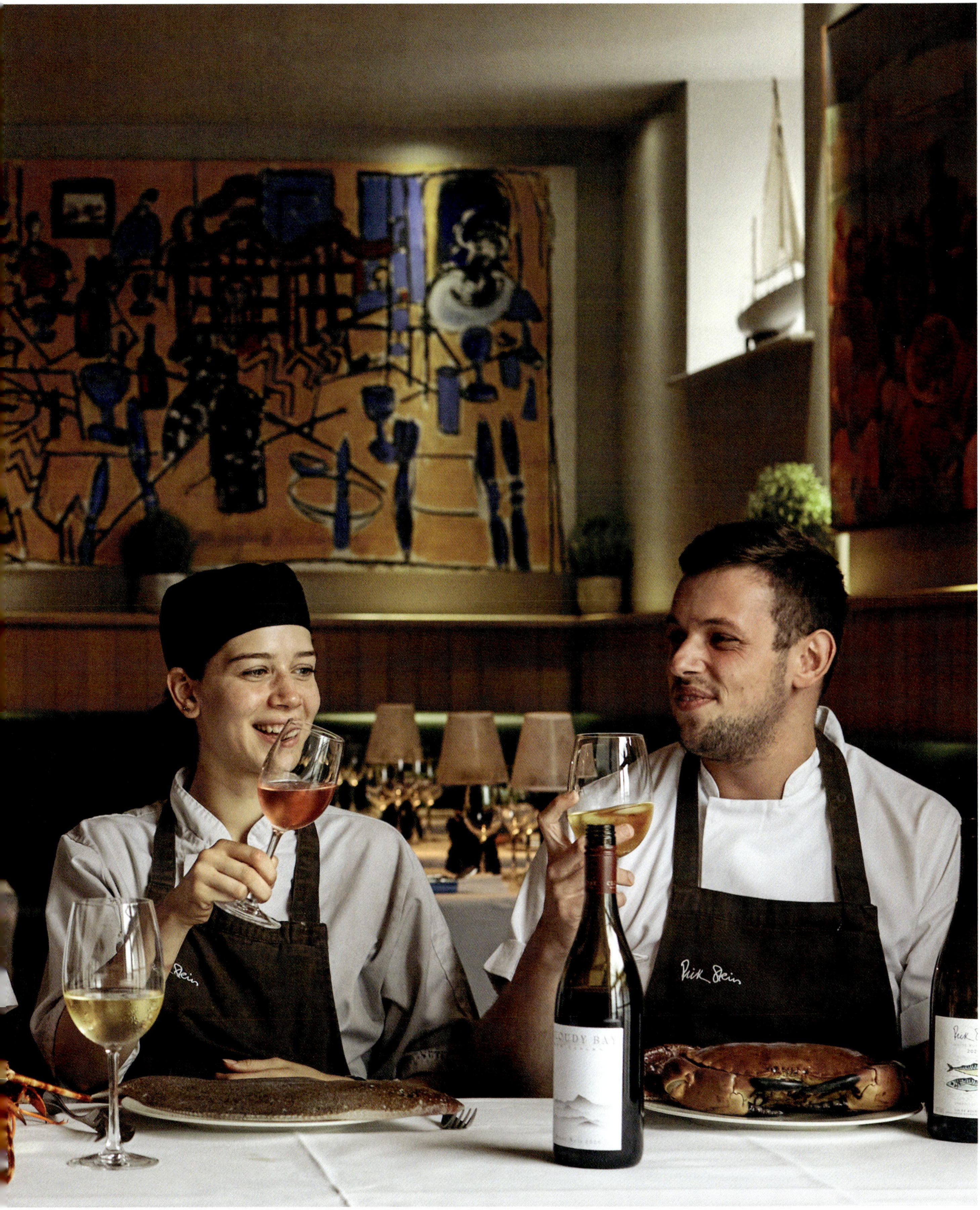
Rick Stein

Charlie's Wine Notes

This is a simple dish that really calls out for a light-touch wine, nothing too exuberant on the fruit but enough to complement the ginger and not be overpowered by the soy. I'd go for a zippy, dry Clare Valley Riesling.

Jack's Chef Notes

The Seafood kitchen has always used steamers – from the old ones that resemble submarine hatches to modern steaming ovens, like Rational. Steaming is a really great way to cook fish – making it the undisputed star of the show.

124   The Seafood Signature Recipes

Steamed bream with garlic, ginger and spring onions

Around 1976, I started trying dishes in some of the less salubrious Chinese restaurants in Soho, London, picking the worst-looking dishes on the menu. One of them was eel in black bean sauce – which, of course, turned out to be totally delicious. Then, I picked up the use of whole, steamed fish with garlic, ginger and spring onions and that's how this bream recipe came about.

Serves 4

2 whole grey bream, each of 450g, cleaned and trimmed
2.5cm fresh ginger root, cut into fine julienne
4 spring onions, trimmed and thinly sliced
2 tablespoons dark soy sauce
2 tablespoons sesame oil
4 garlic cloves, finely chopped

Pour about 2.5cm of water into the bottom of a shallow pan with a well-fitting lid. Put a petal steamer into the pan, bring the water to the boil and then lay the grey mullet on the steamer. Sprinkle the fish with the julienned fresh ginger. Cover with the lid, reduce the heat to medium and steam for 10–12 minutes until cooked through.

Carefully lift the fish off the steamer on to warmed plates (reserve the cooking juices for the next step) and scatter over the sliced spring onions. Keep warm.

Pour 4 tablespoons of the cooking juices into a small pan and add the soy sauce. Place the pan over a medium heat and bring the liquid up to the boil, then pour the sauce over the fish.

Heat the sesame oil in a small pan over a medium heat. Add the garlic, leave it to sizzle for a few seconds, then pour this straight over the fish. Serve the fish whole at the table for four people to share, removing the meat from the bone, as they help themselves.

1975–1984

Grilled lobster with fines herbes

We've had this recipe on the menu since The Seafood opened. We used to get endless supplies of good-value lobster, so I used to chop them in half, put melted butter on them, then grill them and finish them off with fines herbes and a bit of lemon juice. It was a simple preparation, which didn't even need us to take the meat out of the shell. Interestingly, we didn't ever change that recipe, because I have always really liked lobster grilled like that. I remember one day a French couple came in and the lady produced some gold-plated lobster picks from her bag. They were wrapped in a leather case. She used them to take every morsel out of every leg.

Serves 4

4 live lobsters, each of 500g
15g butter, melted
175ml Fish Stock (page 270)
½ teaspoon Thai fish sauce (nam pla)
2 teaspoons lemon juice
50g unsalted butter, cut into small pieces
1 teaspoon chopped chives
1 teaspoon each chopped tarragon, chervil and flat-leaf parsley leaves
salt and freshly ground black pepper

Kill the lobsters painlessly by putting them into the freezer for 2 hours. Bring a large pan of heavily salted water to the boil (about 150g salt to every 5 litres of water). Add the lobsters and bring the water back to the boil. Cook for 15 minutes, then remove and leave to cool. (As an aside, if you had larger lobsters, of up to 1.25kg, they would need a 20-minute boil.)

Lay the lobsters belly-side down on a board and cut them in half.

Remove the stomach sac from each lobster piece (this is a slightly clear pouch that will now be in half), from the head section of each half. Remove the intestinal tract from the tail section by running the knife down the back of the meat and removing it in one piece. (Alternatively, you can cut the tail into thin slices and remove the intestinal tract from each slice with the tip of a small, sharp knife.)

Pre-heat the grill to medium–high. Put the lobster halves on to a baking tray or the rack of the grill pan. Brush the meat with the melted butter and season with a little salt and pepper. Grill for 8–10 minutes until cooked through.

Just before the lobsters are ready, combine the fish stock, fish sauce and lemon juice in a small pan, bring to the boil and boil for 1 minute. A piece at a time, whisk in the butter to build up an emulsified sauce. Stir in all the chopped herbs. Serve the lobster halves with the sauce spooned over (it will melt into the fish).

Charlie's Wine Notes

Grilled lobster and Chardonnay are the best of friends – open the best bottle of white Burgundy that you are happy to pay for and enjoy one of life's greatest pairings. For me, seeing as we are celebrating a big birthday, I'd go for Meursault or Puligny-Montrachet.

Jack's Chef Notes

This is a twist on a classic, using fish sauce to season a typical, French butter emulsion. Fines herbes are classic with lobster – it's the chervil and tarragon flavours that are the match for the shellfish.

The Seafood Signature Recipes

1975–1984

Freshly boiled and dressed crab

We buy our crabs from a lobster-fishing family, the Murts, who have been supplying us for three generations. Grandad Murt's boat was called The Boscastle Belle *(with the same registration as his grandson, Johnny, now uses), and he always caught really good crabs.*

Serves 1–3

1 x 900g live crab per person, or 1 x 1.5–1.75kg live crab to serve 2–3
freshly ground black pepper

FOR THE MUSTARD MAYONNAISE (MAKES 300ML)
1 tablespoon English mustard
1 egg, at room temperature
1 tablespoon white wine vinegar
¾ teaspoon salt
freshly ground white pepper
300ml sunflower oil

First, make the mustard mayonnaise. Put the mustard, egg, vinegar, salt and a few turns of pepper from the white pepper mill into a liquidiser. Turn on the machine, then gradually add the oil through the hole in the lid until you have a thick emulsion. This makes more than you need for this recipe, but the mayonnaise will keep for about 1 week in the fridge. Set aside.

Crabs should be boiled in plenty of water, salted at the ratio of 150g salt to 4.5 litres of water.

Put the crabs into a pan of cold salted water, bring to the boil and simmer – the smaller ones will take 15–25 minutes, the larger ones 20–25 minutes. When the crabs are cooked, lift them out of the water and run them under the cold tap to make them easier to handle. Break off and discard the tail flap and the two flaps that cover the mouth on the under-shell beneath the eyes.

Now, insert the blade of a large knife between the body and the back shell and twist to release the shell. Pull off the feathery-looking gills (or "dead man's fingers") from the body and discard. Remove the stomach sac from the back shell by pressing on the little piece of shell located just behind the eyes. Discard both the bone and the stomach. Empty any excess water out of the back shell.

Cut the body into 4 pieces and crack each of the claw sections with the back of a large knife, but try not to shatter them completely, so that you can reassemble the crab to look much as it was, for serving.

Jack's Chef Notes

We're really proud of our long association with the Murts. There really is nothing better than this simple recipe to show off all their Padstow crab fishery achieves.

Charlie's Wine Notes

You want to be able to taste that delicate crab meat as you're eating this dish, so a classic unoaked Chablis works a treat here.

Take a large plate for each person and put the 4 pieces of the body section back together again. Put the back shell back in place and rearrange any legs or claws that may have fallen off.

If you wish to serve the crab dressed, break the legs away from the body section and discard all but the largest joints. Crack the shells with the back of a knife or a hammer and pick out the white meat from these joints with a crab pick. Break open the claws and remove this meat too, discarding the very thin flat bone from the centre of the claws. Then pick out all the white meat from the little channels in the body section, using a crab pick, taking care not to break off any pieces of wafer-thin shell. Scrape out the brown meat from the back shell, chop it into small pieces if necessary and fold in a little of the mayonnaise and some freshly ground black pepper.

If you want to serve the crab in the back shell, wash the shell out well under cold water. Dry. Spoon the white crab meat into either side of the shell and spoon the brown crab meat down the centre. Serve with the mustard mayonnaise, and some minted new potatoes and a mixed green leaf salad, if you like.

130 The Seafood Signature Recipes

Jack's Chef Notes

It took many years before Rick's desire to have Dover sole filleted at the table was realised – this recipe (see overleaf) is a Seafood classic.

Charlie's Wine Notes

Dover Sole à la Meunière is my absolute favourite dish on the menu. I love it with an old vines' Chenin Blanc from South Africa, which has enough elbow to match the butter in the sauce but not overpower the delicate fish.

The Seafood Signature Recipes

Dover sole à la meunière

I think Dover sole is the best fish in the sea, and à la meunière (with a light dusting of flour – from the "miller's wife", the meunière herself) is the best way to cook it.

Serves 4

50g plain flour
½ teaspoon salt, plus extra to season
10 turns of freshly ground white pepper, plus extra to season
4 whole Dover soles, each of 400–450g, trimmed and skinned (see box, opposite; or ask your fishmonger)
2 tablespoons sunflower oil
100g salted butter
1 tablespoon lemon juice
2 tablespoons chopped curly parsley leaves
1 lemon, peeled and cut into thin slices, to serve

FOR THE GRILLED POTATOES
450g large potatoes, peeled and cut lengthways into 5mm slices
50ml extra virgin olive oil
salt and freshly ground black pepper

Start with the grilled potatoes. Pre-heat the grill to high. Boil the potatoes in a pan of salted water until tender (about 12 minutes), then drain. Lay the potatoes on a grill tray and brush them liberally on both sides with the olive oil. Season with black pepper and grill for about 10 minutes until beginning to turn brown. Keep warm.

Meanwhile, mix the flour with the salt and white pepper. Coat the prepared Dover soles on both sides with the seasoned flour and then knock off the excess.

Heat half of the oil in a large well-seasoned or non-stick frying pan. Add one of the soles, lower the heat slightly and add 10g of the butter. Fry over a moderate heat for 4–5 minutes, without moving the fish, until the underside is richly golden. Baste the fish with the foaming butter.

Carefully turn the fish over and cook it for another 4–5 minutes until golden brown and cooked through, basting throughout. Lift on to a serving plate and keep warm. Repeat with the second fish.

Discard the frying oil and wipe the pan clean. Add the remaining butter and allow it to melt over a moderate heat. When the butter starts to smell nutty and turn light brown, add the lemon juice, parsley and some seasoning. Pour some of this beurre noisette over each fish and serve straight away topped with lemon slices and with the grilled potatoes.

Skinning a whole flat fish

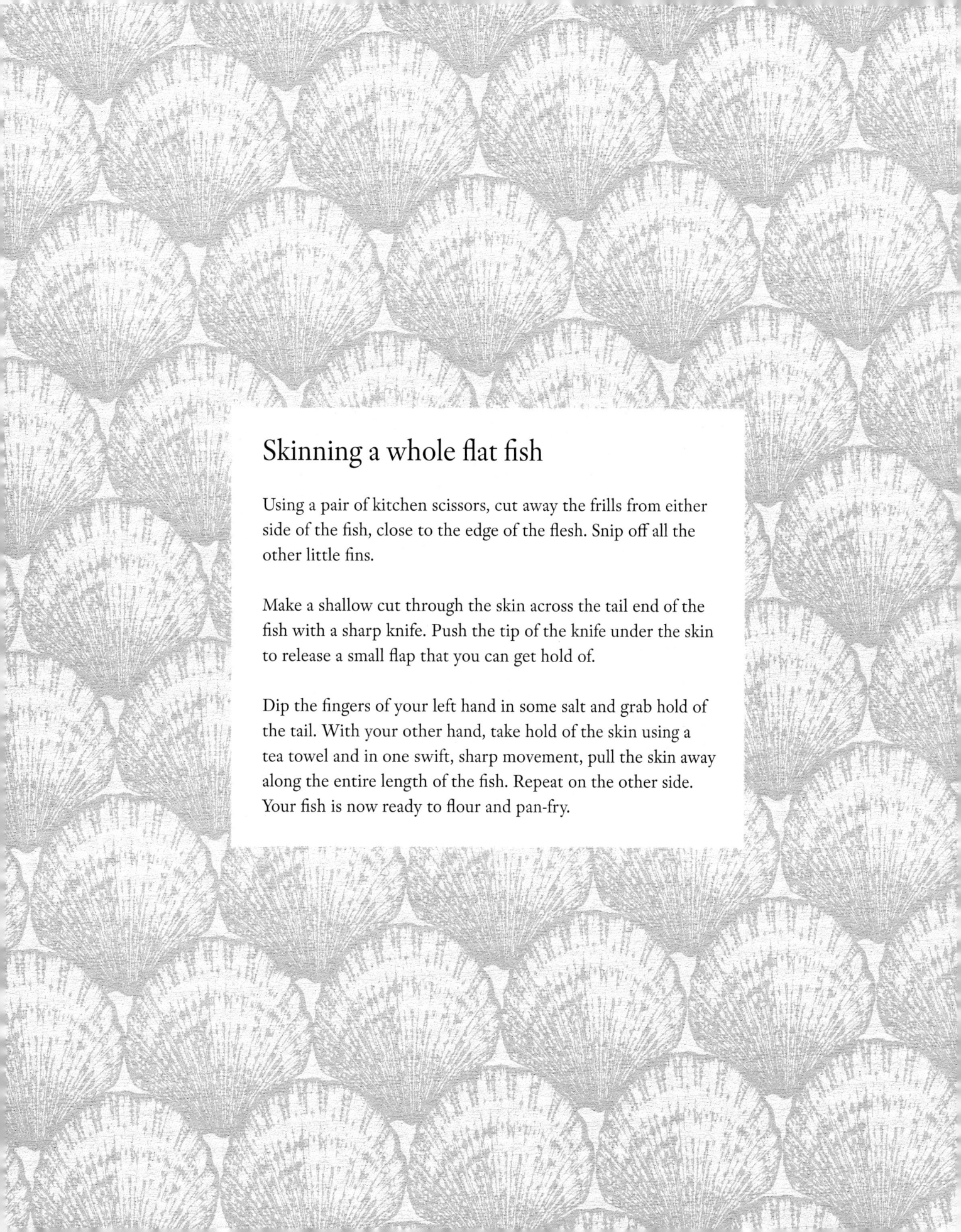

Using a pair of kitchen scissors, cut away the frills from either side of the fish, close to the edge of the flesh. Snip off all the other little fins.

Make a shallow cut through the skin across the tail end of the fish with a sharp knife. Push the tip of the knife under the skin to release a small flap that you can get hold of.

Dip the fingers of your left hand in some salt and grab hold of the tail. With your other hand, take hold of the skin using a tea towel and in one swift, sharp movement, pull the skin away along the entire length of the fish. Repeat on the other side. Your fish is now ready to flour and pan-fry.

1975–1984

Treacle tart with clotted cream ice cream

This was my mother's recipe for treacle tart – I'm fairly confident she will have given it to me scribbled on the back of an envelope – and the reason I like it is that it has just the right ratio of breadcrumbs to syrup, and a good base. It was on the menu at The Seafood Restaurant from the day we opened, which makes it particularly worthy of its place in this book.

Serves 8–10

725g golden syrup (see method overleaf for a measuring tip)
juice of ½ lemon
175g coarse fresh white breadcrumbs
icing sugar, for dusting

FOR THE PASTRY CASE
225g plain flour
½ teaspoon salt
65g unsalted butter, chilled and cut into pieces
65g chilled lard, cut into pieces
1½–2 tablespoons cold water

FOR THE CLOTTED CREAM ICE CREAM
600ml full-cream milk
225g clotted cream
1 vanilla pod, slit lengthways
6 egg yolks
75g caster sugar
crumbled digestive biscuit, to serve (optional)

For the ice cream, put the milk and clotted cream into a pan. Scrape out the seeds from the vanilla pod, add the pod and seeds to the milk and cream and almost bring to the boil. Set aside for 20 minutes.

Cream the egg yolks and sugar together in a bowl. Bring the cooled milk and cream mixture back to the boil, strain it on to the egg-yolk mixture and whisk it in to form a custard. Strain the custard once more back into a clean pan and cook over a gentle heat, stirring constantly, until the custard has thickened and lightly coats the back of a spoon. Pour the custard into a bowl and leave it to cool; then chill it in the fridge until quite cold (overnight, if possible).

Churn the custard in an ice-cream maker until smooth. Transfer to a plastic box, cover and freeze for 6 hours or until needed.

For the pastry, sift the flour and salt into a food processor or a mixing bowl. Add the pieces of butter and lard and work them together, either in the food processor or with your fingertips, until the mixture looks like fine breadcrumbs. Stir in the water with a round-bladed knife (or process very briefly) until it all comes together into a ball, then turn it out on to a lightly floured surface and knead it briefly until smooth. Roll out the pastry and use it to line a loose-bottomed flan tin that measures 23cm across the base and is 4cm deep. Chill the pastry dough for 20 minutes.

...method continued overleaf

The Seafood Signature Recipes 135

Pre-heat the oven to 200°C/180°C fan. Line the pastry case with a crumpled sheet of greaseproof paper and a thin layer of baking beans and bake blind for 15 minutes. Remove the paper and beans and return the pastry case to the oven for 5–6 minutes, or until the edges are biscuit-coloured. Remove and lower the oven temperature to 180°C/160°C fan.

To make the golden syrup easier to measure, stand the tin(s) of golden syrup in a pan of hot water until the syrup has gone liquid. Remove from the pan, pour away the water and dry out the pan. Measure out the 725g of syrup directly into the dried-out pan, then stir in the lemon juice. Tip the breadcrumbs into the pastry case and spread them out evenly. Carefully spoon over the warm syrup and allow it to sink in and saturate the bread. Bake for 25–30 minutes until set and golden brown.

Leave the tart to cool in the tin for 15 minutes, then transfer it to a serving plate. Serve cut into wedges and dusted with icing sugar, with scoops of the clotted cream ice cream (we like to serve our ice cream on a bed of crumbled digestive too).

Jack's Chef Notes

One of my earliest memories of being in The Seafood is seeing Grandma's treacle tart on the menu. I feel she would be thrilled that we're celebrating it here, for our 50th anniversary.

Charlie's Wine Notes

This has me reaching for the port, a nice Tawny. Our friend Sophia at Quinta de la Rosa, on the banks of Portugal's Douro river, does an excellent one.

The Seafood Signature Recipes

ENGLAND

The Good Food Guide
▲ Seafood Restaurant ▮

The Seafood Restaurant has appeared in *The Good Food Guide* for well over forty years. Reading through the entries that straddle the five decades offers a fascinating insight in to the way in which British restaurants have evolved over half a century and how The Seafood Restaurant, in particular, mirrors that evolution in its own unique and inspiring way. It is also a story of a small family restaurant, from its early days cooking locally caught fish with passion, battling the vagaries of hospitality in a small out-of-the-way Cornish village, through to its current celebrated status as one of the world's great culinary destinations.

1981

Richard and Jill Stein's alluringly flowered and fish-netted restaurant may have had to serve longer than it should have done for its first Guide *entry, but people seem sure now that their buying and cooking are as sound as each other. 'The large local mussels in garlic and butter, and their oak-smoked ham with mushrooms in garlic mayonnaise both made delicious beginnings, and we then shared an enormous crawfish which had been shown to us alive and kicking half an hour before it was served. The abundant flesh, though less sweet than a lobster, was beautifully firm, and the salad with fennel and chives added to the overall freshness of impression.' Mr Stein tries to persuade his customers to have their lobsters grilled and buttered straight from the tanks; likewise the Camel oysters (£3-30 for six) are served* nature, *and sea bass or salmon peel with a light butter and chive lemon sauce, a version of beurre nantais. 'Steak with an outdoor flavour' (oak chippings again) is also offered, but the short menu has little else for fish-haters apart from good soups and vegetables, and simple sweets (or cheese with home-made bread). The likeliest wines are the Sancerres and Muscadets in the £6 range, though whites from other regions, such as Poitou and Arbois, and countries (including English Adgestone '76) denote intelligent interest. Blanc de Blancs is £2-40 for half a carafe, the Cornish Cider Company in Penryn supply cider, and there may be Devenish bitter this year. 'Unfussy' and mostly efficient service. More reports, please.*

PADSTOW

1982 *Jill and Richard Stein's restaurant, a whelk's throw from the quayside of this inviting town, is limited in both season and repertoire. But this is no reproach to a chef who, unlike his innumerable counterparts in France, has had to set up a 'vertical' operation, humping his own mussels and digging his own clams before cooking and serving them for – sometimes – as sparse or dégagé clientele.*

1983 *Off-season, Richard Stein still attends the local technical college to hone his culinary skills, despite seven years running this unusual ground-floor restaurant under a block of flats rented out to holidaymakers. 'The raw materials,' he says, 'are more important than high skills in cooking.' The Steins have their own oyster beds at Seamills (£3-90 for a half-dozen), get their soles from the Barbican market in Devon off boats they trust to store fish properly, and their lobsters from a fisherman at Padstow who delivers daily to the restaurant tanks from which you pick your own… . Richard's cooking gets unanimous praise… . A set menu impressed with carrot and coriander soup, whole grilled lemon sole with lobster butter, and strawberry ice-cream topped with strawberry slices… . They are planning to offer a few local cheeses.*

1984 *Richard Stein became the fish correspondent for* Woman's Realm *last year, which is unlikely to distract from his main living because this is a serious fish place. Lobsters start at £9, plates of shellfish are £6-95, or there is a three-course menu at £8. The dining-room is white and well lit. Specialities are bouillabaisse – made without rascasse but with turbot, monk-fish, brill, mullet, mussels and langoustines with a saffron liquor, and the local salmon trout, coated in clotted cream and tarragon, wrapped in puff pastry, baked eleven minutes and served with a reduced wine sauce. Fennel is rampant in these parts and he uses it to cure mackerel which is then served with smoked sea trout and mayonnaise.*

1985–1994

PURPLE TIGER'S KITCHEN SOUNDTRACK

The best-selling album of the decade, Dire Straits' *Brothers in Arms*, is released in May, featuring such enduring classics as "Money for Nothing" and "Walk of Life".

1985 FLOYD ON FISH

David Pritchard, producer for the BBC's *Floyd on Fish*, contacts Rick to ask him if he and the chef/restaurateur/television presenter, Keith Floyd, can visit for an episode of the show.

AUSTRALIA – PART TWO

The Steins head off to Australia over the winter months again – this time stopping in Bangkok for more culinary adventures to provide inspiration for the menu back home.

1989 COOKBOOK OF THE YEAR

English Seafood Cookery wins the prestigious Glenfiddich award for Cook Book of the Year.

1986 AUSTRALIA BOUND

The Steins make their first family trip to Australia, stopping in Singapore and soaking up the food and culture with a mind to introduce what they discover to The Seafood menu when they return.

1988 ENGLISH SEAFOOD COOKERY

Penguin publishes Rick's first book, *English Seafood Cookery*.

DECANTER AWARD

The Seafood Restaurant wins *Decanter*'s Restaurant of the Year.

1992 JACK IN THE KITCHEN

Twelve-year-old Jack gets his first taste of working in The Seafood kitchen, as a kitchen porter.

1990 RICK STEIN'S CAFÉ

Rick and Jill open a café above the Deli.

1993 AT THE CINEMA

Jurassic Park is released and becomes the UK's highest-grossing movie of the decade.

1994 ST PETROC'S HOTEL & BISTRO

Rick and Jill buy St Petroc's, which was already running as a simple hotel. They develop it so that it becomes not only a hotel but also a bistro serving food from Britain and the Mediterranean.

ED ARRIVES IN THE KITCHEN; JACK GOES FRONT OF HOUSE

Ed, aged 15, starts working with Rick in the kitchen at The Seafood – although his calling, ultimately, is in the project management of the business's buildings and renovations. Jack, still at school but working in his spare time, moves front of house, enjoying the opportunity to interact with the customers.

1985–1994

Meurette of lemon sole with Beaujolais

One of the prizes we received at the restaurant gave us the opportunity to visit a number of restaurants in France, including around Lyon. The idea for this dish came from a restaurant in Fleurie (which also gives is name to a Beaujolais wine) where the dish was made with zander, so I just adapted it to work with lemon sole.

Serves 4

350g lemon sole fillets, skin on
25g unsalted butter
1 tablespoon plain flour
salt and freshly ground
　black pepper

FOR THE CROÛTONS
2 slices of white bread
25ml groundnut oil
a knob of butter

FOR THE RED WINE STOCK
25g butter
225g equal quantities of
　carrot, celery, leek and onion
　chopped and mixed together
1 tablespoon brandy
900ml Chicken Stock
　(page 270)
½ bottle of Beaujolais
1 fresh or dried bay leaf
1 thyme sprig or ½ teaspoon
　dried thyme

First, make the croûtons. Using a 2.5cm round cutter, cut out 8 discs from the slices of bread. Heat the groundnut oil in a frying pan over a medium–high heat and fry the bread discs, turning and adding a little knob of butter to the pan to given them a golden colour, until crisp on both sides.

To make the red wine stock, melt the butter in a pan and add the chopped mixed vegetables (known as mirepoix) and fry them until they are just beginning to brown (about 5–6 minutes). Add the brandy and boil off the alcohol before adding the 900ml of chicken stock, along with the Beaujolais, bay leaf and thyme. Bring to the boil and simmer for 30 minutes.

Meanwhile, for the meurette, brown the shallots with the sugar and butter in a shallow pan. Add the 300ml of chicken stock and simmer the shallots gently for about 15 minutes until they are tender, then turn up the heat and reduce the shallots and stock for 10 minutes until you have a shiny brown glaze. Set aside and keep warm.

To make the persillade, finely chop the garlic and parsley together. Set aside.

To make the garnish, cut the bacon into thin strips and fry them gently in the butter, add the mushrooms and continue to fry until soft (about 8 minutes). Season with salt and black pepper, then set aside and keep warm.

...ingredients and method continued overleaf

144　The Seafood Signature Recipes

The Seafood Signature Recipes 145

Charlie's Wine Notes

This is a dish to blow the "Can-I-drink-red-wine-with-fish?" question out of the water. There's a good slug of Beaujolais in the sauce, so a totally appropriate wine match would be that same wine – a slightly chilled Fleurie is just the ticket.

Jack's Chef Notes

During this decade, Beaujolais became very popular, so while this recipe is unusual in its use of red wine, the results are a great success. Rightly so – it's a really hearty dish.

FOR THE MEURETTE
24 shallots, peeled
¼ teaspoon sugar
15g butter
300ml Chicken Stock (page 270)

FOR THE PERSILLADE
1 small garlic clove
1 small bunch of flat-leaf parsley

FOR THE MUSHROOM AND BACON GARNISH
1 rasher of streaky bacon, rind removed
15g butter
225g button mushrooms, quartered

To make the final dish, strain the red wine stock into a shallow pan, bring to the boil and boil rapidly, to reduce the volume by half. Add the fish fillets and cook gently until just tender. This should take about 5 minutes.

In the meantime, mix the butter with the flour to make a paste – this is known as beurre manié. Remove the fillets from the pan and place them neatly on a warmed serving dish. Break the beurre manié into small pieces and stir the pieces, a few at a time, into the red wine sauce. Continue to stir until the sauce thickens. Add the meurette and the mushroom and bacon garnish. Check the seasoning and add a little salt if necessary.

Spread each of the croûtons with an equal amount of the persillade, then spoon the sauce over the fish, top with the croûtons, and serve.

Singapore chilli crab

During the mid-1980s, we made a family visit to Australia and we stopped at Singapore on the way. There, we ate crab that gave me the idea of serving seafood with really spicy sauces – that was something groundbreaking for us at the time, to create a dish that was all about the chilli. I love that the dish asks people to pick through a crab that has been bashed open – we take off the back shell, split up the body section and crack the claws. It's a lot to eat, but it's wonderful and we still have it on the menu today – when we have the capacity for it, and the time for all that eating to be done.

Serves 4

- 2 x 900g live or whole cooked crabs (see pages 248–9)
- 4 tablespoons groundnut or sunflower oil
- 4 fat garlic cloves, finely chopped
- 2.5cm fresh ginger root, finely chopped
- 4 tablespoons tomato ketchup
- 3 medium–hot red chillies, finely chopped
- 2 tablespoons dark soy sauce
- freshly ground black pepper
- 2 spring onions, cut into 5cm pieces and finely shredded lengthways, to serve

If you are using live crabs, turn them on their backs with the eyes facing you. First, drive a thick skewer or a thin-bladed knife between the eyes and into the centre of the crab. Then, lift up the tail flap and drive the skewer through the underside.

For uncooked and cooked crabs, prepare for stir-frying by breaking off and discarding the tail flaps. Break off the claws, then using a large-bladed knife, cut them in half at the joint. Crack the shells with a hammer or the back of the knife. Chop the body section of each crab in half, then gently tug on the legs to pull the pieces away from the back shell. You can use a knife as a lever but the body pieces should come away easily with the legs attached. Turn each piece over and pick off the soft gills (dead man's fingers), then cut them in half again so you have two legs attached to each piece. Discard the back shells or save for stock.

Heat the oil in a large wok. Add the crab pieces and stir-fry for 1 minute. Add the garlic and the ginger and stir-fry for a further 2 minutes. Add about a quarter of the brown meat from the back shell (the remainder will keep in an airtight container in the fridge for up to 2 days, to use in another dish), along with the tomato ketchup, red chillies, soy sauce, 150ml of water and a few turns of black pepper. Cover the wok and simmer the liquid over a medium heat for 5 minutes if the crab is fresh or 2–3 minutes if the crab is cooked. Serve the crab straight away with the shredded spring onions scattered over.

148   The Seafood Signature Recipes

Charlie's Wine Notes

I could talk about off-dry Rieslings for Chilli Crab (see recipe, page 147), but actually what we'd all drink in Singapore would be lots and lots of ice-cold Tiger beers. Perfection.

Jack's Chef Notes

I once saw Dad move from the vegetable section in the kitchen to show the chef on mains, John Walton, how to cook this dish properly – the whole kitchen stopped to watch. When Dad left, we had to cook it for 75 people at once. John cooked better than I've ever seen him cook to get all those covers out.

Jack's Chef Notes

If you've never tried serving oysters, this is a great recipe to start with because they are cooked. As a chef making it in a kitchen, beurre blanc is a very friendly sauce – because it doesn't split.

Charlie's Wine Notes

Raw oysters call for a light white wine, but here, where they are cooked with a rich beurre blanc, a lightly oaked Macon-Chardonnay is far more the thing.

Oysters with beurre blanc and spinach

There was a stage when we had a lot of oysters coming in to the restaurant and poaching them meant that we could make sure we used them at their best – lightly poached and served in the shell with a rich beurre blanc.

Serves 4

boiling water, from a kettle
16 oysters in the shell, well scrubbed
16 spinach leaves, washed and stalks removed

FOR THE BEURRE BLANC
25g finely chopped shallot or onion
1 tablespoon white wine vinegar
1 tablespoon dry white wine
150g unsalted butter, cut into small pieces

Pre-heat the grill to high.

Place a trivet into the bottom of a large pan and pour in about 5cm of boiling water – the trivet should sit above the water level.

Place the oysters on a plate and, carefully, protecting your hands, rest the plate on the top of the trivet.

Cover the pan, place it over a high heat and steam the oysters for about 4 minutes until they are just opened. Remove just the oysters from the pan and open them fully, taking care to save all the juices that come out of them (you'll need them for the beurre blanc). Put the spinach leaves on the plate in the steamer and steam for 2 minutes until wilted. Remove and set aside.

Make the beurre blanc. Put the shallot or onion, vinegar, wine and 50ml of water into a small pan. Add the juice from the oysters and simmer until only 2 tablespoons of liquid are left. Take the pan off the heat and, a few at a time, whisk in the pieces of butter to build up a light emulsion. Keep warm.

Remove the oyster meats from the shells and place a folded leaf of spinach into the base of each shell. Place the shells on to a baking tray and push them very briefly under the grill to warm the spinach. Remove and place the oysters on top. Pour a little beurre blanc over each one and slide the shells back under the grill for about 15–20 seconds to warm the oysters through. Serve immediately.

Pan-fried fillet of monkfish with new-season garlic and fennel

This recipe has stood the test of time; and again it is influenced by a trip to France. This time, I'd found a grocer selling new-season garlic (available during late spring and early summer). It occurred to me that that would make a delicious dish with fennel. The combination works really well with monkfish.

Serves 4

16 large garlic cloves, peeled (new season, if possible)
100g semolina
15g fennel-herb sprigs
100g unsalted butter
2 fennel bulbs, thinly sliced
600ml Fish Stock (page 270)
4 pieces of prepared monkfish fillet, each about 225g
4 tablespoons sunflower oil
2 teaspoons lemon juice
a splash of Pernod
salt and freshly ground black pepper

Slice 2 of the garlic cloves and put them with the semolina and all but 1 fennel sprig into a food processor and blend until you have an aromatic pale-green powder. Set aside.

Cut the remaining garlic cloves lengthways into long, thin pieces. Melt half the butter in a pan, add the fennel bulbs and garlic and fry over a medium heat for 10 minutes to lightly brown. Add half the stock, season, and simmer for 15 minutes until the fennel is tender.

Pre-heat the oven to 200°C/180°C fan. Coat the pieces of monkfish in the semolina mixture.

Heat the oil in an ovenproof frying pan over a medium heat. Add a small knob of the remaining butter and all the monkfish and fry, turning now and then, until golden all over (about 3–4 minutes altogether). Transfer the pan to the oven and bake the monkfish in the hot oven for a further 8 minutes until cooked through.

Remove the pan from the oven, lift the fillets on to a chopping board, and rest them for 4–5 minutes. Cut each diagonally into thick slices, keeping each fillet in shape. Transfer to a plate and keep warm.

Finely chop the remaining fennel herb. Add the sautéed fennel mixture, lemon juice, Pernod, remaining stock and chopped herb to the empty monkfish pan over a high heat. Simmer rapidly to reduce, then add the remaining butter, simmering to melt and combine to make a rich sauce. Adjust the seasoning, if necessary. Lift the fish on to 4 warmed plates and spoon some sauce around each to serve.

Charlie's Wine Notes

Fennel is a tricky ingredient for wine pairing – the herbaceous and aniseed qualities don't sit well next to purely fruity wines. And monkfish is a meaty fish, so we need a wine with lots of weight. I'd go for a Chardonnay, but maybe a more taut style... perhaps even from an English producer, like the brilliant Danbury Ridge in Essex.

Jack's Chef Notes

Monkfish was an under-appreciated fish in the 1980s, when Dad first brought it on to the menu. This dish is a favourite of the chefs, because it requires perfect braising of the fennel and garlic, perfect sauce work with the emulsion, and then cooking the monkfish to the perfect 50°C, resting it, and the satisfaction of slicing it, knowing it is just right.

The Seafood Signature Recipes

1985–1994

Bourride of red mullet, gurnard and fresh salted cod

In 1978, during a trip to Saint Tropez, I had a bourride – properly made, this Provençal fish stew is really quite a thing and I immediately loved everything about it. All that garlic just works. The croûtons in this recipe come from a tip given to me by the late Keith Floyd, who was the first to suggest to me topping each one with spicy, homemade harissa. Using salted cod lifts the flavours to make this extra-delicious.

Serves 4

200–250g skin-on red mullet fillet
200–250g skin-on gurnard
200–250g fresh salted cod (see box, page 157; or buy it salted from your fishmonger)
2 tablespoons olive oil
1 onion, chopped
1 small leek, cleaned and chopped
½ fennel bulb, chopped
4 garlic cloves, chopped
2 thick strips of orange zest
2 tomatoes, sliced
1 bay leaf
1 thyme sprig
1.2 litres Fish Stock (page 270)
½ teaspoon salt
12 fresh mussels, beards trimmed

Make the aïoli. Add the garlic, salt, egg yolk and lemon juice to a large bowl. Combine using a whisk or an electric hand-held mixer, then very gradually whisk in the olive oil to make a thick mayonnaise-like sauce. Set aside.

For the bourride, first cut all the fish into 50g pieces. Set aside.

Heat the oil in a large pan and, when hot, add the onion, leek, fennel, garlic and orange zest and fry gently without colouring for 5 minutes. Add the tomatoes, bay leaf, thyme, fish stock and salt, bring to the boil, then lower the heat and simmer for 30 minutes.

While the tomato mixture is cooking, make the croûtons. Heat the oil in a frying pan over a medium–high heat. Add the bread slices and fry on both sides until crisp and golden. Spread the croûtons with harissa, and keep warm.

Add the fish pieces to the tomato sauce and simmer gently for 5 minutes to cook through. Add the mussels for the last 3 minutes of the cooking time, cooking them through (discard any that don't open), then carefully lift out all the fish and divide it between 4 warmed serving dishes. Keep warm.

FOR THE CROÛTONS

2 tablespoons olive oil
4 x 2.5cm-thick slices of baguette, cut on the slant
1 recipe quantity of Harissa (page 270)

FOR THE AÏOLI (MAKES 175ML)

4 garlic cloves, peeled and mashed or grated
½ teaspoon salt
1 egg yolk, at room temperature
2 teaspoons lemon juice
175ml extra virgin olive oil

Strain the cooking liquor through a fine sieve into a clean pan, pressing out as much liquid as you can with the back of a ladle.

Whisk a ladleful of the cooking liquor into the bowl with the aïoli. Stir this mixture into the pan containing the strained cooking liquor and cook it over a low heat until slightly thickened – aim for the consistency of single cream. Do not let it boil.

Pour the sauce equally over the servings of fish. Serve each portion topped with a croûton.

Jack's Chef Notes

Bourride might be a classic fish stew, but this version is restaurant-ified and is thickened with the aïoli, which makes it really special to eat – although for a chef it can be tricky to get right.

Charlie's Wine Notes

Many Provençal locals drink Bandol rosé with bourride, which works really well. I'd personally go for a Provençal white, though, perhaps from Luberon.

The Seafood Signature Recipes

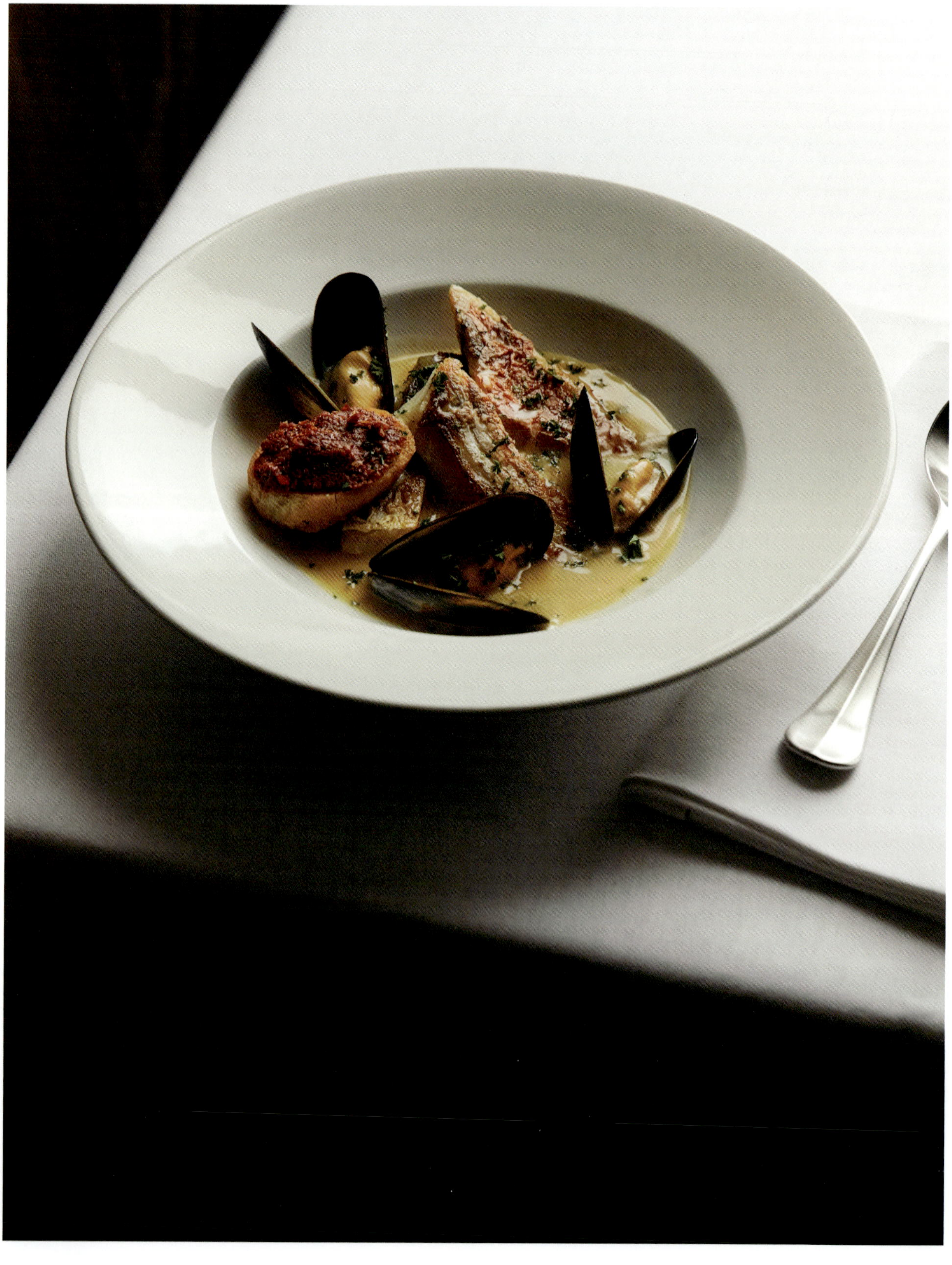

Salting fresh cod

Pour a 1cm-deep layer of salt over the base of a shallow plastic container. Put a thick piece of unskinned cod fillet on top and cover the fish with another thick layer of salt. Cover the container and refrigerate overnight.

The next day, lift the now-rigid piece of cod out of the salt and rinse under cold water.

Put it into a large bowl and cover with lots of fresh water. Leave to soak for 1 hour. (Commercially produced salt cod will be almost completely dried out and needs much longer soaking.) Rinse off the excess salt and leave to soak in lots of cold water for 24–48 hours, depending on its thickness, changing the water now and then.

Drain the cod and remove the skin and bones. Simmer gently in water for 5 minutes, then lift out and drain well. Use as instructed in the recipe.

1985–1994

Cod and mussel chowder

A "classic" American chowder varies according to region and ours is inspired by wonderful trips to New England, where the chowders come with a milk base and potatoes, salt pork, cod and some kind of shellfish – often lobster or clams. We use mussels, which are so abundant on our own Cornish coastline.

Serves 4

20 fresh mussels
30g butter
60g salt pork, cut into small dice
120g onions, diced
300ml whole milk
120ml double cream
1 bay leaf, sliced (preferably a fresh one)
240g potatoes, cut into 5cm dice and not washed (you need the starch to thicken the liquid)
120g skinless cod fillet, cut into 5cm pieces
salt and freshly ground black pepper
a small amount of chopped flat-leaf parsley, to serve
2 water biscuits, crushed, to serve

Clean the mussels and open them by placing them in a pan with a splash of water and steaming them over a high heat with a lid on the saucepan. As soon as the mussels open, take the pan off the heat and drain the mussels through a colander, saving the cooking liquor in a bowl underneath.

When the mussels have cooled enough to handle, remove the meats from the shells and take out the beards. Discard the shells and beards and set the meats aside.

Melt the butter in a large frying pan over a medium–high heat. Add the diced pork and fry for 5–6 minutes, stirring occasionally, until it is beginning to brown. Then, add the onions and fry for 3–4 minutes until soft.

At the same time, pour the milk and cream into a large saucepan and add the bay leaf. Place the pan over a medium heat, tip in the potatoes and bring them to the boil. Simmer until firm but not raw (about 10–12 minutes). Add the pork and onions and the reserved cooking juice from the mussels and simmer for another 5 minutes. Season with salt, if necessary, and black pepper.

Add the cod pieces and simmer for 4–5 minutes until the fish is cooked, then remove the pan from the heat and add the mussels (it's important that you don't continue to cook at this point, or you will toughen the mussels up).

Pour the chowder into a serving tureen or 4 warmed bowls and finish with the chopped parsley and crushed water biscuits.

The Seafood Signature Recipes

Jack's Chef Notes

This is a real winter warmer – wholesome East Coast American comfort food of the kind that really sets you up for the colder months of the year.

Charlie's Wine Notes

I'm a fan of the texture and thrust of a good white Bordeaux for our Cod and Mussel Chowder. They are a great match.

The Seafood Signature Recipes

1985–1994

Mackerel recheado

In the mid-1980s, before the boys were in school, we went on family holidays to Goa, often returning to the same hotel year after year. There, the owner gathered a really good brigade of chefs, and I'd spend time in the kitchen with them, watching them cook (I even encouraged one or two to come to Cornwall). The dish I liked best was pomfret with a sort of masala – so I reinvented it at home, with mackerel, and we still have it on the menu today, albeit with a slightly simplified masala. Tied together with bits of cotton string, it looks beautiful – I don't know another British restaurant that serves it that way. It works really well.

Serves 4

4 large mackerel, each about 275–350g, backbone removed
seasoned flour, for dusting
groundnut or vegetable oil, for frying
Kachumber Salad, to serve (page 271)
lemon wedges, to serve

FOR THE MASALA PASTE
½ teaspoon cumin seeds
2 teaspoons coriander seeds
1 teaspoon peppercorns
½ teaspoon cloves
¼ teaspoon turmeric
½ teaspoon salt
½ teaspoon sugar
5 red chillies
3 garlic cloves
a walnut-sized piece of tamarind, seeded
5cm fresh ginger root
2 tablespoons red wine vinegar

For the masala paste, grind together the cumin seeds, coriander seeds, peppercorns, cloves, turmeric, salt and sugar in a pestle and mortar, spice mill or very clean coffee grinder. If using a pestle and mortar, add the chillies, garlic, tamarind, ginger and wine vinegar and pound to a paste. Otherwise, combine the dry and wet ingredients in a liquidiser using a little water to loosen the paste, but not turn it to liquid.

Pre-heat the oven to its highest setting.

Apply a generous layer of masala paste to the insides of the fish. Reassemble each fish and secure each in two places with tied string. Dust the fish with the seasoned flour and shake off any excess.

Heat the oil in a roasting tin on the hob over a medium heat and fry the mackerel on one side until they turn deep brown (about 3–4 minutes). Turn the fish over and bake them in the oven for about 8 minutes until cooked through.

Serve the fish tied, snipping the string at the last moment, with the kachumber salad and a lemon wedge on the side.

Charlie's Wine Notes

In 2007, with Sharp's brewery, we came up with the perfect beer to match with oily fish: Chalky's Bite, named for our beloved family Jack Russell (see page 45). The beer has since won award after award. It's a Belgian-style beer with added fennel and works wonders with Mackerel Recheado.

Jack's Chef Notes

This recipe is a classic starter at The Seafood, and for me is such a lovely reminder of our many trips to India. My top tip is that it is important to have a pair of sharp scissors to snip the string.

The Seafood Signature Recipes

Grilled scallops in the shell with toasted hazelnut and coriander butter

The first scallops I had were in Australia, during my round-the-world trip in 1966. I really like cooking scallops that are still stuck to the half shell – that way, you get the real deal. This recipe provides a very pleasing combination of toasted hazelnuts with coriander and butter. The flavours really work together – which is probably why this dish arrived on the menu after my trip and has never really left.

Serves 4

12 prepared scallops in the shell (see box, page 164)
25g unsalted butter, melted

FOR THE TOASTED HAZELNUT AND CORIANDER BUTTER
20g unblanched hazelnuts
75g unsalted butter, softened
2 tablespoons chopped coriander leaves
2 tablespoons chopped flat-leaf parsley leaves
½ shallot, roughly chopped
1 teaspoon lemon juice
salt and freshly ground black pepper

Pre-heat the grill to high.

For the toasted hazelnut and coriander butter, spread the hazelnuts over a baking tray and toast them under the grill for 4–5 minutes, shaking the tray now and then, until they are golden brown. Tip them into a clean tea towel and rub off the skins, then put the nuts into a food processor.

Add the softened butter and the coriander, parsley, shallot and lemon juice, and season with a good pinch of salt and some pepper. Blend together until semi-smooth.

Put the scallops on to a large baking tray (do them in batches, if necessary) and brush the meats with the melted butter. Season with a little salt and pepper, then grill for 1½ minutes.

Drop a generous teaspoonful of the hazelnut and coriander butter on to each scallop and return them to the grill for a further 1½ minutes until they are cooked through. Serve 3 scallops per person.

Charlie's Wine Notes

The natural sweetness of scallops is the perfect accompaniment to an oaked Chardonnay, especially when it comes with the hazelnut butter. I'd go Aussie, from the Margaret River region, south of Perth.

Jack's Chef Notes

We have always served scallops in the shell, even when that went out of fashion in the 1990s, when everyone else was pan-frying them. Like all trends, shells have come full circle and are now back in vogue.

The Seafood Signature Recipes

Preparing scallops

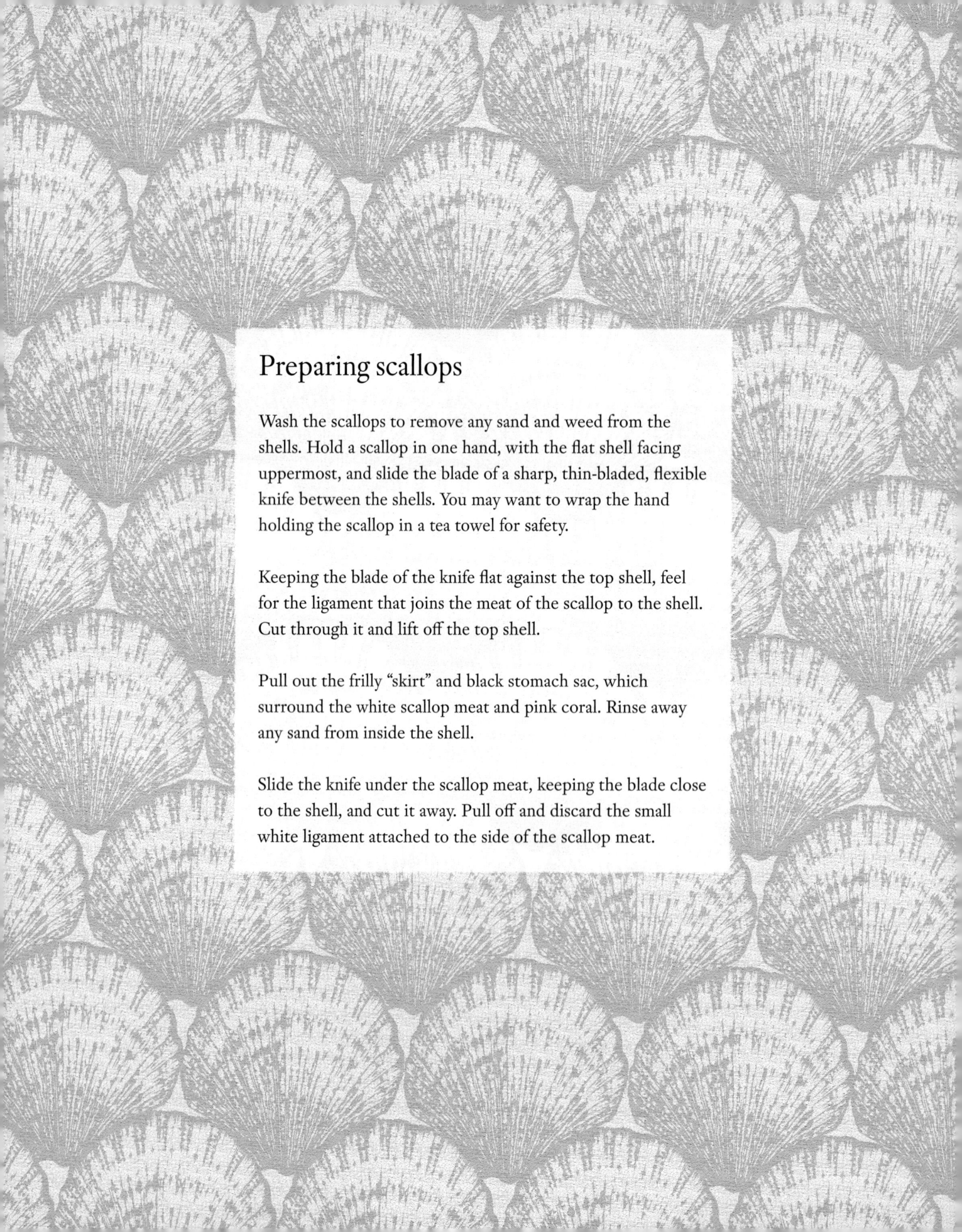

Wash the scallops to remove any sand and weed from the shells. Hold a scallop in one hand, with the flat shell facing uppermost, and slide the blade of a sharp, thin-bladed, flexible knife between the shells. You may want to wrap the hand holding the scallop in a tea towel for safety.

Keeping the blade of the knife flat against the top shell, feel for the ligament that joins the meat of the scallop to the shell. Cut through it and lift off the top shell.

Pull out the frilly "skirt" and black stomach sac, which surround the white scallop meat and pink coral. Rinse away any sand from inside the shell.

Slide the knife under the scallop meat, keeping the blade close to the shell, and cut it away. Pull off and discard the small white ligament attached to the side of the scallop meat.

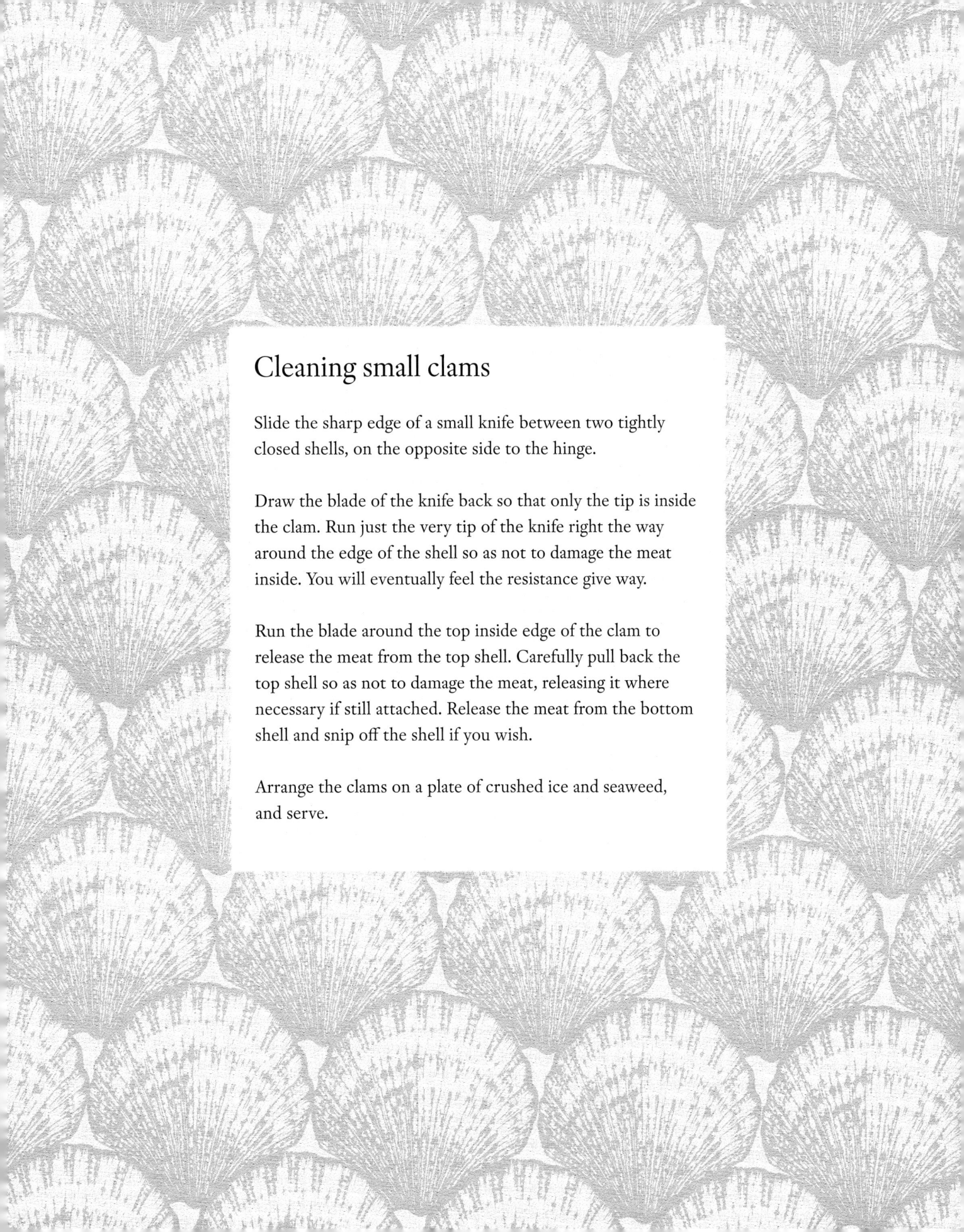

Cleaning small clams

Slide the sharp edge of a small knife between two tightly closed shells, on the opposite side to the hinge.

Draw the blade of the knife back so that only the tip is inside the clam. Run just the very tip of the knife right the way around the edge of the shell so as not to damage the meat inside. You will eventually feel the resistance give way.

Run the blade around the top inside edge of the clam to release the meat from the top shell. Carefully pull back the top shell so as not to damage the meat, releasing it where necessary if still attached. Release the meat from the bottom shell and snip off the shell if you wish.

Arrange the clams on a plate of crushed ice and seaweed, and serve.

Hot shellfish with garlic and lemon juice

This recipe is inspired by the dishes I had on holiday in Venice, with our great friend Bill Baker, who spent time after graduating taking tourists on discovery tours of the city (and would later become a giant in the wine world). There, we visited a restaurant named Corte Sconta ("Hidden Courtyard") where they serve up small shellfish pulled from the lagoon. It suits our Padstow "lagoon" perfectly – we have mussels and winkles in abundance; they are the cornerstones of our food.

Serves 4

8 cooked Dublin Bay prawns or Mediterranean prawns (crevettes)
32 winkles
4 whelks
24 fresh mussels, cleaned
50ml dry white wine
20 cockles, washed
16 small clams, such as carpetshell, cleaned (see box, page 165)
8 Pacific oysters
85ml extra virgin olive oil
2 garlic cloves, finely chopped
1 medium–hot red Dutch chilli, seeded and chopped
juice of ½ lemon
1 handful of flat-leaf parsley leaves, chopped

Heat 5cm of water in a large saucepan with a lid, to steam all of the ingredients in the saucepan steamer. Re-heat the Dublin Bay prawns, and the winkles and whelks if they are already cooked, for 2–3 minutes.

If the winkles and whelks are raw, drop them into separate pans of boiling salted water and cook the winkles for 1 minute and the whelks for 4 minutes. Drain and keep warm.

Put the mussels into a pan with the white wine. Cover and cook over a high heat for 3–4 minutes until they have opened (discard any that remain shut). Lift out the cooked mussels with a slotted spoon, and transfer them to a bowl. Cover and keep warm. Repeat with the cockles, small clams and oysters, using the same cooking liquor. The oysters will not open fully, so finish opening them with a short, thick-bladed knife.

Make a dressing by combining the olive oil, garlic, chilli and lemon juice and warm through for 2–3 minutes, finishing with the parsley.

Arrange the warm shellfish on a large, warmed serving platter. Bring the dressing to the boil, then pour it over the shellfish and serve with plenty of French bread.

Charlie's Wine Notes

This is my favourite starter on our menu and I always drink a textbook classic French Sancerre or Pouilly-Fumé with it – crisp and light to match the shellfish.

Jack's Chef Notes

I'd say this is the signature starter at The Seafood Restaurant. This recipe simplifies the dressing for making at home, but in the restaurant we take the liquor from steaming the shellfish and quickly reduce it with the other dressing ingredients.

The Seafood Signature Recipes   167

VICTORIA
Carol Shields The Stone Diaries
PETER CAREY The Fat Man in History
'Tis
FRANK McCOURT

The Kindness of Strangers
RODDY DOYLE A Star Called Henry
Red Earth and Pouring Rain Vikram Chandra

Charlie's Wine Notes

Ice cream and Pedro Ximénez sherry are the perfect match – no other explanation needed.

Jack's Chef Notes

This is the perfect example of something that happens all the time in restaurant kitchens: mishaps can be the creation of fantastic new dishes. These days we serve the ice cream with a dark chocolate, orange and pistachio biscotto on top – but back in the day, just the ice cream was innovation enough.

170   The Seafood Signature Recipes

Crème brûlée ice cream

This recipe – a very rich custard ice cream, studded with sweet caramel pieces – was a happy accident, from around the mid-1980s. I was making crème brûlée under the Salamander (our restaurant grill), because I preferred it that way to using a blow torch, and got distracted. By the time I came back to my desserts, the cream was split and the sugar on top was rock hard. I didn't want to waste it all, so I suggested we scoop everything into the ice-cream machine and see what happened. This was the result.

Serves 8

200ml whole milk
375ml double cream
1 teaspoon vanilla extract
5 egg yolks
120g caster sugar

Put the milk, cream and vanilla extract into a pan over a medium heat and bring the liquid slowly to the boil.

Meanwhile, beat the egg yolks with 50g of the caster sugar until pale and creamy. Gradually beat in the hot milk and cream, then return the mixture to the pan and cook over a gentle heat until you have a custard that is thick enough to coat the back of the spoon. Do not let it boil or it will curdle.

Pour the custard into a shallow, ovenproof dish measuring about 25cm by 25cm – the custard should be about 2.5cm deep and come near the top of the dish. Leave to cool, then cover the surface with a layer of greaseproof paper (to stop a skin forming) and chill for about 6 hours, or until set.

Pre-heat the grill to its highest setting. Remove the custard from the fridge and sprinkle with the remaining caster sugar. Put it under the grill for about 5 minutes until the sugar has caramelised. Alternatively, if you have a blowtorch, you can achieve the same results by playing the flame across the top of the sugar. Remove from the grill (if necessary), and leave to cool.

Break up the caramel topping here and there with the handle of a kitchen knife and stir the pieces into the creamy mixture below. Transfer the mixture to an ice-cream maker and churn according to the manufacturer's instructions, until firm. Transfer to a freezerproof container and store in the freezer until needed.

ENGLAND

The Good Food Guide

▲ Seafood Restaurant 🍾

1986 An uncomplicated, now very popular fish restaurant. The enormous seafood platter arrives loaded with mussels, prawns, king prawns, whole crab and so on, all virtually untampered with by the kitchen. The supply lines are Real Food in the best sense – lobsters, crabs and crawfish from local fishermen; mussels, cockles and winkles from the Camel estuary; oysters and clams from Porth Navas in Cornwall; langoustines from the Irish Sea via Newlyn in summer or overnight train from Loch Fyne in Argyll in winter... . This plain cooking is typical. 'I dislike dishes such as lobster thermidor because they smother the flavour of the fresh lobsters,' says Mr Stein. Thermidor is hence employed only with lesser fish. But even so the kitchen can cook elegant dishes – salmon steak in puff pastry with a Muscadet and herb sauce recalls the great days of the Horn of Plenty at Gulworthy.

1988 This is one of the great fish restaurants, right on the quay, in case anyone should doubt the freshness of the produce. Padstow is in an area of outstanding natural beauty, reached via some outstandingly steep and twisted narrow streets, and its fleet still puts out. The atmosphere is relaxed and unpretentious, almost like the Walnut Tree Inn at Llanddewi Skirrid, but spacious, white, full of healthy plants and invariably busy with variously dressed customers. What the long menu does, it does brilliantly, because fish dishes are best when they are simple and Rick Stein's genius is to keep them that way, which is not to say plain... . The menu changes daily, which Mr Stein says has completely galvanised the kitchen.

1989 Rick Stein has developed into one of the most sensitive and creative fish cooks in the country. In the mood of the late 1980s the décor offers a sense of light and space with bright white walls and plenty of daylight. The feel is almost Mediterranean. In June a delicatessen selling charcuterie and cooked dishes opened. Bedrooms overlooking the harbour have been added. All of this has grown from the small upstairs above a night-club in the late 1970s, and the extra rating point is well earned. The place retains an easy-going seaside character with art posters and a loyal following of smart and unsmart; young and old. The menu is a grand sweep of modern thinking on fish cookery... . There is an understanding here of flavours and textures that extends to desserts such as fine strawberries in a sweet tart case filled with Chantilly cream and served with a port and black peppercorn sauce, or poached pear sliced onto a nest of puff pastry, served with lime ice-cream. Espresso coffee. 'Happiest meal I've had in a long time.'

1990 This has been a good year for the Steins. Rick's book on fish was given the Glenfiddich Award for the best cookbook of the year; their restaurant was variously be-laureated. Hardly surprising, for by any standards it is exceptional. Padstow is a small north Cornish fishing town now much prettified and improved... . The cooking is as up-to-date as Alastair Little's, Simon Hopkinson's or anyone else's in London. It has many ideas that amuse by their intelligence; it joins simple and direct flavours together to great effect; it does not seek to impress by complexity... . The staff are young, local and cheerful. When the place is full, they run.

1993 Rick Stein Inc. grows and grows. The shop and bakery (round the corner in downtown Padstow) have been refurbished and extended, there is talk of a coffee-shop, a new book is due, and the restaurant is now open for lunch every day. The Seafood shows that real restaurants – busy, good, bright and humming with every sort of life – can exist in Britain, and can make money.

1995–2004

TASTE OF THE SEA
Rick's first TV programme, *Taste of the Sea*, airs on the BBC, putting The Seafood Restaurant firmly on the destination-dining map. Both the TV programme and the accompanying book win awards.

GOOD HOTEL GUIDE
The Seafood Restaurant and rooms win the Good Hotel Guide's Cesar Award.

1995 ST DECAMON'S
The Steins buy St Decamon's, next door to St Petroc's, enabling them to add rooms to the hotel.

1996 A NEW KITCHEN
Rick and Jill buy the property behind The Seafood Restaurant, enabling them to dismantle the old kitchen, extend to create a new one, and increase the size of the restaurant.

EGON RONAY GUIDE

The Seafood Restaurant wins *Egon Ronay*'s Restaurant of the Year.

CAFÉ EXPANSION

Within four years, the café has outgrown its small space and so Rick and Jill buy the next-door building in Middle Street and expand, introducing a far more substantial menu and adding three rooms above.

1998 AT THE CINEMA

Titanic is released in the UK and becomes the UK's highest-grossing movie of the decade.

HOTEL & RESTAURANT MAGAZINE

The Seafood Restaurant wins *Hotel & Restaurant Magazine*'s Seafood Restaurant of the Year – an achievement it repeats for the following three years, and again in 2003.

2000 STEIN'S COOKERY SCHOOL

In May, Stein's cookery school opens on the harbour front to host teaching events and cookery demonstrations.

2001 ST EDMUND'S HOUSE

St Edmund's House opens in June, following a year of renovation, to offer luxury accommodation in the heart of Padstow, just behind The Seafood Restaurant.

2002 AA AWARDS

The Seafood Restaurant wins the AA's prestigious Seafood Restaurant of the Year Award.

2003 NEW YEAR HONOURS

Rick is awarded an OBE for services to Cornwall in The Queen's New Year Honours List.

STEIN'S PATISSERIE

Head Pastry Chef Stuart Pate joins The Seafood Restaurant and helps establish Stein's Patisserie on Lanadwell Street the following year, just a stone's throw from the harbour.

JACK BACK AT THE SEAFOOD

After university and a gap year, Jack returns to The Seafood in October to learn to be a chef.

2004 STEIN'S FISH & CHIPS

Rick's dream of opening a fish-and-chip shop comes true in March, when Stein's Fish & Chips opens on the South Quay, serving fish fried to order, with homemade chips, mushy peas and tartare sauce.

PURPLE TIGER'S KITCHEN SOUNDTRACK

The best-selling album of the decade, James Blunt's *Back to Bedlam*, is released in October, pipping to the post other contenders from the decade, including *White Ladder* by David Gray (1998) and *Parachutes* by Coldplay (2000).

Fish pie

I grew up eating my mother's fish pie, which was very like this one, although she didn't use smoked haddock (but I love its smokiness) and I avoid using salmon. For a long time, I felt the restaurant didn't need staples like fish pie – I felt they weren't restaurant-y enough. But it's not true – hearty dishes are exactly what we need sometimes.

Serves 4

1 small onion, thickly sliced
2 cloves
1 bay leaf
600ml whole milk
300ml double cream
450g skin-on cod fillet
225g undyed smoked haddock fillet
4 eggs
100g butter
3 tablespoons plain flour
5 tablespoons chopped flat-leaf parsley
freshly grated nutmeg
1.25kg floury potatoes, such as Maris Piper or King Edward, peeled and quartered
1 egg yolk
salt and freshly ground white pepper

Stud a couple of onion slices with the cloves. Put these in a large pan with the bay leaf, 450ml of the milk, and the cream, cod and smoked haddock. Bring the liquid just to the boil, then simmer for 8 minutes. Lift the fish out on to a plate and strain the cooking liquor into a jug. Set both aside, leaving the fish until it is cool enough to handle.

Meanwhile, hard-boil the eggs for just 8 minutes. Drain them and leave to cool. Peel the cooled eggs, and cut them into chunky slices.

Break the cooled fish into large flakes, discarding the skin and any stray bones. Sprinkle the flakes over the base of a shallow 1.75-litre ovenproof dish. Arrange the egg on top.

Melt 50g of the butter in a pan over a medium heat. Add the flour and cook for 1 minute. Off the heat, gradually stir in the reserved cooking liquor. Return the pan to the heat and bring the liquid to the boil, stirring all the time. Simmer gently for 10 minutes to cook out the flour, then remove the pan from the heat once more, stir in the parsley and season with nutmeg, salt and white pepper. Pour the sauce over the fish and leave to cool. Chill in the fridge for 1 hour.

Meanwhile, boil the potatoes for 25–30 minutes until tender. Drain them, then tip them back into the pan and mash with the rest of the butter and the egg yolk. Season with salt and freshly ground white pepper. Beat in enough of the remaining milk to form a soft, spreadable mash. Pre-heat the oven to 200°C/180°C fan.

Spoon the potato over the filling and mark the surface with a fork. Bake for 35–40 minutes until piping hot and golden brown on top.

Jack's Chef Notes

This is a classic fish pie that came back on to the menu after Dad made *Seafood Lovers' Guide* for TV, at around the turn of the millennium. Like he says, sometimes comfort is everything we're looking for.

Charlie's Wine Notes

Talk about comfort. I don't mess around with matches when it comes to fish pie – reach for a complementary, buttery Chardonnay.

Jack's Chef Notes

Vanilla and fish might be an unusual pairing, but it works so well. In the restaurant, we clarify the butter further than most – so that it goes slightly nutty.

Charlie's Wine Notes

Sea bass is a delicate fish that suits wines with a light touch. We also have the vanilla to contend with here. For those reasons, I'd go for a fine Soave from the Veneto, in Italy.

180   The Seafood Signature Recipes

Fillets of sea bass with vanilla butter vinaigrette

This is one of Jack's favourite dishes, and was inspired by a visit to Paris, when I had lobster, painstakingly picked from the shell, dressed in exactly this way. The thing that's special about the dressing is that it is made with clarified butter and vinegar rather than olive oil or vegetable oil, which gives it an extra richness. You don't need a lot of it, so it's crucial to get the balance right, including the amount of vanilla.

Serves 4

125g unsalted butter
4 sea bass fillets, about 100g each, skin on
½ vanilla pod
50ml vermouth
2 teaspoons white wine vinegar
1 shallot, peeled and halved
150ml Fish Stock (page 270)
25g peeled, seeded and diced tomato
1 tablespoon coarsely chopped chervil
¼ teaspoon salt, plus extra to season the fish
6 turns of the black pepper mill, plus extra to season the fish

First, clarify the butter. Place the butter in a small pan and leave it over a very low heat until it has melted. Skim off any scum from the surface and pour off the clear (clarified) butter into a bowl, leaving behind the milky white solids that will have settled in the bottom of the pan.

Brush both sides of the sea bass fillets with a little of the clarified butter and season on both sides with salt and pepper. Set aside. Pre-heat a lightly oiled ridged griddle until very hot.

To make the dressing, split the vanilla pod open lengthways, scrape out the seeds with a small teaspoon and very finely chop the pod. Put the seeds and the pod into a small pan with the vermouth, vinegar and shallot. Place the pan over a high heat and bring the liquid to the boil. Boil for a few minutes until reduced to about 1 tablespoon.

Add the fish stock and boil once more until reduced to about 3 tablespoons. Remove the shallot halves, then add the remaining clarified butter, and the tomato, chervil, salt and pepper and keep the dressing just warm over a very low heat.

Make sure your griddle is hot and add the fish fillets, skin-side down. Cook for 1 minute, then flip them over and cook for 30 seconds on the other side, pressing down on the top of each fillet in turn with the back of a fish slice to help mark them with the lines from the griddle. Lift the fillets each on to 4 warmed plates and spoon the dressing around each piece of fish to serve.

1995–2004

Mussels with black beans, garlic and ginger

This has been on the menu since the mid-90s. Stir-frying the mussels in a really hot wok gives them a lovely smoky flavour. The black beans bring a delicious savouriness and the 1-2-3 of soy, rice wine vinegar (or sherry) and stock is really versatile – you can use it on any seafood: scallops, razor clams... anything.

Serves 4

- 1 teaspoon Chinese salted black beans, rinsed
- ¼ teaspoon caster sugar
- 2 tablespoons groundnut oil
- 4 garlic cloves, finely chopped
- 15g fresh ginger root, peeled and finely chopped
- 3 spring onions, trimmed and thinly sliced, white and green parts separated
- 1.75kg mussels, cleaned
- 1 tablespoon dark soy sauce
- 2 tablespoons Chinese rice wine or dry sherry
- 3 tablespoons Chicken Stock (page 270)
- 1 teaspoon arrowroot or cornflour (optional)
- 1 tablespoon chopped coriander leaves

Mash together the black beans and sugar.

Put the groundnut oil into a wok or large, deep frying pan and heat until very hot. Over a high heat, add the garlic, ginger and mashed black beans and stir-fry until the smell of hot ginger and garlic rises (about 1–2 minutes). Add the white of the spring onions and stir-fry for a few seconds. Add the mussels, soy sauce, rice wine or sherry and the stock. Cover and steam the mussels for about 3–4 minutes until they open up (discard any that stay shut).

If you prefer a thicker sauce, remove the mussels to a serving dish. Mix the arrowroot or cornflour with a little cold water to make a paste, add it to the sauce and bring to the boil, stirring to thicken.

Pour the sauce over the mussels, then scatter over the coriander and green spring onions, and serve.

Jack's Chef Notes

Mussels go so well with Asian flavours and this is one of my all-time favourite seafood dishes – simple to cook and eat but complex in flavour and a real crowd-pleaser.

Charlie's Wine Notes

There's a huge amount of flavour going on here, and I'm more inclined to beer than wine. I'd go for a new-style IPA, with plenty of flavourful American hops to match the elements in the dish.

The Seafood Signature Recipes

The Seafood Signature Recipes 183

Bouillabaisse

In the late '90s, I made a number of trips to Provence and ate bouillabaisse, which I loved, many times. But I realised that if I wanted to put this famous fish soup on the menu at The Seafood, not having small, whole rockfish, which make the dish so special in places like Marseille, meant I would need to simplify and modify it. So this is my version, which has been, apart from complaints from some purists, very popular.

Serves 8

4 small monkfish tails, each about 175–200g
12 mussels, beards trimmed
4 gurnard, each about 250–300g
4 John Dory, each about 250–300g
2 cooked lobsters, each about 500g
150ml olive oil
1 onion, chopped
½ leek, cleaned and sliced
3 carrots, peeled and diced
½ small fennel bulb, finely chopped
a pinch of crushed dried chillies
1kg skinless conger eel or pollack, cut into small chunks
100g tomato purée
100ml dry white wine
a bouquet garni of thyme, bay leaves and flat-leaf parsley
4–5 garlic cloves, chopped
½ teaspoon saffron strands
½ teaspoon mild curry powder
salt, freshly ground black pepper and cayenne pepper

When you're ready to make the bouillabaisse, prepare all the fish and make a stock. Skin the monkfish tails and remove the fillets, and fillet the gurnard and John Dory. Break off the legs and claws of the lobsters and set aside the thinner legs to make the stock. Crack the shells of the claws with the back of a knife and break at the joints into smaller pieces. Cut the rest of the lobster in half lengthways, detach the head from the tail and cut each tailpiece across into three evenly sized pieces. Put the fish fillets and lobster pieces on to a tray, cover with cling film and keep chilled until needed.

Now make a fish stock by putting the fish bones, lobster legs and 2.25 litres of water into a large pan. Bring to the boil, then reduce the heat and leave to simmer gently, uncovered, for 20 minutes. Strain the liquid into a clean pan. You should have about 2 litres of stock. If not, make it up with a little water. Set aside.

For the soup, heat the oil in a large pan. Add the vegetables and crushed dried chillies and cook gently for 20 minutes until soft but not coloured. Add the conger eel or pollack and fry briskly with the vegetables for 3–4 minutes. Add the tomato purée and white wine and the 2 litres of fish stock. Bring to the boil, add the bouquet garni, garlic, saffron, curry powder and a pinch of cayenne pepper and leave to simmer very gently, uncovered, for 1 hour.

Meanwhile, make the rouille and the croûtons. To make the rouille, cover the slice of bread with the fish stock or water and leave to soften. Squeeze out the excess liquid and put the bread into a food processor with the harissa, and the garlic, egg yolk and ¼ teaspoon of salt. Blend until smooth. With the machine still running, gradually

Jack's Chef Notes

The chefs have a love/hate relationship with this recipe – they love to eat it, but it can be hard to cook. And some of the pronunciations over the years have been comical.

Charlie's Wine Notes

So many options here. Similarly to the Bourride (see page 154), a Bandol rosé would match well, or even a white Rhône blend.

FOR THE ROUILLE
  (MAKES ABOUT 300ML)
25g slice of day-old crustless white bread
a little Fish Stock (page 270) or water
2 tablespoons Harissa (page 270)
3 fat garlic cloves, peeled
1 egg yolk
¼ teaspoon salt
250ml olive oil

FOR THE CROÛTONS
a little olive oil, for shallow frying
12 thin slices of baguette
2–3 garlic cloves, peeled

TO SERVE
100ml rouille (see above)
25g finely grated Parmesan
450g small potatoes (optional)

add the oil until you have a smooth, thick mayonnaise-like mixture. (If you prefer, you can make this well in advance – it will store in the fridge for up to 1 week.)

For the croûtons, heat the oil in a frying pan, add the slices of bread and fry on both sides until golden brown. Drain on kitchen paper, then rub one side of each croûton with garlic. Keep warm.

Pre-heat the oven to 150°C/130°C fan. Pass the soup through a sieve into a clean pan, pressing through as much of the liquid as you can with the back of a ladle. Return the soup to a wide-based, shallow, clean pan, season with salt, pepper and more cayenne pepper, and bring back to a simmer. (If you want to serve the fish with small potatoes, add them to the soup to cook for 20 minutes until tender.)

Add the monkfish fillets and the mussels and cook for 1 minute. Then add the gurnard and John Dory fillets and the pieces of lobster, making sure that they are fully submerged. Simmer for 2 minutes. The fish will be slightly undercooked at this point, but the mussels should have opened (discard any that are shut).

Carefully lift the fish fillets and lobster pieces out of the soup on to a warmed serving plate, ladle over a small amount of the soup, cover with foil and keep warm in the oven – don't leave them any longer than 10 minutes. Scoop out the potatoes (if using) and keep warm.

Ladle the soup into warmed bowls. Serve as a first course with the croûtons, rouille and Parmesan. Serve the fish as a main course, with more rouille and the small potatoes that you cooked in the soup.

The Seafood Signature Recipes

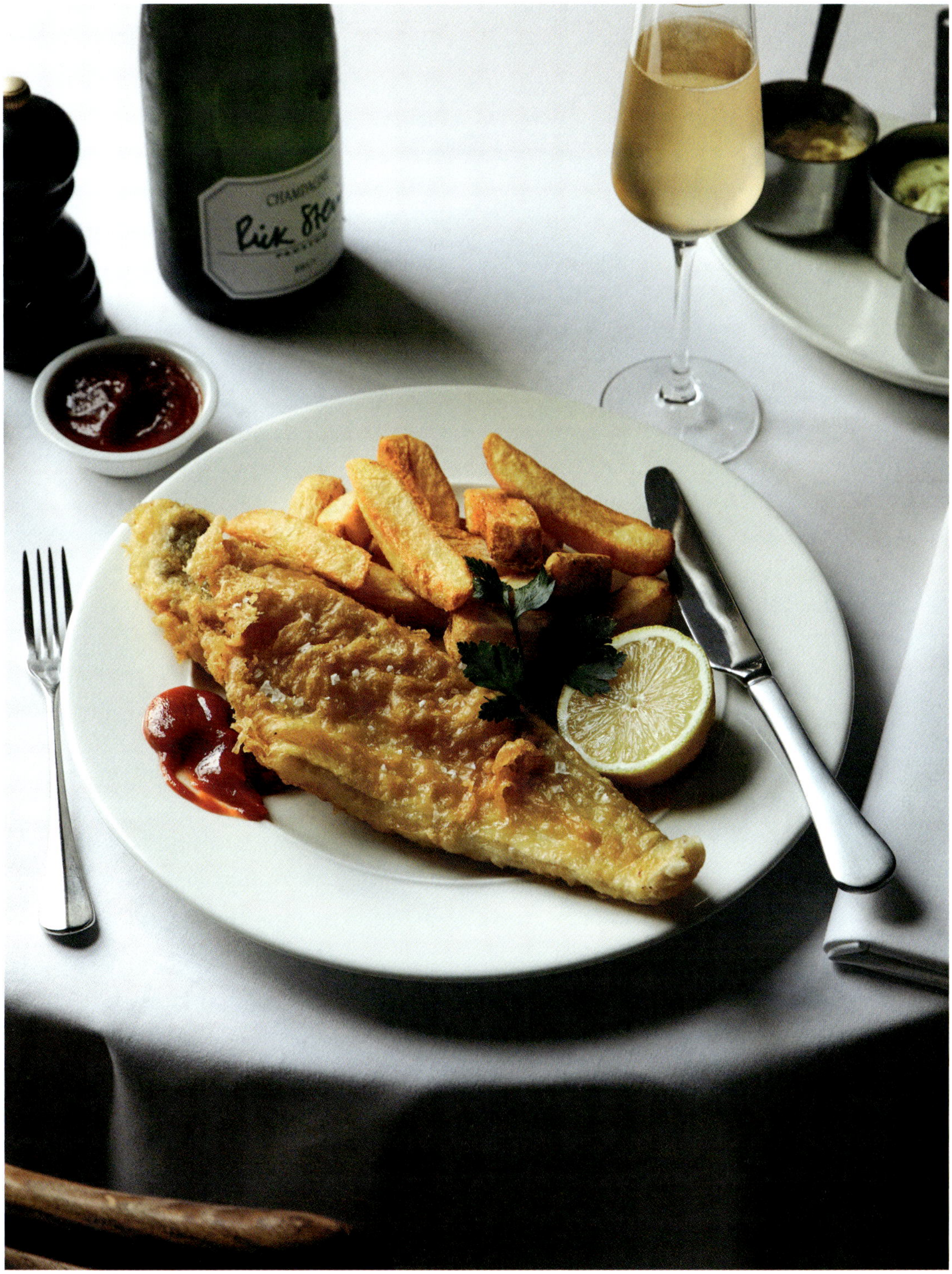

1995–2004

Fish and chips with tartare sauce

In the restaurant, we deep-fry our fish in beef dripping, which gives a flavour I love. I find its smell comforting too – maybe because it reminds me of roast dinner and Yorkshire pudding. For this recipe, though, we're sticking with vegetable oil – dripping makes hard work of cleaning up afterwards because it solidifies once it cools. When we first put fish and chips on the menu at the restaurant, we wondered if we would be able to charge restaurant prices for traditionally takeaway food, but the beef-dripping batter, double-fried chips and homemade tartare make sure it is worth it.

Serves 4

240g plain flour
1 teaspoon salt, plus extra to season
3½ teaspoons baking powder
270ml ice-cold water
900g floury potatoes, such as Maris Piper
sunflower oil, for deep-frying
4 haddock fillets, each of 180g; or 180g-pieces of thick cod fillet, cut from the head end, not the tail
freshly ground black pepper
ketchup, lemon wedges and mushy peas, to serve (optional)

Make the tartare sauce. To do this, you need to first make a mustard mayonnaise (which, in itself, goes particularly well with crab). Put the mustard, egg yolks, vinegar, salt and pepper into a mixing bowl and place the bowl on a folded tea towel (this is just to stop it slipping). Using a wire whisk, beat the oil into the egg mixture a little at a time, until you have incorporated it all and the sauce is emulsified. Once you have added about the same volume of oil as the original mixture of egg yolks and vinegar, you can add oil more quickly. Once your mayonnaise is ready, stir through the remaining ingredients until evenly combined.

To make the batter, mix the flour, salt and baking powder with the ice-cold water until smooth. Transfer the batter to the fridge and keep it cold – you'll need to use it within 20 minutes.

Pre-heat the oven to 150°C/130°C fan. Line a baking tray with plenty of kitchen paper and set aside.

Peel the potatoes and cut them lengthways into chips that are 1cm thick. Pour some sunflower oil into a large deep pan until the pan is about a third full and heat it to 130°C on a cooking thermometer. Drop half the chips into a frying basket and cook them in the oil for about 5 minutes until tender when pierced with the tip of a knife but not coloured. Lift them out and drain off the excess oil. Repeat with the rest of the chips and set aside.

The Seafood Signature Recipes

Jack's Chef Notes

Every so often, young chefs forget to close the bottom vent on our special beef-dripping fryer, causing a flood of lard, which is a nightmare to clean. The Seafood moves between hake, haddock and cod for our fish and chips. We are currently using haddock.

Charlie's Wine Notes

The best wine match for the crispy batter, salt, vinegar and special beef dripping is a great English sparkling made just up the river from the restaurant by our great friends at Camel Valley. The fizz works so well with the fat from the beef dripping; it lifts it off the palate.

FOR THE TARTARE SAUCE

1 tablespoon English mustard, at room temperature
2 egg yolks, at room temperature
1 tablespoon white wine vinegar, at room temperature
¾ teaspoon salt
few turns of the white pepper mill
300ml groundnut or sunflower oil
1 teaspoon finely chopped pitted green olives
1 teaspoon finely chopped gherkins
1 teaspoon capers, drained and finely chopped
1 teaspoon chopped chives
1 teaspoon chopped flat-leaf parsley

To fry the fish, heat the oil to 160°C. Season the fillets with salt and pepper and then dip them into the batter. Fry the fish, two pieces at a time, for 7–8 minutes until crisp and golden brown. Lift out the fish fillets and drain them on the paper-lined tray. Keep the fried fillets hot in the oven while you cook the other two.

Raise the temperature of the oil to 190°C and cook the chips in small batches for about 2 minutes until they are crisp and golden. Lift them out of the pan and give them a shake to remove the excess oil, then drain them on kitchen paper and keep them hot while you cook the rest. Sprinkle with salt and serve them with the deep-fried fish and tartare sauce.

1995–2004

Roast tronçon of turbot with Hollandaise sauce

The tronçon of turbot is our signature dish and it has been on the menu for ever. So, while arguably the recipe deserves a place in the earlier decades of the book, its place is secure wherever we choose to put it.

Serves 4

25g unsalted butter
4 tronçons of turbot, each about 225–275g
85ml Fish Stock (page 270)
1 teaspoon chopped fines herbes: parsley, French tarragon, chives, chervil
¼ teaspoon Thai fish sauce (nam pla) or a pinch of salt
juice of ½ lemon
sea-salt flakes and freshly ground black pepper

FOR THE HOLLANDAISE SAUCE
2 egg yolks
225g clarified unsalted butter (see page 198 for the technique), warmed
1½ tablespoons lemon juice
a good pinch of cayenne pepper
¾ teaspoon salt

Pre-heat the oven to 230°C/210°C fan.

Melt a small piece of the butter in a large, ovenproof frying pan over a medium–high heat and when it is foaming, add the tronçons of turbot, cooking them quickly on either side until lightly browned. Season the white sides with salt and pepper, turn them dark-side up and season once more. Transfer the frying pan to the oven and roast for 15 minutes until cooked to 55°C on a cooking thermometer.

Meanwhile, for the Hollandaise, put 2 tablespoons of water and the egg yolks into a stainless steel or glass bowl and set the bowl over a pan of simmering water, making sure that the base of the bowl is not touching the water. Whisk until voluminous and creamy. Remove the bowl from the pan and gradually whisk in the clarified butter until thick and mousse-like. Whisk in the lemon juice, cayenne pepper and salt. (Alternatively, use the quick version in the note below.) Set aside.

Combine the fish stock, fines herbes, Thai fish sauce or salt, lemon juice and the remaining butter in a small pan and bring to the boil. Arrange the tronçons on 4 warmed plates and just cover the top of each tronçon with the fines herbes sauce. Spoon the Hollandaise sauce over one end of each tronçon. Serve with some plainly boiled new potatoes and your favourite simply steamed green vegetable.

Note: For quick Hollandaise sauce, put the egg yolks, lemon juice and water into a liquidiser. Turn it on, then slowly pour the warm, melted butter through the lid. Season with cayenne pepper and the salt.

Jack's Chef Notes

Serving turbot on the bone was decades ahead of its time. Plus, there's nothing quite like making a 12-yolk hollandaise over a bain marie in the biggest bowl you've ever seen – a proper workout before each service. Now we use a Thermomix, but I do enjoy it when the machine isn't working and we have to go back to the elbow grease.

Charlie's Wine Notes

The talisman of The Seafood Restaurant menu, this is such a decadent dish that it absolutely has to be served with white Burgundy – the richer and fleshier, the better.

The Seafood Signature Recipes

Charlie's Wine Notes

For as long as I can remember, Dad's note for this dish on the menu (as in his introduction) has said "The idea is that you eat an oyster, take a bite of the sausage, then a good gulp of cold white wine like Muscadet." So, it has to be Muscadet.

Jack's Chef Notes

The chefs were sceptical of serving sausages and oysters together, but Dad was right, and once the dish came on the menu, we were all converts.

Oysters Charentais

I looked up on the Internet the origins of this dish and the only reference I found was me. However, in the Charente region of France, where I picked up this recipe, oysters and sausages are a thing. In the restaurant we make our own sausages. I like the idea that you eat an oyster and you bite into some sausage – like the ritual of salt, tequila, lemon... only in this case, you finish off with a glass of cold Muscadet or something similar. This is a perfect dish if you're looking for a bite more substantial than just oysters, but not so substantial as to feel over-full.

Serves 4

16 Pacific oysters
lemon wedges, to serve

FOR THE SAUSAGES
350g skinned belly pork, roughly chopped
75g chorizo sausage, chopped
½ teaspoon each of salt, paprika, freshly ground black pepper, thyme leaves and cayenne pepper
100g caul fat

Put all the sausage ingredients except for the caul fat into a food processor and process into a coarse paste. Scrape the mixture into a bowl. Cut the caul into 12 x 10cm squares. Divide the sausage mixture into 12 pieces, each about the size of a golf ball, and shape them into small sausages. Wrap each one in a piece of the caul fat.

Twenty minutes before serving, carefully open the oysters (see box, page 194), taking care not to lose too much of the liquor. Divide them equally between 4 serving plates.

Pre-heat the grill to high. Grill the sausages, turning them now and then, until lightly browned and cooked through (about 6–8 minutes). Put 3 of the sausages on to each plate and serve immediately with a wedge of lemon for squeezing.

Opening oysters

Wrap the hand you intend to use to hold the oyster in a tea towel. Hold the oyster in that hand and push the point of a knife into the oyster's hinge.

Work the knife and oyster backwards and forwards, applying a little pressure. The hinge will break open quite easily. Slide the knife under the top shell and sever the ligament that joins the oyster to the shell.

For the recipe on the previous page, take care to try to keep as much of the juice inside the shells as possible.

Myrtle's turbot

The late, great Myrtle Allen at Ballymaloe House in County Cork was a Food Hero of mine and was more influential than anyone else in stressing the importance of great produce simply prepared. The recipe is very easy, so if you can get a suitably sized turbot, you must try it and marvel at what a fantastic fish it is when cooked on the bone. We used to do this with smallish turbot, big enough for two people.

Serves 4

1 x 1.5kg turbot
½ small bunch of thyme
½ small bunch of flat-leaf parsley
½ small bunch of chives
75g butter
salt and freshly ground black pepper

Pre-heat the oven to 200°C/180°C fan.

With a sharp knife, cut through the skin on the top (dark) side only, all the way around the fish close to the frill-like fins. Season on top with some salt and pepper.

Pour 600ml of water into a roasting tin large enough to hold the turbot. Put the fish in the tin and bake for 30 minutes.

Meanwhile, finely chop the picked herbs.

Gently melt the butter in a small pan, stir in the chopped herbs and set aside.

Remove the fish from the oven and carefully peel away and discard the top skin. Transfer the fish to a warmed serving dish.

On the hob over a high heat, reduce the remaining cooking juices until just a few tablespoons remain, and add the liquid to the pan of herb butter, stirring to emulsify to a sauce. Pour the sauce over the white flesh of the turbot. Serve with plenty of boiled new potatoes.

Charlie's Wine Notes

I can't look past a decent white Burgundy for turbot – it is the king of the sea.

Jack's Chef Notes

When the new range was put in, we were able to roast a whole turbot in a turbot kettle to create a really simple, beautiful dish (and I miss it). Whole turbot is now very popular in Michelin-starred restaurants, so once again, The Seafood was ahead of the curve.

The Seafood Signature Recipes 197

Warm salad of seared monkfish and tiger prawns with a fennel butter vinaigrette

I think the most important thing about this dish is the dressing, which makes everything taste lovely because it has butter in it. Here, it's perfect with the monkfish and prawns, but it would go with any fish, and probably meat too.

Serves 4

2 thin monkfish fillets taken from a small monkfish tail, each about 100g
12 unpeeled raw tiger prawns
2 tablespoons olive oil
1 tablespoon lemon juice
1 teaspoon salt
½ teaspoon crushed black peppercorns
½ teaspoon crushed fennel seeds
½ teaspoon finely shredded pasilla chilli
a pinch of dried chilli flakes
3 tablespoons sherry vinegar
100g clarified butter (see below)
1 large plum tomato, skinned, seeded and diced
2 tablespoons coarsely chopped fennel herb
125g mixed baby green salad leaves

FOR THE CLARIFIED BUTTER
175g salted butter

First, make the clarified butter. Place the butter in a small pan and leave it over a very low heat until it has melted. Then, skim off any scum from the surface and pour off the clear (clarified) butter into a bowl, leaving behind the milky white solids at the bottom.

Trim away any membrane from the outside of the monkfish fillets. Twist the heads off the tiger prawns, if necessary, then peel them, leaving the last tail segment in place.

Mix together the olive oil, lemon juice, salt, peppercorns, fennel seeds, pasilla chilli and chilli flakes in a shallow dish. Add the monkfish and turn it once or twice in the mixture.

Heat a heavy-based frying pan over a high heat. Lift the monkfish out of the flavoured oil and cook over a high heat for 2 minutes until browned on one side. Add the prawns and turn the monkfish. Cook for a further 2 minutes until both are cooked through and the prawns are lightly browned. Lift the monkfish and prawns out on to a plate.

Take the pan off the heat and leave it to cool slightly. Add the sherry vinegar, the remaining flavoured oil and the 100g of clarified butter to the pan and stir to release all the flavours in the pan.

Tip the diced tomato and chopped fennel herb into a small bowl, stir in the flavoured butter and season to taste with salt and pepper.

To serve, slice the monkfish diagonally into 1cm-thick slices. Arrange the salad leaves, monkfish and prawns in the centre of 4 large plates and spoon the tomato dressing around the edge.

Jack's Chef Notes

Serving a warm salad was very much of this era and this is a particularly good one – and, as Charlie says, a great barbecue dish.

Charlie's Wine Notes

I love this dish, especially if it's cooked on the barbecue. Wine-wise, I'd go for a textural, peachy Albariño.

Charlie's Wine Notes

It would be rude not to have a Armagnac here wouldn't it? I'd go 10-year-old Bas Armagnac.

Jack's Chef Notes

This tart is one of Dad's favourites – prunes and Armagnac are, quite simply, a classic combination.

Prune tart with Armagnac

When I was a boy, prunes were the sort of low-level thing served with rice pudding. This dish, though, came as a result of my TV series, in which I journeyed from Bordeaux to Marseille by canal. En route, we stayed in Agen, which produces fantastic prunes that are so moist and heavy. This tart really does rely on having a good, juicy prune. Try Californian if you can't find any from Agen.

Serves 6

FOR THE PASTRY
100g plain flour
65g chilled butter, cut into pieces
25g caster sugar
½ tablespoon beaten egg
1 tablespoon cold water

FOR THE FILLING
2 eggs
65ml double cream, plus extra to serve
4 tablespoons vanilla sugar (see Note), or use caster sugar and a few drops of vanilla extract
3 tablespoons ground almonds
2 tablespoons Armagnac or Cognac
2 tablespoons cold water
25g butter, melted
175g Agen prunes or other good-quality, moist pitted prunes
icing sugar, for dusting
vanilla ice cream or double cream, to serve

First, make the pastry. Put the flour and butter into a food processor and blend until the mixture looks like fine breadcrumbs. Add the sugar and blend for a few seconds. Mix the beaten egg with the cold water. Turn on the machine and pour the egg through the feed tube – after a couple of seconds the mixture will start to stick together in small lumps. Switch off the machine, tip the dough into a bowl and bring it together gently into a ball. Chill for 30 minutes before use.

Roll out the pastry on a lightly floured surface until it is large enough to line a lightly greased 21cm loose-bottomed flan tin (2.5cm deep) with a slight overhang. Prick the base with a fork and chill the pastry case for 20 minutes. Pre-heat the oven to 220°C/200°C fan.

Line the pastry case with a sheet of crumpled greaseproof paper, then cover the base with a generous layer of baking beans. Bake blind for 15 minutes, then remove the beans and paper and return the pastry to the oven for a further 3–4 minutes until pale golden. Set aside while you make the filling, but leave the oven on.

Put the eggs, cream, sugar, almonds, Armagnac or Cognac and water into a bowl and whisk until smooth. Stir in the melted butter.

Arrange the prunes in a single layer over the base of the pastry case, then pour the batter over the top. Trim the pastry edge and bake the tart for 25–30 minutes until set and lightly golden. Remove from the oven and leave to cool slightly, then dust with icing sugar and serve with a scoop of vanilla ice cream or a little unwhipped double cream.

Note: To make vanilla sugar, slit a vanilla pod open and put it in a jar of caster sugar (about 500g sugar). Leave for 1 week before use.

ENGLAND

The Good Food Guide

Seafood Restaurant ▲ 🍾

1996 Rick Stein is a seafood missionary, gathering converts from all over the country for his simple, good fresh fish and shellfish. It is cooked only as much as it needs to be, and accompanied by a straightforward sorrel or hollandaise sauce, or perhaps an emulsion of olive oil, garlic and lemon juice. ... The excellence of the cooking elicits praise: for mouclade with leeks, 'one of the best dishes we have eaten anywhere in this country', for a 'truly superb' bourride of John Dory, brill and salt-cod, and for soft-shell crab, chargrilled squid, beautifully textured steamed brill with a beurre blanc, and grilled mackerel with lemon grass and coriander. Even the dishes that have to be 'mucked about with' work well, thanks to freshness and distinctive flavours: a rich hot tureen of tan-coloured shellfish soup, and crawfish ravioli with basil and spinach that was judged 'sublime, a truly fantastic dish'. One pair of reporters confessed that 'until this meal we had never realised how truly memorable lobster can be'.

1997 'A seafood restaurant of exceptional quality, with attentive service, delightful ambience and marvellous food,' enthused one reporter. On form, this is undoubtedly one of the best fish restaurants in Britain. A conservatory bolted on to the front faces out across the breakwater, and the bright dining-room is enlivened with colourful modern paintings, feeling more cosmopolitan than its fishing-village location might suggest. Cooking is often simple and straight-forward: the best way with fish... . The restaurant's casualness – find where to sit in the conservatory, pour your own wine – is not to everybody's taste. The Seafood does not have the gestures of a grand restaurant; it has something more important: an atmosphere in which people can enjoy themselves without fuss. To take delight in such a naturally informal environment, and to eat such honest food, is something the Guide supports wholeheartedly.

1998 *Everybody wants to eat here, not surprisingly given the honest enthusiasm with which Rick Stein promotes the simple pleasures of eating fresh seafood. As a fishy messiah he is unequalled – satellite operations include nearby St Petroc's, a delicatessen and a café… . The food is 'almost disarmingly simple' and generally free of distracting flourishes. It goes its own way, directed by ultra-fresh supplies and intelligent treatment.*

2003 *Mirrors enlarge, and pictures enliven, this fresh, white-painted dining room. A new executive chef, Roy Brett, now oversees all three kitchens (see entries above for St Petroc's Bistro and Rick Stein's Café), plus the bakery and deli. This leaves Rick himself free to develop new recipes and source supplies. More fish now comes from dayboats; he has also managed to find elvers (to one reporter's delight), and might serve ormers (abalone) with cuttlefish, shiitake and enoki mushrooms… . The kitchen has no difficulty balancing innovation against the simple treatment that the best fish so often deserves.*

2004 *'A really wonderful meal, enhanced by knowledgeable and interested staff' is a typically enthusiastic endorsement of Rick Stein's flagship restaurant. It consists of a small conservatory at the front for drinks, and a modern, bright dining room with white walls and colourful abstracts of a foodie nature. Although sightings of the man himself are rarer these days, the food nevertheless bears the imprint of his 30 or more years of cooking and of his global travels, taking in anything from plain oysters via stir-fried mussels with black beans, to monkfish vindaloo with pilau rice.*

Given the wide range of customers – including families with children hacking away at whole lobsters – the menu offers an obligingly broad spectrum of dishes, including a warm salad of tuna with cannellini beans, and deep-fried local cod – 'fresh as a daisy, with excellent batter' – served with big, well-made chips, proper mushy peas, and a dollop of good tartare sauce. Moist, steamed fillet of hake comes with an unctuous sauce verte and large, soft Spanish butter beans, while a simply presented spider and velvet crab risotto stole the show for one visitor: the flavour 'terrific', the whole beautifully balanced, indeed 'one of the best seafood risottos I can recall tasting'.

2005-2014

2005 STEIN'S DELI AND STEIN'S GIFT SHOP

During the first few months of the year, the deli relocates to a new building on South Quay, and the shop in Middle Street becomes an upmarket gift shop.

NEW SHAREHOLDERS

Ed, Jack and Charlie are invited to the Board as shareholders.

2009 THE CORNISH ARMS

The Cornish Arms at St Merryn joins The Stein Group – establishing itself firmly as a local village inn with great real ales from St Austell Brewery and good, unfussy pub food. Ed Stein oversees the project to completion.

2007 BRYN COTTAGE AND PROSPECT HOUSE

In April, one-bedroomed Bryn Cottage welcomes its first guests. Prospect House opens later the same year, offering a further four rooms just up the road from St Petroc's.

2008 REFURBISHMENT AT THE SEAFOOD RESTAURANT

Major works complete at The Seafood Restaurant, including a remodelled conservatory, a new seafood bar and two further bedrooms above.

JILL STEIN INTERIORS

Inspired by all the work she has done refurbishing The Seafood Restaurant and the rooms above it, Jill launches herself into interior design, founding her own business, Jill Stein Interiors.

2011 PURPLE TIGER'S KITCHEN SOUNDTRACK

The best-selling album of the decade, Adele's *21*, is released in January, featuring such classics as "Rolling in the Deep" and "Someone Like You". It sells over five million copies in the UK alone, and 32 million copies worldwide.

AT THE CINEMA

Skyfall is released and becomes the UK's highest-grossing movie of the decade and the first in the UK to take over £100 million at the Box Office.

STEIN'S FISHERIES

Stein's Fisheries opens on South Quay – our own fishmonger selling fresh fish, shellfish and pre-prepared seafood dishes.

2013 NEW YEAR HONOURS

Jill is awarded an OBE for services to Hospitality in The Queen's Birthday Honours List.

2012 STEIN'S AT TREVONE FARM

Jill launches her three individually designed holiday properties in the village of Trevone.

AUTOBIOGRAPHY

Rick publishes his autobiography, *Under a Mackerel Sky*.

2014 MARTINDALE

Jill's eight-bedroomed traditional Cornish cottage, Martindale, opens in the village of Penrose, just 6 miles from Padstow.

RICK STEIN, WINCHESTER

The first venture outside of Cornwall, The Seafood Restaurant finds a second home in Winchester, Hampshire.

Jack's Chef Notes

Scoring and cooking the squid to get the right colour is really important with this dish. The sauce is so well balanced – it's the kind of sauce chefs will put on staff tea to increase the flavour.

Charlie's Wine Notes

A light and aromatic dish, this salad needs something equally light as a pair... I'm thinking a crisp and fresh Vinho Verde from Portugal.

Squid, mint and coriander salad with roasted rice

This is a memorable dish for me – the result of our trip to Thailand in 1986. It was an early means to show off the excellence of the great squid we have in Cornwall in a simple and fresh way. It's also quite hot with red chilli. The crisp, roasted rice was something I'd never come across before, giving a pleasing crunch to the salad.

Serves 4

225g prepared small squid
2 tablespoons groundnut oil
a good pinch of cayenne pepper
2 tablespoons long-grain rice
1 Romaine lettuce heart, cut across into wide strips
4 spring onions, trimmed, halved and finely shredded
a handful of mint leaves
a handful of coriander sprigs
salt and freshly ground black pepper

FOR THE DRESSING
1 red finger chilli, thinly sliced into rings
50ml white wine vinegar
juice of 1 lime
2 tablespoons Thai fish sauce (nam pla)
½ teaspoon caster sugar
1 lemongrass stalk, outer leaves removed and the core very finely chopped

Cut along one side of each squid pouch and open it out flat. Score the inner side into a diamond pattern with the tip of a small, sharp knife, then cut the squid into 5cm squares. Separate the tentacles, if large. Season with a little salt and pepper.

Start the dressing: in a bowl cover the chilli slices with the vinegar and leave them to steep for 30 minutes.

Meanwhile, heat the oil in a wok. Add the squid and stir-fry for 2 minutes. Transfer the squid to a plate, sprinkle with the cayenne and leave to cool, but don't refrigerate.

While the squid is cooling, heat a small, heavy-based frying pan over a high heat. Add the rice and toss for a few minutes until it is richly browned and smells nutty. Tip the rice into a mortar or mug and pound it with a pestle or the end of a rolling pin to break it up. Don't grind it into fine powder.

To serve, toss together the lettuce, spring onions, mint and coriander and spread the salad out on a large oval platter. Scatter over the squid and any oil left in the pan.

Lift the chilli slices out of the vinegar (keep the vinegar for the next time). Mix the slices with the rest of the dressing ingredients and 2 tablespoons of water. Spoon this over the squid and sprinkle with the roasted rice. Serve straight away.

Monkfish vindaloo

Over time, working in television taught me that if I wanted to develop the menu at The Seafood, we would need to venture further than recipes from Britain and France. It was a risk – the food critic Christopher Driver had been vocal about how The Good Food Guide wasn't interested in restaurants that put foreign foods on their menu. Nonetheless, I had a sense that it was important that we kept challenging ourselves, and encouraging our guests to love things that they might not find elsewhere. It felt right to move things forward. Putting on the menu Indian and Thai dishes that I had picked up from my travels really worked, and monkfish vindaloo, which I'd first had in Goa in the late 1980s, was a perfect match.

Serves 4

60ml vegetable oil
1 onion, chopped
2 tomatoes, roughly chopped
1 teaspoon salt
4 medium–hot green chillies, halved lengthways
900g skinned monkfish tail, sliced across into steaks of 2.5cm thick
coconut vinegar or white wine vinegar, to taste

FOR THE VINDALOO CURRY PASTE
40g dried Kashmiri chillies
1 teaspoon black peppercorns
1½ teaspoons cloves
7cm cinnamon stick
1 teaspoon cumin seeds
1 teaspoon turmeric powder
1 small onion, chopped
40g fresh ginger root

For the vindaloo paste, soak the chillies in warm water for 20 minutes. Put the peppercorns, cloves, cinnamon and cumin seeds into a mortar or spice grinder and grind to a fine powder. Tip the powder into a mini food processor and add the drained chillies, the turmeric, onion, ginger, garlic, tamarind, sugar and vinegar. Blend to a smooth paste.

Once your paste is ready, make the curry. Heat the 60ml of vegetable oil in a large, deep frying pan over a medium–high heat. Add the onion and fry over a moderate heat for 10 minutes until softened and translucent.

Stir in the vindaloo paste and fry gently for 5 minutes. Add the tomatoes, 300ml of water and the salt, and leave the sauce to simmer for 20 minutes, giving it a stir every now and then.

Add the green chillies with the monkfish and simmer for 10 minutes, turning the fish once, until the fish is cooked through. Add more vinegar and salt to taste.

Jack's Chef Notes

In the restaurant, when we're making a batch of monkfish vindaloo, the onions alone take about 4 hours. It's not as spicy as you might expect, as it's inspired by a traditional Goan/Portuguese recipe. The key is in the salt and vinegar.

Charlie's Wine Notes

I'm a beer-and-vindaloo fan and The Seafood's vindaloo is great with an IPA or a wheat beer.

40g garlic (about 8 cloves), peeled
50g tamarind paste
1 teaspoon caster sugar
2 tablespoons coconut vinegar or white wine vinegar

FOR RICK'S EVERYDAY PILAU RICE
315g basmati rice
1 teaspoon vegetable oil
2 cloves
3cm cinnamon stick
1 green cardamom pod, cracked
1 bay leaf
¼ teaspoon salt
350ml boiling water

While the curry is cooking, wash the rice, then soak it for 30 minutes in cold water. Heat the teaspoon of oil in a saucepan over a medium heat and fry the spices and bay leaf for 30 seconds until they smell aromatic. Drain the rice from its soaking water and add it to the spice mixture with the salt; stir a little. Add the boiling water and bring the liquid back to the boil, then cook over a very low heat with the lid on for 10–12 minutes until all the water has been absorbed. Serve with the curry.

212 The Seafood Signature Recipes

The Seafood Signature Recipes 213

Indonesian seafood curry

In 2008, while we were filming Far Eastern Odyssey *in Bali, I came across this dish, by a Swiss-German chef called Heinz von Holzen who had a cookery school there and had amassed recipes from all over the world. We filmed him making the curry, which was based on an Indonesian spice paste called basa gede. Whereas in Bali the curry would be traditionally cooked slowly, over a long time, this version is adapted for the way we cook in Europe – making a fragrant sauce from the paste with ginger, garlic, lemongrass and coconut, and producing something far speedier but no less tasty. I've changed the fish, but kept his principles for a really hot and spicy curry.*

Serves 4

FOR THE INDIAN SPICE PASTE (BASA GEDE; MAKES ABOUT 200G)
1½ teaspoons black peppercorns
½ nutmeg
25g candle nuts, macadamia nuts, cashew nuts or roasted peanuts
1 teaspoon sesame seeds
60g shallots, roughly chopped
25g fresh ginger root, peeled and roughly chopped
40g galangal (or extra ginger), peeled and roughly chopped
15g fresh turmeric root, peeled and chopped, or 1 teaspoon turmeric powder
3 fat lemongrass stalks, core chopped
20g (about 4) garlic cloves, peeled

First, make the spice paste. Put the peppercorns, nutmeg, nuts and sesame seeds into a spice grinder and grind to a fine powder. Tip the powder into a mini food processor, add all the remaining ingredients and blend everything into a very smooth paste. Like most pastes, this one will keep perfectly in the fridge in a clean jar for a week. After that, they progressively lose their fragrance. To store for longer, spoon the paste into small pots or ice-cube trays, cover and freeze.

For the salad (ingredients overleaf), bring a large pan of salted water to the boil. Add the green beans and cook for 2 minutes until just tender. Drain and refresh under cold water, then dry the beans well and put them into a bowl. Heat the oil in a small pan over a high heat, add the shallots and fry for about 4–5 minutes until crisp and golden.

Using a slotted spoon, lift out the crispy shallots on to kitchen paper. Add the garlic to the pan on the heat and do the same. Add the chopped red chilli and fry for just a few seconds. Add the fried shallots, garlic and chilli to the beans in the bowl, along with the coconut, beansprouts, lime leaves and sliced bird's-eye chilli. Toss to combine, and set aside.

...ingredients and method continued overleaf

Charlie's Wine Notes

An off-dry Gewürztraminer from Alsace complements the aromatic elements of this dish, and the sweetness offsets the spice of the curry.

Jack's Chef Notes

This is our top-selling dish. The green bean salad that we serve alongside is unusual in that it uses shrimp paste in the dressing, but it all works so well together.

2 medium–hot red chillies,
   seeded and roughly chopped
3 red bird's-eye chillies,
   roughly chopped
1 teaspoon shrimp paste
1 tablespoon palm sugar
1 teaspoon salt
3 tablespoons vegetable oil
juice of ½ lime

FOR THE GREEN BEAN AND
   COCONUT SALAD
250g fine green beans, cut into
   pieces
6 tablespoons vegetable oil
1 shallot, sliced
2 garlic cloves, sliced
1 medium–hot red chilli,
   seeded and chopped
150g fresh coconut,
   finely grated
100g beansprouts
2 makrut lime leaves, shredded
2 red bird's-eye chillies,
   thinly sliced

Prepare the squid by holding the body in one hand and the head in the other and gently pull the head away from the body, taking the milky-white intestines with it. Remove the tentacles from the head by cutting them off just in front of the eyes. Discard the head. Squeeze out the beak-like mouth from the centre of the tentacles and discard. Separate the tentacles if they are large. Reach inside the body and pull out and discard the clear, plastic-like quill. Pull off the two fins from either side of the body pouch, then pull away the brown, semi-transparent skin from the body and fins. Wash out the body pouch with water. The squid is now ready to use.

Put the squid, prawns and chunks of fish into a shallow bowl and sprinkle with the salt, some white pepper and the lime juice. Mix together well. Add half the spice paste and rub it well all over the pieces of seafood.

Heat the oil in a large pan over a medium heat. Add the remaining spice paste and fry gently for 2–3 minutes until it starts to smell fragrant. Add the lime leaves, lemongrass and stock and simmer for 1 minute.

Add the pieces of fish (not the squid or the prawns) to the pan and leave to cook for 1 minute, then turn them over and cook for a further minute. Add the coconut milk, together with the squid and prawns, and simmer for 2 minutes. Season to taste with a little more salt and lime juice.

FOR THE CURRY

250g medium squid (pouch about 18cm long)

12 large raw prawns, peeled (see box, page 218; or buy ready-peeled)

400g fish fillets, such as monkfish, John Dory, gurnard or sea bass, cut into 3–4cm chunks

1 teaspoon salt

1 tablespoon lime juice, plus extra to taste

200g Indonesian spice paste (see page 214)

2 tablespoons vegetable oil

4 makrut lime leaves, torn into small pieces

2 fat lemongrass stalks, halved and bruised

120ml Asian chicken stock (page 271) or shop-bought chicken stock

250ml full-fat coconut milk

freshly ground white pepper

FOR THE DRESSING

½ teaspoon shrimp paste

4 teaspoons lime juice

1 tablespoon vegetable oil

2 teaspoons palm sugar

½ teaspoon salt

For the dressing, blend the shrimp paste with the lime juice in a small bowl, then whisk in the oil, sugar and salt. Pour the dressing over the salad, then toss everything together well.

Serve the curry with the salad alongside.

Peeling prawns

Hold the body of each prawn in one hand and firmly twist off the head with the other. Save the heads for making stock (see recipe, page 270), if you wish.

Break open the soft shell along the underbelly of each prawn and peel it away from the flesh. (You can leave the last tail segment of the shell in place for some recipes, but for this curry, you'll need to remove it.)

Run the tip of a small sharp knife along the back of the prawn and pull out the intestinal tract if dark and visible, but this is not always essential.

Charlie's Wine Notes

Delicately fried seafood in a light batter, like our Fritto Misto (see recipe, overleaf), needs a light-touch wine with plenty of zip. A Gavi di Gavi would work really well here, with its citrus-fruit tang.

Jack's Chef Notes

Chefs will flock to a fritto misto – it's the kind of dish we eat when we are on holiday; a great chef's long-lunch dish.

The Seafood Signature Recipes

Fritto misto of scallops, prawns and squid with lemon

This dish represents a turning point for us – after we had rebuilt the kitchen in the mid-90s and so had more space at The Seafood and more chefs on hand, we were able to perfect our fritto misto, making it worthy of its Italian roots. Everything has to be fried to order and then served quickly so that it arrives at its best. I absolutely love it and we serve it to this day.

Serves 4

8 prepared scallops (see box, page 164)
100g prepared squid (see method, page 216)
12 large, raw, headless prawns, peeled and de-veined (see box, page 218)
1 litre olive oil
75g plain flour, seasoned with salt and black pepper
2 lemons
salt
aïoli, to serve (page 222)

Pre-heat the oven to 150°C/130°C fan and line a large baking tray with plenty of kitchen paper.

Detach the coral from each scallop and slice it in half lengthways (this prevents the corals exploding during cooking). Then slice the scallop meat horizontally in half as well. Cut the squid across into thick rings. Season all the seafood with a little salt.

Pour the oil into a large saucepan and heat to 190°C on a cooking thermometer, or until a small piece of white bread dropped into the oil browns and rises to the surface in 1 minute.

Toss the fish in the seasoned flour and deep-fry in batches for 30 seconds–1 minute at a time, until the floury coating is just beginning to be tinged with brown. Lift out the cooked fish with a slotted spoon, arrange it on the baking tray and keep it hot in the oven while you cook the rest.

Slice each lemon across into chunky halves and serve with the seafood for squeezing over, with aïoli on the side for dipping.

Grilled cod with aïoli and butter beans

I developed this classic dish based on the Provençal dish aïoli garni, which is served cold and made using salt fish. I wanted a warm version for our menu, and fresh cod, so that it could become a main meal. The sauce, of which there is quite a lot, has power, but isn't overpowering.

Serves 4

50g dried butter beans
4 eggs
1 fennel bulb
4 skin-on cod fillets, each about 175–200g
melted butter, for brushing

FOR THE SAUCE
50g unsalted butter
225g finely chopped mixed carrot, leek, celery and onion
1 tablespoon Cognac
10g dried mushrooms
1 tablespoon balsamic vinegar
¼ medium–hot red chilli, seeded and chopped
2 tablespoons olive oil
1 teaspoon Thai fish sauce (nam pla)
600ml Fish Stock (page 270)
½ teaspoon salt
4 basil leaves, finely sliced

Bring the butter beans to the boil in a large pan of salted water. Simmer gently until very soft (about 90 minutes). Remove from the heat and keep warm in the cooking liquid.

While the beans are simmering, make the aïoli (see ingredients, overleaf). Put the garlic cloves on to a chopping board and crush them under the blade of a large knife. Sprinkle them with the salt and then work them with the knife blade into a smooth paste. Scrape the garlic paste into a bowl and add the egg yolk and the lemon juice. Using an electric hand mixer, whisk everything together and then very gradually whisk in the olive oil to make a thick mayonnaise-like mixture. Refrigerate until needed.

To make the sauce, melt half the butter in a large pan over a medium–high heat. Add the mixture of carrot, leek, celery and onion and sweat for 5–6 minutes until soft. Add the Cognac and let it boil. Then add all the rest of the sauce ingredients, except the remaining butter and the basil leaves. Simmer for 30 minutes, then pass the sauce through a fine sieve into a clean pan. Bring it back to the boil, then reduce the heat and simmer until reduced to about 150ml.

Boil the eggs for 7 minutes. Drain, remove the shells and keep warm.

Remove the outer leaves of the fennel but don't cut off the tops. Slice the bulb into thin sections, then cook in salted water until just tender. Drain and keep warm.

...ingredients and method continued overleaf

FOR THE AÏOLI (MAKES
ABOUT 175ML)
4 garlic cloves, peeled
½ teaspoon sea salt
1 egg yolk
2 teaspoons lemon juice
175ml extra virgin olive oil

Pre-heat the grill to high. Brush the pieces of cod on both sides with melted butter and place, skin side up, on a greased baking tray or the rack of the grill pan. Grill for 8 minutes or until just cooked through. The cooking time will depend on the thickness of the fillets.

Place the cod on 4 warmed plates. Drain the butter beans and divide them equally between the plates. Add the fennel, then cut the eggs in half and put two halves on each plate. Add a spoonful of aïoli to each serving.

Bring the sauce to the boil and whisk in the last 25g of butter, then add the basil leaves. Pour the sauce over the beans and fish and serve.

Jack's Chef Notes

When you make the aïoli for this dish, it's important to sprinkle the chopped garlic with sea salt, then to use the back of the knife to squish it to get all of the garlic juices out.

Charlie's Wine Notes

Dad makes his aïoli the correct way – with lots and lots of garlic. So, as garlic is the main element here, we want something like a Bourgogne Aligoté, which will match that garlic spice, while being rich enough to complement the cod.

The Seafood Signature Recipes 223

2005–2014

Sashimi of salmon, tuna, sea bass and scallops

After watching me create mackerel sashimi on the television, the Japanese Ambassador in London suggested I visit Japan and learn to make a more traditional style. He explained that Japanese cooks would never use raw mackerel, because of a parasite that lives in the fish in Japanese waters (in Japan, mackerel is always cured). It was an offer too good to refuse. There, I learned to fillet fish for sashimi with the freshest fish imaginable. This dish is the result of that trip, and a much-loved and enduring addition to The Seafood menu.

Serves 4

90g piece of skinned salmon fillet, pin bones removed
90g piece of sea-bass fillet, skinned and pin bones removed
90g piece of tuna fillet
4 scallops, out of the shell, corals removed (see box, page 164)

TO SERVE
1 x 7.5cm piece daikon radish (mooli), peeled, then finely cut lengthways into long, thin shreds on a mandoline
wasabi paste
Japanese pickled ginger
100ml dark soy sauce, for dipping
micro shiso leaves

To prepare the sashimi, carefully trim away the brown meat from the skinned side of the salmon fillet. Then, using a super-sharp knife, neatly trim up all the fish fillets to remove any thin pieces of fish, then cut each one across into 5mm-thick slices. Cut each scallop horizontally into 3 slices.

To serve, arrange each type of fish attractively on each plate, overlapping the slices, and add the daikon, a hazelnut-sized amount of wasabi, and the pickled ginger.

Divide the soy sauce between 4 dipping saucers and arrange one sauce on each plate. Top the daikon with a few micro shiso leaves, then serve with chopsticks.

Charlie's Wine Notes

Dry Sake works so well with sashimi. We've been recommending it to our customers to enjoy with this dish for years – and there's definitely no reason to change now.

Jack's Chef Notes

We had a chef, Koji, who came to The Seafood during his seventh year of ten years of training to be an *itamae* (master sushi chef). It was the summer and he surfed and made sushi and sashimi – we all learned a lot from him, perfecting the techniques that Dad would also learn in Japan.

The Seafood Signature Recipes 225

Grilled whole sea bass with Pernod and fennel

This is one of my absolute favourites. I particularly love anything that goes with our homemade mayonnaise. Flavouring the mayo with fennel, which we pick in Padstow, works really well with the fish, and sea bass especially. It's one of the few herbs that barbecues really well, tucked into the cavities of the fish to give that lovely aniseed scent. Sprinkling the fish with Pernod to bring out the aniseed has always been a hit.

Serves 4

1 large sea bass, about 1.5–1.75kg
25ml olive oil
1 large bunch of fennel sprigs
2 teaspoons Pernod, pastis or Ricard
salt and freshly ground black pepper
salad leaves and lemon wedges, to serve

FOR THE FENNEL MAYONNAISE (MAKES 300ML)

2 egg yolks, at room temperature
2 teaspoons white wine vinegar
½ teaspoon salt
300ml olive oil
3 teaspoons Pernod
1 teaspoon chopped chives
1 tablespoon finely chopped fennel bulb

Light the barbecue at least 45 minutes before you intend to grill your fish – this will give the coals time to fire up and then die down to hot ash, so that you cook the fish rather than incinerate it as soon as it hits the grill. Ideally, use a barbecue grilling basket, which sandwiches the fish between the wires to secure it on top of the barbecue. If you don't have one, creating a bed of fennel herbs on which to rest the fish is a good alternative.

First, make the mayonnaise. If you're making it by hand, put the room-temperature egg yolks with the vinegar and salt into a mixing bowl. Place the bowl on a tea towel to stop it slipping. Using a wire whisk, lightly whisk everything together to break up the egg. Still using the whisk, a few drops at a time, beat the oil into the egg mixture until you have incorporated it all. (Once you have added the same volume of oil as the original mixture of egg and vinegar, you can add the oil a little more quickly.) Continue until you have an emulsified, creamy mayo. If you're using a food processor or liquidiser, put the whole egg, vinegar and salt into the machine, turn it on and then slowly add the oil through the hole in the lid until you have a thick emulsion.

Once you have your basic mayo, stir through the rest of the ingredients to fully incorporate. Set aside until you're ready to serve.

Trim and scale the bass, then slash it three or four times on each side, cutting down to the bone. Brush the fish liberally with the olive oil both inside and out, then season with salt and pepper.

Push several fennel sprigs into the gut cavity. Lay more sprigs on one side of your grilling basket and lay the fish on top, placing more on the top of the fish before closing the basket.

Place the basket carefully over the charcoal, grilling the fish for about 12 minutes, taking great care to avoid over-charring. If the sea bass seems to be blistering too much, move it to a cooler part of the barbecue. Just before turning the fish to cook the second side, sprinkle it liberally with the Pernod, pastis or Ricard, then turn it over and grill for a further 12 minutes until cooked through. Take the fish off the grill.

Serve the bass with the fennel mayonnaise, a wedge of lemon, a handful of salad leaves, and a large bowl of boiled potatoes.

Jack's Chef Notes

Whole-fish cooking was really coming back into fashion around this decade. This one is great on the chargrill in the kitchen, or on the barbecue in the garden – or on the beach.

Charlie's Wine Notes

Pernod and fennel bring strong flavours to this dish. As a result, I like the aromatic and texture quality of a blend of Sauvignon and Sémillon here – perhaps one from a good producer in Australia's Hunter Valley.

228　The Seafood Signature Recipes

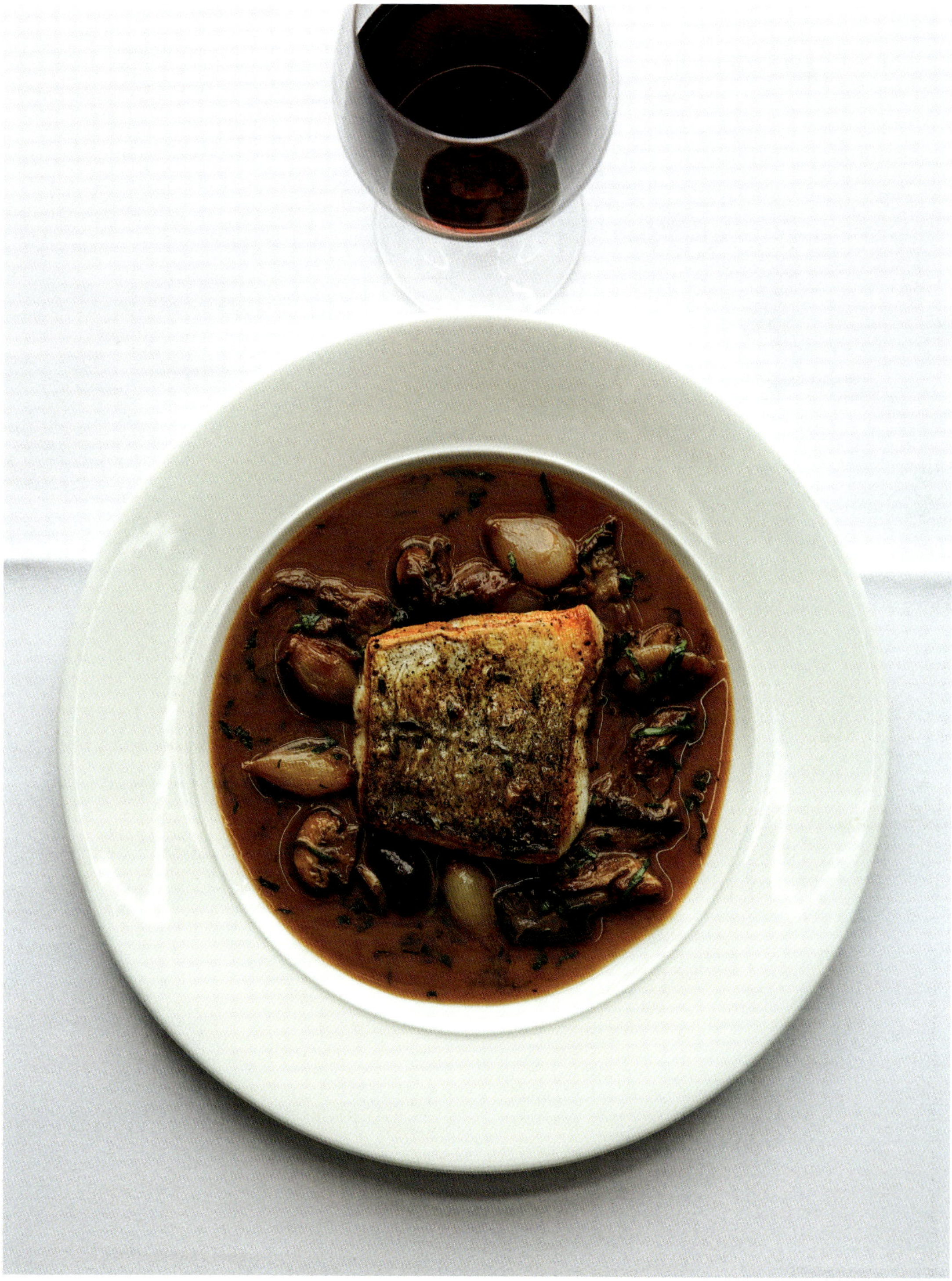

A casserole of hake with shallots and wild mushrooms

With wild mushrooms and red wine bringing earthy robustness, this dish is perfect for autumn. The first two decades of the millennium saw hake stocks increase thanks to managed recovery, and now Cornish hake is one of our most sustainable fish.

Serves 4

15g dried porcini mushrooms
150ml warm water
90g unsalted butter
12 small shallots, peeled but left whole
½ teaspoon caster sugar
8 garlic cloves, peeled but left whole
900ml Chicken Stock (page 270)
1 thick slice of cooked ham, cut into small dice
1 carrot, chopped
1 leek, chopped
1 celery stick, chopped
½ onion, chopped
2 teaspoons balsamic vinegar
2 thyme sprigs
50ml red wine
4 skinless hake fillets, each about 175g
100g wild mushrooms, sliced
salt and freshly ground black pepper

Soak the dried porcini in the warm water for 30 minutes.

Meanwhile, melt 25g of the butter in a shallow pan (large enough to fit the fillets of hake side by side), over a medium heat. Add the shallots, sugar and garlic and fry until lightly browned. Barely cover the contents of the pan with some of the chicken stock, then add the ham, and ¼ teaspoon each of salt and pepper. Simmer gently for about 25 minutes until both the shallots and garlic are tender.

Then, turn up the heat and boil rapidly until the stock has reduced to a thick, sticky glaze, shaking the pan now and then so that the onions and garlic become well coated. Remove the onions and garlic from the pan to a plate and keep warm. Set the pan to one side, unwashed.

Melt another 25g of the butter in a medium pan over a medium heat. Add the carrot, leek, celery and onion and fry for about 10 minutes until nicely coloured. Add the remaining chicken stock, along with the balsamic vinegar, 1 thyme sprig, the red wine and the soaking liquor from the dried mushrooms and simmer for 20–30 minutes. Then, strain the flavoured stock through a fine sieve into a jug and discard all the vegetables.

Jack's Chef Notes

This is a really complex sauce and rich in flavour. I have always said that if the Michelin inspector was in, this is the dish I'd want them to order.

Charlie's Wine Notes

Like the meurette recipe (see page 144), this is a prime example of a fish dish that can go really well with red wine. I've paired this well with a juicy Bardolino.

Heat a small knob of the remaining butter in a frying pan. Add the hake fillets, skin-side down, and cook for about 1 minute, until lightly browned. Season with salt and pepper and put the fillets side-by-side in the pan you used for glazing the shallots. Pour over the stock, add the second thyme sprig, cover and simmer for 5 minutes to cook the fish.

Meanwhile, melt another 15g of the butter in the frying pan, add the soaked porcini and the wild mushrooms and fry briskly for 2–3 minutes. Season with a little salt and pepper.

Remove the cooked hake from the pan and keep it warm. Boil the remaining liquid until reduced and well-flavoured (about 10 minutes, to a single-cream consistency), then whisk in the remaining butter. Stir in the mushrooms.

Put the hake on to 4 warmed plates. Add the glazed shallots and garlic, spoon over the sauce, and serve.

Grilled Dublin Bay prawns with a Pernod and olive oil dressing

I introduced this recipe to the menu when we began getting really delicious langoustines from Scotland and I loved the idea of cutting them lengthways, which is such a beautiful way to present them. It's adapted from a recipe by the mid-20th-century British cook Elizabeth David, who inspired my cooking in lots of ways – not least with this sauce. I think she must have come up with a version quite late on in her lifetime – the soy sauce in it is the giveaway. The dish has become a regular feature on the menu; we still make it to this day.

Serves 4

16 large or 24 smaller cooked Dublin Bay Prawns
2 small shallots, finely chopped
½ tablespoon roughly chopped tarragon
½ tablespoon roughly chopped flat-leaf parsley
1 teaspoon Dijon mustard
1 teaspoon dark soy sauce
85ml extra virgin olive oil
1½ tablespoons lemon juice
1 teaspoon Pernod
50g butter, melted
salt and freshly ground black pepper

Pre-heat the grill to high.

Cut the Dublin Bay prawns open lengthways and use a teaspoon to scoop out the creamy contents of the heads and any red roe. Put this into a small bowl and stir in the shallots, tarragon, parsley, mustard, soy sauce, oil, lemon juice, Pernod and salt and pepper to taste.

Place the halved prawns cut side up on a baking tray or the rack of the grill pan and brush with the melted butter. Season lightly with salt and pepper and grill for 2–3 minutes until the shells as well as the meat are heated through.

Put the prawns on 4 serving plates and spoon over a little of the dressing. Divide the rest of the dressing between 4 dipping saucers or small ramekins, and serve.

Charlie's Wine Notes

Finding a pairing for this dish means taking account of that Pernod dressing with its strong anise. I'd go for a special Vermentino from the Italian island of Sardinia.

Jack's Chef Notes

The dressing on this dish is really interesting because it uses the tomalley found inside the Dublin Bay prawns, with soy and lemon juice to create a thick vinaigrette that is absolutely delicious.

The Seafood Signature Recipes

2005–2014

Chocolate fondant

This has been on The Seafood's menu for nearly 20 years. It was adapted from a French recipe, by our wonderful pâtissier Stuart Pate, who was not only the head pastry chef at The Seafood, but also ran a pastry unit at our production kitchen, which baked most of the products for Stein's Patisserie in Lanadwell Street.

Makes 5

125g unsalted butter, plus extra (softened) for greasing the moulds
4 teaspoons cocoa powder, plus extra for dusting
125g 70% dark chocolate, broken up
60g caster sugar
3 whole eggs
3 egg yolks
vanilla ice cream, to serve

FOR THE WHITE CHOCOLATE CRUMB (OPTIONAL)
360g white chocolate drops

FOR THE CARAMEL SAUCE (OPTIONAL)
100g caster sugar
150ml double cream
15g unsalted butter
a pinch of salt

YOU WILL NEED
8cm-diameter foil fondant moulds x 5

Brush the moulds with the softened butter, then dust them with a light layer of cocoa powder. Place them in the fridge while you make the fondant.

Put the butter and dark chocolate in a bowl placed over a pan of hot water (a bain-marie) until all of the chocolate and butter have fully melted. Stir to combine, then remove the bowl from the heat and stir in the cocoa powder, beating until there are no lumps.

In a separate bowl, mix together the sugar, eggs and egg yolks by hand with a balloon whisk for 4–5 minutes. Do not over-whisk as, if you do, the pudding will collapse when you cook it. The mixture should be light and voluminous.

Once the chocolate and butter have cooled down to body temperature, add the egg mixture and stir until fully combined. Again, take care not to over-mix.

Spoon the fondant mixture equally into the prepared moulds (you should get about 120g per tin). Leave to set in the fridge overnight.

If you're making the white chocolate crumb, pre-heat the oven to 160°C/140°C fan. Line a baking tray with silicone paper and evenly spread out the white chocolate drops. Bake the drops in the oven for about 12–15 minutes until lightly caramelised. Leave to cool, then use your hands to break up the chocolate into a crumb. Store the crumb in an airtight container in the freezer until you're ready to use.

...method continued overleaf

Charlie's Wine Notes

Chocolate is quite a hard match for wine, but there's a delightful sparkling, sweet red from Piedmont called Brachetto that really works.

Jack's Chef Notes

This classic dessert was created by French chef Michel Bras. It's the ultimate crowd-pleaser… so much so that, at the end of the night, the chefs will eat any that customers haven't ordered.

To make the caramel sauce, put the sugar into a small pan with 60ml of water and place it over a low heat. When the mixture comes to the boil, boil rapidly until the syrup turns to a rich, amber-coloured caramel. Remove the pan from the heat and add the cream (be careful – it will spit), then stir in the butter and salt. Return the pan to a low heat and stir until all the caramel has dissolved into the sauce. Leave to cool, then set aside until you're ready to serve.

To finish the fondants, pre-heat the oven to 200°C/180°C fan. Bake the fondants for 8–10 minutes until the outside is firm (the inside should still be runny).

Gently turn out the fondants on to individual serving plates (you can carefully run a knife around the inside of the mould, if you need, but the fondant should release without). Sprinkle the top of each with a little white chocolate crumb and serve with a spoonful of caramel and a scoop of vanilla ice cream. (You will have caramel and crumb left over – the caramel will keep in the fridge for up to 2 weeks; the crumb will store in an airtight container for 2 or more weeks.)

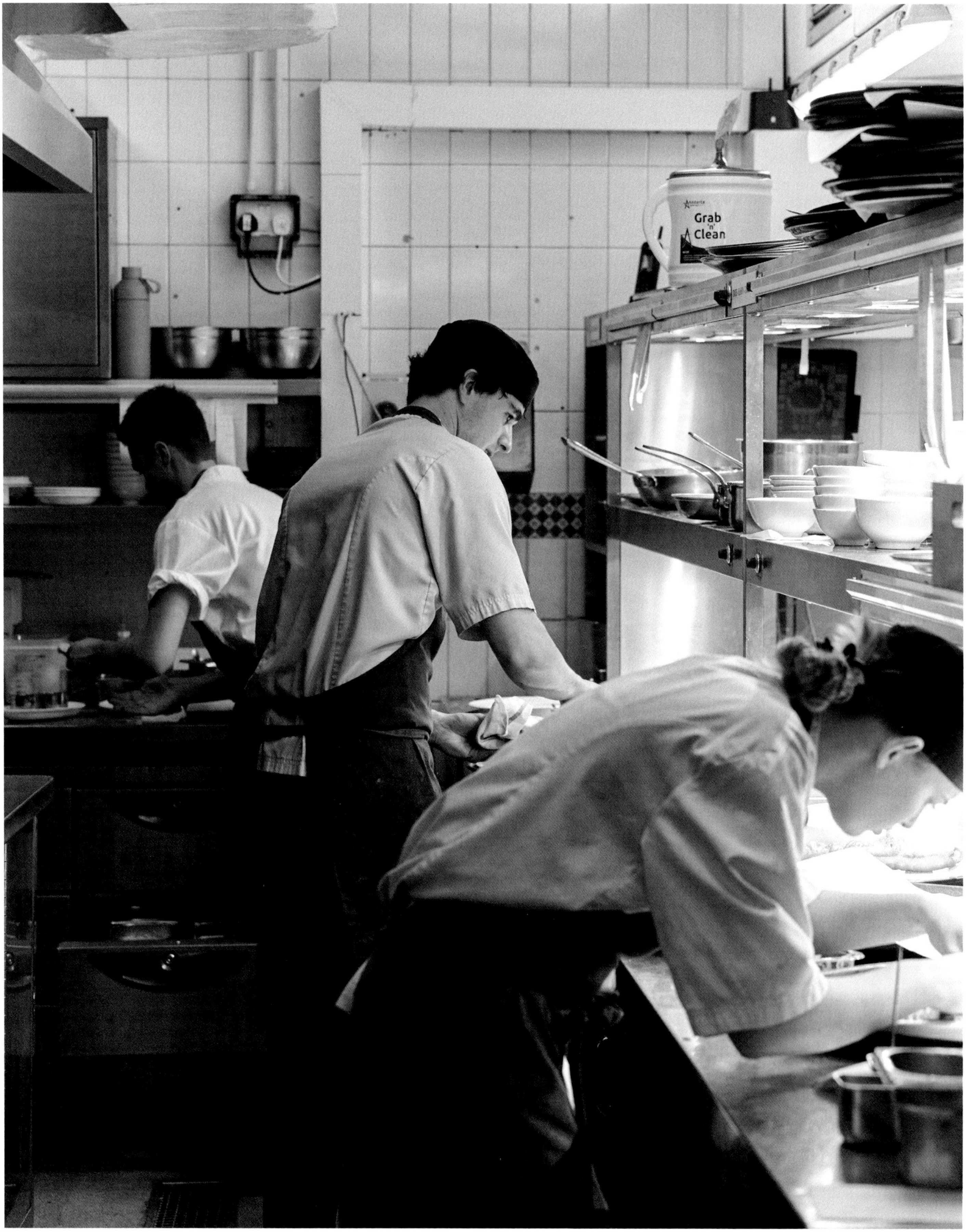
Grab 'n' Clean

ENGLAND

The Good Food Guide

▲ Seafood Restaurant 🍾

2005 There are three Stein-owned establishments in Padstow listed in the Guide, and his name also adorns a deli, pâtisserie, gift shop, cookery school and now a fish 'n' chip shop, but this is the original venture, and remains the flagship. A spacious, white-walled place with a conservatory out front, the atmosphere is enlivened by bright modern pictures and the cheery, infectious attitude of the staff. A wealth of piscatorial choice is offered, of unimpeachable freshness, as befits the location, and there is an appealing mix of traditional simplicity and the influence of foreign climes. Thus, langoustines on ice, or potted shrimps might preface a main course such as chargrilled fillet of sea bass with tomato butter and vanilla vinaigrette, or fillets of Dover sole with stir-fried red peppers, asparagus and wild garlic with a soy and sesame oil dressing... . Platters of fruits de mer, served naturally with mayonnaise and shallot vinegar, offer a crash course in marine biology, and the five-course tasting menu (including coffee) is fulsomely praised, producing perhaps oysters with spicy sausage, grilled langoustines, poached skate, sea bass, and a passion-fruit pavlova. That some thought goes into desserts is evidenced by the take on bread-and-butter pudding, made from saffron cake and served with stewed rhubarb on the side.

2007 The big, white double room on the Padstow quay-side benefits from bold, statement-making modern paintings and admirably slick service. It's the place, as if you needed reminding, that put this charm-laden Cornish fishing village on the map, and made its proprietor a star. Fish and shellfish of exemplary freshness are still the main draw, with simpler dishes showing up best. Seared red mullet might begin, with chargrilled Dover sole seasoned with sea salt and lime to follow, or perhaps a classic fish pie with cod, smoked haddock and minty peas.

PADSTOW

2009 A £2.5m refit has given Rick Stein's flagship restaurant a fresh new look, and brought a seafood bar to its heart. Here you can order anything from the menu without booking, and watch the preparation of seafood platters, sushi and sashimi. Although Rick Stein is no longer in the kitchen he is still an effective ambassador for his restaurants. This, his first, opened in 1975 and continues to reflect his passion for fish brought straight to the kitchen from the boats that tie up within sight of the restaurant. As Stein puts it, this is not supposed to be a temple of gastronomy, it's a relaxed environment in which to enjoy exhilaratingly fresh fish. The general thrust of the cooking is towards simplicity, but this does not mean predictability; flavours come from all over the world, so alongside classics like oysters, 'fruits de mer' or fish and shellfish soup with rouille and Parmesan, starters could include crab, ginger and coriander broth or Chinese-style steamed scallops. Main courses reflect a similar scope: fish and chips, monkfish vindaloo, Singapore chilli crab, and chargrilled whole Dover sole with sea salt and lime are typical players. Despite the changes to the interior there is a comforting sense of continuity; the same paintings are back on the walls and a buzzy, unbuttoned atmosphere prevails.

2014 The Seafood Restaurant has upped its game judging by the number of glowing reports received this year. The spacious, smart but unfussy dining room exudes an easy, informal ambience, while service strikes precisely the right balance: attentive and personal. Reporters not only applaud the breadth to the menu with its influences from the Med, Asia and the USA, but also highlight the classics of fish and shellfish soup, roast tronçon of turbot (rich, meaty and very fresh turbot roasted on the bone, served with a slick of hollandaise) and Padstow lobster, grilled or steamed, with mayonnaise. There has been praise, too, for 'lovely briny Palourde clams straight out of the estuary outside'; 'zingy, fresh-tasting' crisp smoked mackerel with green mango and papaya salad, Thai holy basil and bird's eye chilli and passion fruit pavlova with crème Chantilly.

2015-2025

2015 RICK STEIN, FISTRAL

April sees the opening of a new Stein restaurant in Newquay, Cornwall, on the famous surf beach at Fistral.

2016 RICK STEIN'S SEAFOOD BAR AND FISHMONGERS

The casual seafood bar opens in May, nestled beside the quay in Padstow – a place to enjoy small plates and a glass of wine.

RUBY'S BAR

Ruby's Bar, on Broad Street, just around the corner from St Petroc's and designed by Jill, Ed and Ed's wife Kate, opens in July.

PURPLE TIGER'S KITCHEN SOUNDTRACK

The best-selling album of the decade is Ed Sheeran's ÷, released in March. The album's accompanying tour became the highest-grossing musical tour of all time.

2018 NEW YEAR HONOURS

Rick is awarded a CBE in The Queen's New Year Honours List, for services to the economy.

WORLD ON A PLATE

Jack publishes his first book, *World on a Plate*.

RICK STEIN, SANDBANKS

Sandbanks, in Dorset, overlooking Poole Harbour, opens in November.

CHARLIE JOINS THE SEAFOOD

After eight years with Vintner in London, Charlie joins the company as Wine Buyer for The Seafood and the rest of the group.

AT THE CINEMA

Star Wars: The Force Awakens is released and becomes the UK's highest-grossing movie of the decade.

RICK STEIN, MARLBOROUGH

Marlborough, Wiltshire is the next stop for a new Seafood Restaurant, in October.

2017 RICK STEIN, BARNES

Acquired in 2016 and then refurbished in 2017, Barnes, London, opens to critical acclaim.

2019 WINE, DINE & STEIN

Jack and Charlie's joint television venture hits the UK's TV screens.

2020 LOCKDOWN

Like all restaurants, The Seafood Restaurant has to close its doors, triggering the launch of *Steins at Home* so that customers can enjoy pre-prepared meal kits of restaurant favourites, such as Lobster Thermidor and Indonesian Seafood Curry, as well as ordering afternoon teas. (*Rick Stein Meal Kits* are still available to order through Dishpatch.) When finally the restaurant re-opens, it does so with the launch of the *Rick Stein* App as a safe and simple way to browse the menu and pay on a smartphone. Jill describes the pandemic as the hardest time to have hit The Seafood in its fifty-year history.

TOP 100 BEST COMPANY

The Stein Group achieves a Top 100 Best Large Company to work for, an accolade it repeats in 2022 and 2025.

2021 STEIN'S COFFEE SHOP

Charlie Stein collaborates with Tom Sobey, founder of Cornwall-based Origin Coffee, to open Stein's Coffee Shop in the space that had been the Patisserie, in heart of the Padstow.

STEIN'S ONLINE FISHMONGER

In October, Rick and the team launch a quay-to-door website, enabling anyone anywhere in the country to order fresh fish and have it delivered to their home, with recipes and ideas too.

THE CORNISH ARMS: SHEPHERD'S HUTS

Summer at the Cornish Arms welcomes guests to five individually designed shepherd's huts overlooking the Cornish countryside, each designed by Jill, Ed and Kate.

2023 BEST CHEF AWARD FOR JACK

Jack Stein wins *Food Magazine*'s Best Chef of the Year reader award.

MOST INFLUENTIAL WOMEN

Jill is featured in CODE's Top 100 Most Influential Women in Hospitality.

2024 LIFETIME ACHIEVEMENT

Rick is awarded the Fortnum & Mason Special Award, a lifetime achievement award recognising his decades of work in food/cookery publishing and television.

FOOD SERVICE AWARD

The Seafood Restaurant is honoured to receive the AA Food Service Award for 2024 – a truly wonderful achievement by its remarkable staff.

2025 THE SEAFOOD RESTAURANT TURNS 50

Jack's Chef Notes

Creating a risotto in a restaurant kitchen usually requires two steps. First, we three-quarters cook the rice and put it in a blast chiller, which cools it quickly. Then, when an order comes in, we take the risotto out of the chiller and it takes only 4 minutes to finish.

Charlie's Wine Notes

We have to go Italian here, so I'm choosing a Chardonnay from Sicily to complement the lobster and stand up to the richness of the risotto. I'd go for Planeta Chardonnay, which we have had on The Seafood wine list for years.

The Seafood Signature Recipes

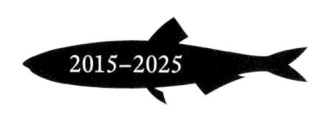

Poached lobster risotto

I love lobster in the shell, but of course lobster is an incredibly expensive ingredient, so we wanted to offer something that gave a really good portion, but made it more accessible. The options are generally lobster and pasta or lobster and rice, so this is our risotto – lobster and rice – made with a delicious stock from the lobster shell. It was inspired by a trip to France for TV, travelling around the villages, cooking in the top part of a double-decker bus. I'm not sure things can get more idyllic.

Serves 4 as a starter or 2 as a main

1 cooked lobster, about 500g
2 tablespoons olive oil
1 shallot, finely chopped
2 garlic cloves, finely chopped
200g Carnaroli or Arborio risotto rice
150ml dry white wine
1 tablespoon softened butter
tarragon fronds, to garnish
salt and black pepper

FOR THE LOBSTER STOCK AND REDUCTION
lobster shell, chopped
1 onion, chopped
4 garlic cloves, chopped (no need to peel)
50g butter
100ml dry white wine
500g tomatoes, chopped
a small handful of French tarragon, roughly chopped
1.5 litres Fish Stock (page 270)
1 teaspoon salt
1 tablespoon Cognac
squeeze of lemon juice

Remove the meat from the lobster, reserving the shell for the stock. Slice the body meat and keep the claw meat as chunky as possible.

For the stock, put the shell in a pan with the onion, garlic and 20g of the butter. Cook for about 5 minutes over a medium heat, stirring occasionally, then add the wine, tomatoes, tarragon and fish stock and bring to the boil. Add the salt and leave to simmer for 40 minutes. Pass the stock through a fine sieve over another large pan and discard the solid ingredients. Keep most of the stock for the risotto, but set aside 200ml for the reduction.

For the risotto, heat the oil in a pan over a medium–high heat, add the shallot and garlic and cook for 5–6 minutes until soft. Add the rice and stir to coat, then add the wine. Let it bubble and be absorbed by the rice, then, a ladleful at a time, add the hot stock. Keep stirring, allowing each ladleful to be absorbed before adding the next. When you have added all the liquid, taste and season.

Finish the lobster reduction. Put the reserved 200ml of stock into a clean pan with the Cognac and bring it to the boil. Reduce it by three-quarters, then whisk in the remaining 30g of butter to form a sauce that coats the back of a spoon. Add a squeeze of lemon juice.

Heat the tablespoon of butter in a frying pan over a medium–high heat. When it's foaming, add the lobster meat and warm it through. Serve the risotto topped with lobster meat and spoon the reduction around it. Garnish with fresh tarragon (if you prefer, you can deep-fry the tarragon in oil at 180°C for 30 seconds, to make it crisp).

2015–2025

Crab with wakame salad and wasabi mayonnaise

These days our kitchen at The Seafood Restaurant brims with culinary excellence from all over the world. Japan features regularly, and this dish, the idea for which I brought home with me after travelling and filming in Japan, is one that keeps coming back.

Serves 4 as a first course

½ cucumber, peeled if you prefer
40g dried wakame seaweed
225g fresh white crab meat (see box, page 248; or buy just the meat, ready-picked)
4 teaspoons fresh brown crab meat
1 tablespoon bonito flakes

FOR THE WAKAME DRESSING
½ teaspoon dashi granules
40ml warm water
2 teaspoons rice wine vinegar
½ teaspoon white sugar
1 teaspoon dark soy sauce

FOR THE WASABI MAYONNAISE
2 egg yolks, at room temperature
2 teaspoons white wine vinegar
2 teaspoons wasabi paste
300ml rapeseed oil
½ teaspoon salt

Cut the cucumber half in half lengthways and scoop out the seeds with a teaspoon. Cut across to create thin slices.

For the wakame dressing, dissolve the dashi granules in the warm water and mix with the rest of the dressing ingredients.

Add the cucumber and wakame seaweed to the bowl with the dressing, and mix together well. Chill.

To make the mayonnaise, mix the egg yolks, white wine vinegar and wasabi paste together in a bowl. Using a wire whisk, a few drops at a time gradually beat in the oil, until you have incorporated it all. Season with the salt.

To serve, pile the white crab meat on to 4 cold plates, then put a teaspoon of the brown crab meat and a tablespoon of the wasabi mayonnaise alongside. Put a handful of the cucumber and wakame seaweed next to the crab meat, sprinkle the bonito flakes on top of the seaweed, and serve.

Charlie's Wine Notes

We don't want to overpower the crab with this pairing, but we are also matching the wasabi mayo... so I'm thinking a crisp Grüner Veltliner from Austria.

Jack's Chef Notes

During the last 10 years everyone has started experimenting with Japanese flavours, so this take on a classic crab salad uses bonito flakes, wasabi and rice wine vinegar.

The Seafood Signature Recipes

Removing the meat from a crab

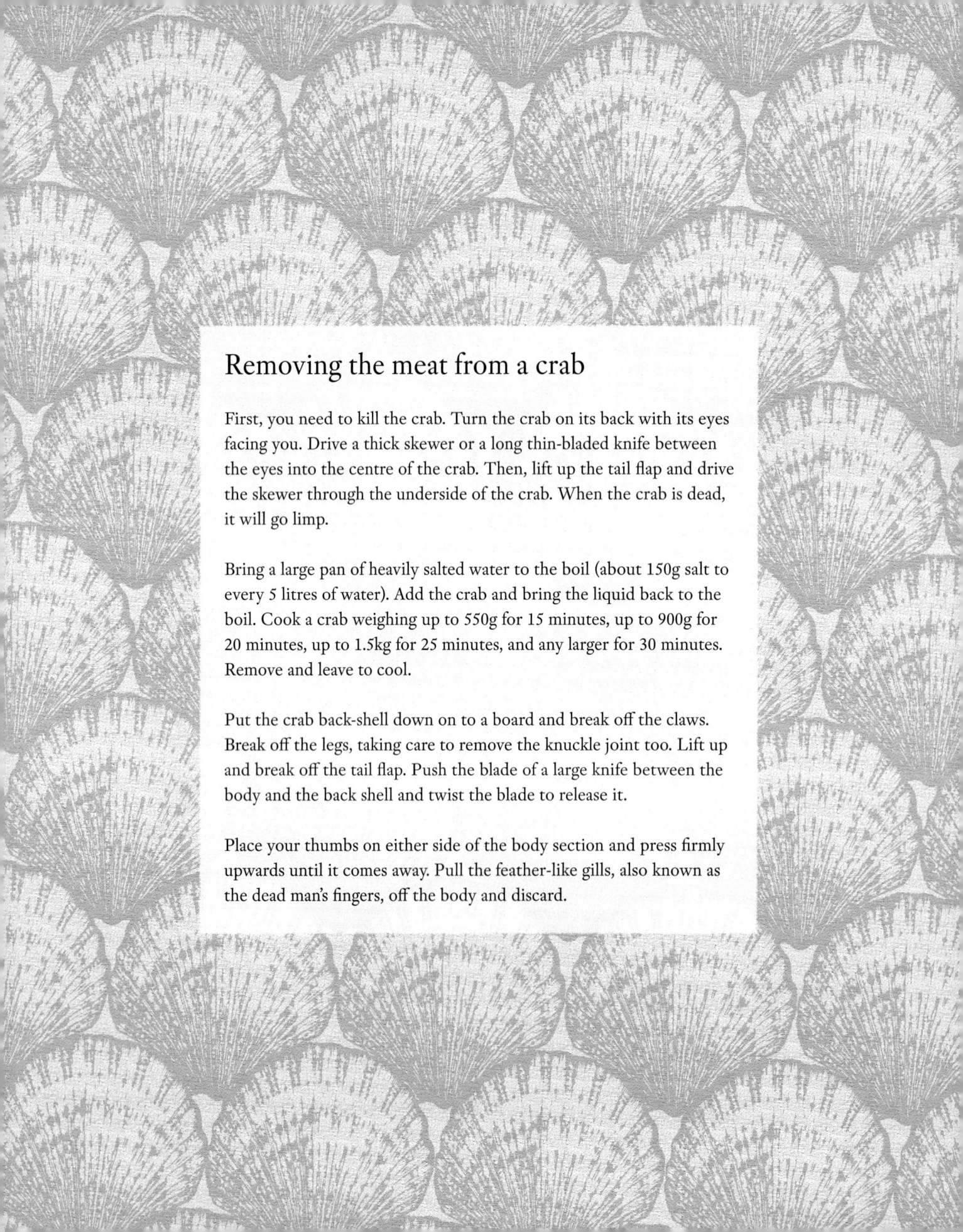

First, you need to kill the crab. Turn the crab on its back with its eyes facing you. Drive a thick skewer or a long thin-bladed knife between the eyes into the centre of the crab. Then, lift up the tail flap and drive the skewer through the underside of the crab. When the crab is dead, it will go limp.

Bring a large pan of heavily salted water to the boil (about 150g salt to every 5 litres of water). Add the crab and bring the liquid back to the boil. Cook a crab weighing up to 550g for 15 minutes, up to 900g for 20 minutes, up to 1.5kg for 25 minutes, and any larger for 30 minutes. Remove and leave to cool.

Put the crab back-shell down on to a board and break off the claws. Break off the legs, taking care to remove the knuckle joint too. Lift up and break off the tail flap. Push the blade of a large knife between the body and the back shell and twist the blade to release it.

Place your thumbs on either side of the body section and press firmly upwards until it comes away. Pull the feather-like gills, also known as the dead man's fingers, off the body and discard.

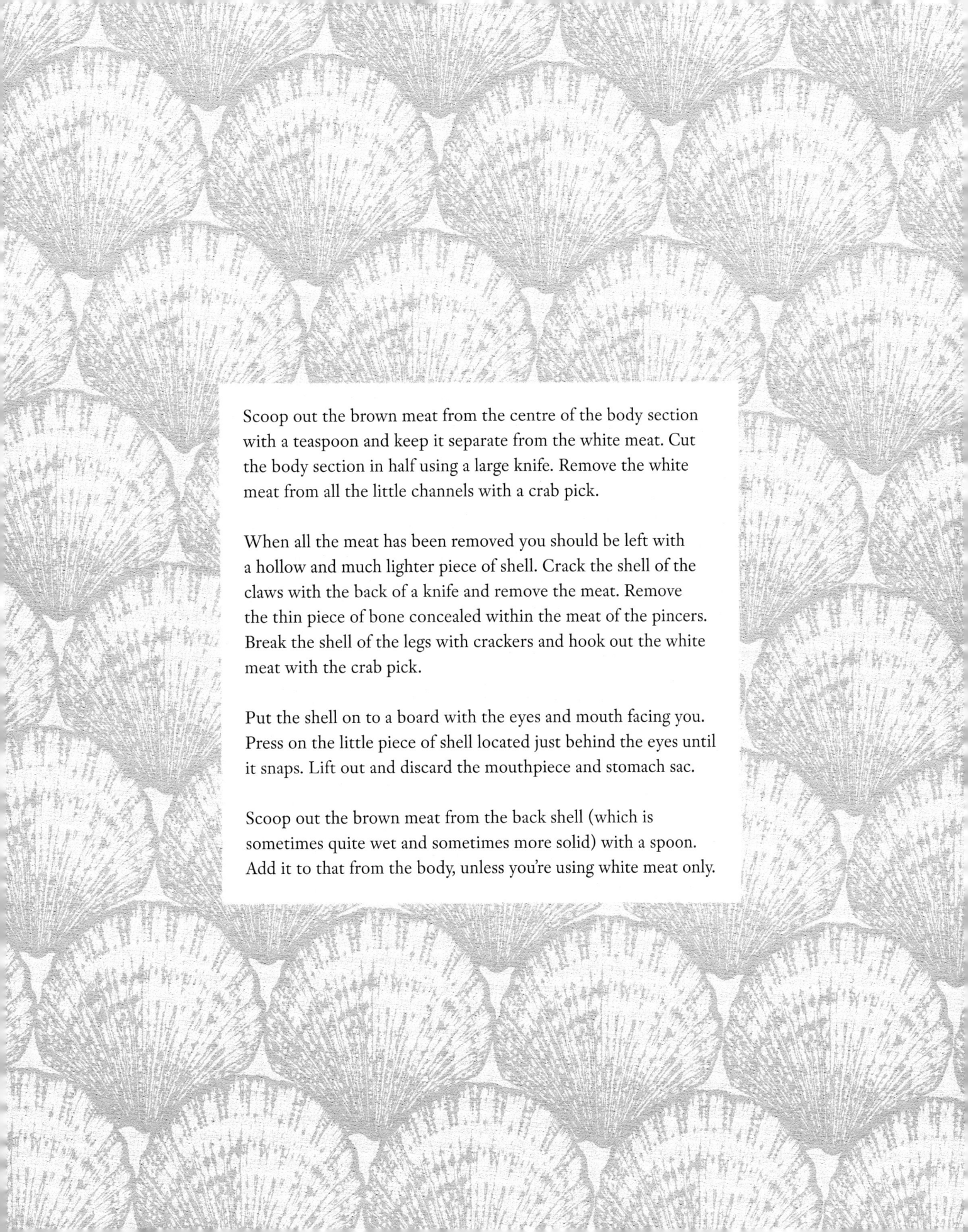

Scoop out the brown meat from the centre of the body section with a teaspoon and keep it separate from the white meat. Cut the body section in half using a large knife. Remove the white meat from all the little channels with a crab pick.

When all the meat has been removed you should be left with a hollow and much lighter piece of shell. Crack the shell of the claws with the back of a knife and remove the meat. Remove the thin piece of bone concealed within the meat of the pincers. Break the shell of the legs with crackers and hook out the white meat with the crab pick.

Put the shell on to a board with the eyes and mouth facing you. Press on the little piece of shell located just behind the eyes until it snaps. Lift out and discard the mouthpiece and stomach sac.

Scoop out the brown meat from the back shell (which is sometimes quite wet and sometimes more solid) with a spoon. Add it to that from the body, unless you're using white meat only.

Marinated tuna with passion-fruit, lime and coriander

Marinating fish is instinctive to me and I'd loved the way Raymond Blanc had served marinated salmon, so with a need to find a starter for a New Year's Eve party in Sydney, I came up with this, a riff on a Peruvian ceviche.

Serves 4

400g tuna loin fillet, about 3cm thick
2 small, ripe and wrinkly passion-fruit, each about 35g
1 tablespoon lime juice
3 tablespoons sunflower oil
1 medium–hot green chilli, seeded and finely chopped
1 teaspoon caster sugar
1½ tablespoons finely chopped coriander
½ teaspoon salt
½ teaspoon freshly ground black pepper

Put the piece of tuna loin fillet on to a board and slice it across, in very thin slices. Lay the slices, side by side but butted close up together, over the base of four 25cm plates. Cover each one with cling film and set aside in the fridge for at least 1 hour, or until you are ready to serve.

Shortly before serving, make the dressing. Cut the passion-fruit in half and scoop the pulp into a sieve set over a bowl. Rub the pulp through the sieve to extract the juice, then discard the seeds left in the sieve. You should have about a tablespoon of juice in the bowl. Stir in the lime juice, sunflower oil, green chilli, sugar, coriander, salt and pepper.

To serve, remove the plates from the fridge and uncover them. Spoon over the dressing and spread it over the surface of the fish with the back of the spoon. Leave for 10 minutes before serving.

Jack's Chef Notes

A ceviche is a South American preparation of marinated raw fish, using citrus juices. It's so easy to prepare at home and is great to kick off a dinner party, just as Dad did, but I also love it as an appetiser for a barbecue.

Charlie's Wine Notes

This dish is packed with flavour – passion-fruit, coriander and lime. The perfect match is an exuberant Kiwi Sauvignon Blanc, which has its own passion-fruit and lime intensity.

The Seafood Signature Recipes

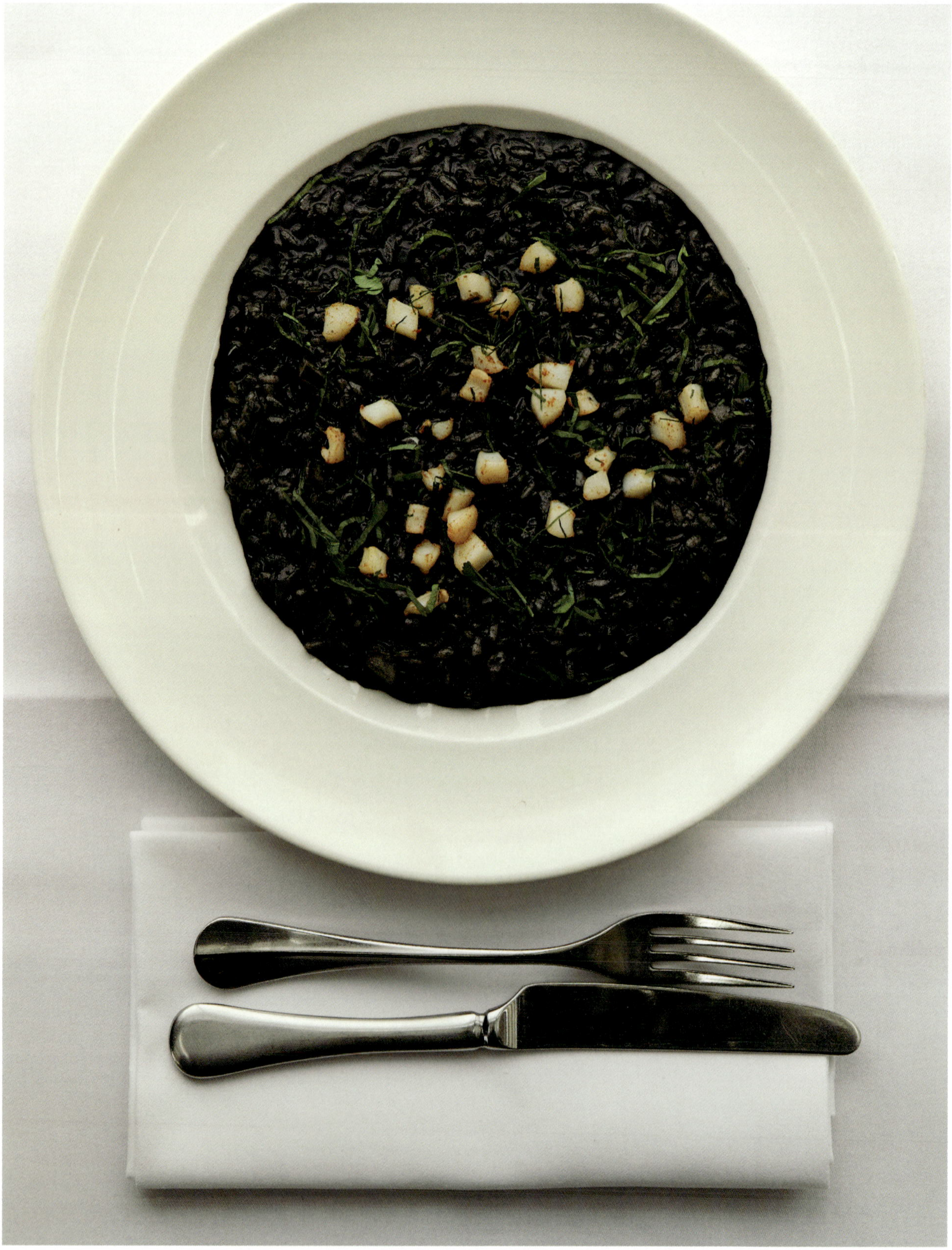

Black risotto

Using Parmesan in seafood dishes is controversial, but in this case (and in the case of the cuttlefish risotto I enjoyed in Croatia, as part of a crew lunch), it works. So much so that we never take this dish off the menu.

Serves 4–6

400g prepared cuttlefish
90ml olive oil, plus extra
  to serve
1 small shallot, chopped
2 garlic cloves, chopped
350g Arborio or Carnaroli rice
100ml white wine
1.2 litres hot Fish Stock
  (page 270)
4 x 4g cuttlefish ink sachets
1 tablespoon freshly
  grated Parmesan
salt and freshly ground
  black pepper
30g butter
a small handful of flat-leaf
  parsley, chopped

Separate the tentacles of the cuttlefish, set aside, then cut the body into 1cm squares.

Heat the olive oil in a large frying pan over a high heat and sauté the cuttlefish, both body and tentacles, for 2 minutes until lightly golden at the edges. Reserve a little of the cuttlefish body to garnish, then reduce the heat a little, add the shallot and garlic and cook for 2 minutes to soften.

Add the rice and fry it in the oil for 2 minutes, then add the white wine. Bring to a simmer to allow this to evaporate before adding the first ladle of hot fish stock. When this has been absorbed, add the next ladle, and so on, stirring after each addition, until nearly all the stock has been absorbed and the rice is cooked, about 15–16 minutes. At this point add the sachets of ink to the pan.

Season with the grated Parmesan and some salt and pepper, and stir in the butter. Serve drizzled with a little olive oil and sprinkled with the reserved cubes of cuttlefish and the chopped parsley.

Jack's Chef Notes

In more recent years we have started to look at the world's more under-appreciated fish for our menu. Cuttlefish is a great example – it is an inexpensive alternative to squid, has more ink to colour the risotto and holds together well in the dish.

Charlie's Wine Notes

This ink-laden risotto is all about richness. An Etna Bianco gives weight and texture, but also a vein of acidity that cuts straight through the fulsomeness of the dish.

Ragout of sautéed turbot with serrano ham, spring vegetables and pea shoots

We originally brought this dish on to the menu to use up any vegetables that were in season at Trerethern Farm, where Ross Geach, a former head chef, grows some of our produce. In the winter, we make a cream-based version. Using miso and chicken stock to add body to a sauce was something I learned in Sydney.

Serves 4 as a first course

40g fresh or frozen peas
60g courgettes, thinly sliced
100g small asparagus, cut on the diagonal into 1cm pieces
250g turbot fillet, skinned, cut into 6–7cm pieces
1 tablespoon vegetable oil
40g unsalted butter
40g serrano ham, cut into strips
10g preserved lemon, finely chopped
200ml Chicken Stock (page 270)
1 teaspoon white miso paste
30g pea shoots
salt

Blanch the vegetables all together in boiling salted water, scooping them out as follows: peas and courgettes after 30 seconds; and asparagus after 60 seconds.

Season the turbot pieces with a little salt. Heat the vegetable oil and ½ teaspoon of the butter in a frying pan over a moderate heat. Add the turbot pieces and fry for 3–4 minutes until cooked.

Put a small pan over a medium–high heat. Add the ham and leave it to sizzle for a few minutes to render the fat. Add the preserved lemon, chicken stock and miso paste, bring the liquid to the boil, add the rest of the butter and boil rapidly for a minute to emulsify the butter and reduce the volume of the sauce a little.

Stir in the vegetables, warm them through and pour the sauce into 4 warmed soup bowls. Top with the turbot pieces and finish with the pea shoots.

Charlie's Wine Notes

A light Burgundy from Macon or even a Chablis will work well here.

Jack's Chef Notes

We use peas, courgettes and asparagus for this recipe, but actually any combination of vegetables will work. Make sure the fat on the serrano ham is well rendered before you continue with the next stage in the method.

The Seafood Signature Recipes

Seared scallop succotash

This dish is nearly always on the menu at The Seafood Restaurant. I love it. It was invented by Camilla Waite, one of our pastry chefs, during a time when we were encouraging our chefs to develop new recipes for the restaurant. This worked really well – it's a classic American succotash, but with crab and scallops, served in the shell.

Serves 4

12 mussels
50ml dry cider
12 scallops, in the shells
25g butter
50ml double cream
60g white crab meat
a handful of finely chopped chives, to serve

FOR THE SUCCOTASH BASE
50g butter
1 garlic clove, diced
2 shallots, diced
1 carrot, diced
1 leek, diced
1 celery stick, diced
1 x 160g tin of sweetcorn, drained, juice reserved
salt and freshly ground black pepper

First, make the succotash base. Place the butter in a saucepan and add the garlic, shallots, carrot, leek and celery. Cook over a low heat for about 5–6 minutes until soft but not coloured. Turn off the heat and stir in the sweetcorn. Season the base with salt and pepper and set aside.

Heat a pot over a high heat. Add the mussels and cider and cover with a lid. After 1 minute check that all the mussels have opened (discard any that have not). Remove the pot from the heat and drain away the liquid. Remove the mussels from their shells and set all of them aside. Discard the shells.

Take the scallops out of their shells (see box, page 164; reserve the shells). Place a pan over a medium–high heat and, when hot, add the butter and a little salt. Once the butter has melted, add the scallops and cook them on one side only for 2–3 minutes – you want them to be nicely coloured – then, turn them over, take the pan off the heat, and leave them to just finish cooking in the residual heat.

Add a ladle of the juice from the sweetcorn, along with the double cream to the succotash base. Add the mussels and the crab meat. Adjust the seasoning, if necessary, and cook over a medium heat, until the succotash is thickened (about 3–4 minutes).

Replace the scallops into their curved shells and spoon the succotash, mussels (3 per portion) and crab meat over them, scattering with the chives to finish.

Charlie's Wine Notes

We are matching for the sweetness of the scallops and the sweetcorn here, so I'd go for Chardonnay from a hot country in the New World – Australia or South Africa, for example.

Jack's Chef Notes

The base of this dish has cream in it, so you can make it in advance, even the day before you intend to serve. Make sure to pan-fry the scallops on one side for three-quarters of the time, then rest them to finish, as you want to serve them medium–rare.

Clams with XO sauce, spring onions and coriander

When Jack was working in Sydney, he used to go to a restaurant in China Town called Golden Century and they would do XO clams with pipis, a type of shellfish. This is the version he brought home, and this XO sauce works really well with European clams. It's a complicated sauce with lots of chilli and dried seafood, but it is so moreish.

Serves 4 as a first course

3 tablespoons vegetable oil
30g fresh ginger root, grated or chopped
20g garlic (about 4 cloves), grated or chopped
1 red chilli, thinly sliced (remove the seeds for less heat)
2 teaspoons fermented black beans, chopped
1 teaspoon caster sugar
2 tablespoons XO sauce (I like Lee Kum Kee)
1.5kg fresh clams or pipis, washed in cold water
2 tablespoons Shaoxing wine or dry sherry
1 tablespoon soy sauce
1 tablespoon cornflour, slackened with a little water
6 spring onions sliced
a handful of coriander, roughly chopped

Heat the oil in a wok over a high heat. Add the ginger, garlic, chilli, black beans, sugar and XO sauce and sauté for 1–2 minutes to soften.

Add the clams, Shaoxing wine and soy sauce, cover the wok with a lid and cook over a high heat for 2 minutes, shaking the pan a couple of times, until the clams are cooked through. Check to see the clams are opened (discard any that aren't), then stir in enough of the cornflour mixture to thicken the sauce to coat the back of a spoon.

Add the spring onions and coriander, toss a few times and serve.

Jack's Chef Notes

Making XO sauce from scratch is quite an involved and lengthy process, but happily you can buy it ready-made from Asian supermarkets, or online. Choose the best quality you can find.

Charlie's Wine Notes

XO sauce, with its many full flavours, is, without doubt, a wine-killer. So, I'd go for a wheat beer here instead.

The Seafood Signature Recipes 259

Pan-fried trout with cucumber, dill and potato salad

This recipe comes from our head chef, Pete Murt, who wanted to create a light and refreshing dish using chalkstream trout. The crispy skin gives a textural balance against the salad and mayonnaise.

Serves 4

4 chalkstream trout fillets, each about 160g, skin on
4 teaspoons olive oil
salt and freshly ground black pepper

FOR THE DILL OIL
200ml olive oil
100g dill, tender fronds picked

FOR THE MUSTARD MAYONNAISE
1 egg, at room temperature
1 tablespoon English mustard
1 teaspoon salt
1 teaspoon white wine vinegar
300ml sunflower oil

First, prepare the dill oil – you'll need to do this the day before you intend to cook. Place the olive oil in the freezer for 1 hour. Put the dill into a blender, add the frozen oil and blitz for 2 minutes until fully combined. If you have a chinois, suspend it over a bowl; if you don't have one, line a sieve with a muslin cloth and suspend this over the bowl. Pour in the dill mixture and leave it to drain overnight.

To prepare the mustard mayonnaise, blend the egg, mustard, salt and vinegar in a food processor. With the motor running, gradually add the oil in a slow trickle until it is all incorporated.

Pre-heat the oven to 220°C/200°C fan.

Season the trout fillets and drizzle them with the olive oil. Heat a non-stick pan over a medium heat. When hot, place the trout fillets skin side down in the pan and fry for about 1–2 minutes until the skin is golden brown. Carefully transfer the fillets to a baking tray and bake them in the oven for a further 2 minutes or so, until cooked through – exactly how long will depend on the thickness of the trout pieces. The fish is ready when the centre is just warm, but still quite pink in the middle.

Meanwhile, make the salad. First, cook and cool the potatoes. Put the potatoes in a pan of salted water over a high heat. Bring to the boil, then reduce the heat and simmer until the potatoes are cooked through and tender to the point of a knife – about 10–15 minutes, depending on the size of your potatoes. Drain and leave to cool completely, then quarter the potatoes lengthways.

FOR THE CUCUMBER, DILL
    AND POTATO SALAD
120g new potatoes
1 fennel bulb
2 cucumbers
2 teaspoons dill oil
2 teaspoons white wine vinegar
1 teaspoon extra virgin
    olive oil
pinch of salt
a handful of mint, leaves picked
4 dill sprigs, to serve

Thinly slice the fennel using a mandoline and place it in iced water to crisp up. Peel one of the cucumbers into ribbons. Peel the second cucumber and slice it in half lengthways. Scoop out the seeds using a spoon and discard. Chop the flesh of the halved cucumber into 5mm cubes. Place them in a microwaveable tub with 100g of the dill oil. Microwave on full power for 20 seconds to just warm.

Mix all the salad ingredients together, apart from the dill sprigs.

Divide the salad equally between 4 serving plates, and garnish each serving with a dill sprig. Place the trout alongside, and then serve with the mayonnaise.

Charlie's Wine Notes

Trout is a delicate river fish and, when cooked simply like Pete does here, it wants a wine that is light-bodied. I would opt for a Grüner Veltliner or even an English Bacchus.

Jack's Chef Notes

River trout is perfect in this dish, but you can use salmon or sea trout instead, if you prefer. We did use to poach the fish in olive oil, but pan-frying is easier.

262 The Seafood Signature Recipes

The Seafood Signature Recipes 263

Razor clams with persillade butter

Razor clams pair really well with garlic and parsley butter and this dish is a great way to cook with an under-used shellfish. The pickled shallots give a lovely acidity and the pine nuts a crunch. Finished with the borage flowers, it's a very pretty dish to serve.

Serves 4

12 razor clams
50ml vegetable oil
a little salt

FOR THE PERSILLADE BUTTER
2 tablespoons chopped chives
2 tablespoons chopped curly parsley
2 tablespoons chopped chervil
100g unsalted butter, slightly softened
1 garlic clove
1 teaspoon lemon juice
3 pinches of salt

To make the butter, blanch all of the herbs in boiling water for 20 seconds and refresh them in a bowl of iced water. Drain off the water and put the herbs into a food processor. Cut the butter into chunks and add them to the herbs along with the garlic. Blitz until well mixed, then add the lemon juice and salt and blitz again.

Wrap the butter in cling film to form a sausage shape (a ballotine) about 5cm in diameter, and tie the ends. Refrigerate for at least 1 hour, but preferably overnight.

Meanwhile, make the pickled shallots. Put the cider vinegar into a pan along with the sugar and salt. Add the sliced shallots, thyme, star anise, juniper berries and black peppercorns. Bring to the boil over a high heat, then remove from the heat and leave to cool.

Pre-heat the oven to 240°C/220°C fan.

Now cook the clams. Pour water into a clean saucepan (use one that has a lid) to a depth of about 1cm. Bring the water to the boil and immediately add the clams. Put on the lid and let the clams steam over a low heat for 3 minutes. Take the clams out of the pan and, when cool enough to handle, remove the clams from the shells.

FOR THE PICKLED SHALLOTS
150ml cider vinegar
25g caster sugar
1 tablespoon salt
2 shallots, thinly sliced crossways
2 thyme sprigs
1 star anise
3 juniper berries
3 black peppercorns

TO GARNISH
15g toasted pine nuts
12 borage flowers

Heat the vegetable oil in a large frying pan over a medium–high heat. Add the clams and pan-fry until they are a light caramelised brown on the underside (about 1–2 minutes). Flip on to the other side for a quick flash fry over a high heat. They should be cooked through.

Remove the clams from the pan and cut off the ends and the dark brown "stomach". Slice each clam into three long pieces. Sprinkle a pinch of salt over them.

Clean the shells with warm water and spoon the butter into them, then place the clams back on top, dividing the pieces equally between the shells. Place the shells on a baking tray and transfer them to the oven for 1–2 minutes to melt the butter.

To serve, arrange 3 clams on each plate. Place a few pickled shallot slices on top and garnish with pine nuts and borage flowers.

Charlie's Wine Notes

Razor clams need a wine with bags of acidity, but we also need to accommodate the richness of the persillade butter. So, I'd go for a 100% Alvarinho Vinho Verde, which has the texture to match.

Jack's Chef Notes

Borage flowers are in season from around early summer until early autumn and they make such a delicate addition to this dish. We get ours from Trerethern Farm, owned by one of The Seafood's former head chefs.

Jack's Chef Notes

Mum has always wanted to bring back classic puddings for the modern era and this is exactly that – a classic summer dessert, beautifully served in individual portions for a modern touch.

Charlie's Wine Notes

A wine that is overly sweet will dominate a summer pudding, so a lightly sweet Moscato d'Asti from Piedmont, Italy, is my choice here.

The Seafood Signature Recipes

Summer pudding

It's very tempting when putting together a pudding menu to focus on creamy things, special Michelin-starred-type desserts, and hearty British staples like bread-and-butter pudding. In order to balance that out, we've recently felt we needed something summery, fruity and light on our dessert menu – this gorgeous summer pudding is it.

Serves 4

115g caster sugar
pared zest of 1 small lemon
225g raspberries
115g red currants
90g blackcurrants
25g white currants (or more red currants if you can't get white)
4–6 thin slices of white bread from a large loaf, crusts removed
double cream, to serve
fresh berries, to decorate (optional)

YOU WILL NEED
150–200ml individual pudding moulds x 4

Put the sugar and 75ml of water into a pan and leave them over a low heat until the sugar has dissolved. Add the pared lemon zest, bring to the boil and simmer for 5 minutes. Remove the zest and blend 1½ tablespoons of the sugar syrup with 50g of the raspberries. Press the mixture through a sieve into a bowl to remove the seeds. Add the red currants, blackcurrants and white currants to the remaining syrup in the pan and simmer for 2 minutes. Remove from the heat and stir in the remaining 175g of raspberries and the sieved raspberry sauce.

Tip the fruit into a sieve set over a bowl to collect the syrup. Dip the slices of bread briefly into the syrup and set two aside for the lids. Use the other slices of bread (you may not need them all) to line the bases and sides of the four pudding moulds, overlapping the pieces slightly to make sure there are no gaps.

Spoon in the fruit equally between the moulds and then spoon ½ tablespoon of the remaining syrup over each portion. Cover each neatly with the reserved syrup-dipped bread, then wrap the tops of the puddings with cling film. Place a small plate on top of each and secure that with something heavy (a tin of beans is good) to weigh the plate down. Transfer the weighted moulds to the fridge to chill overnight, along with any remaining syrup.

To serve, carefully run a knife around the inside edge of each pudding mould. Invert each pudding on to a serving plate, spoon over any remaining syrup and serve with double cream, and with fresh berries, if you wish.

ENGLAND

The Good Food Guide

Seafood ▲ Restaurant

2016

When The Seafood Restaurant opened, Harold Wilson was still PM – Rick Stein's place celebrated 40 years of service in 2015. The Stein brand grew out of Padstow and into living rooms via the TV and printed page, and continues to grow (with restaurants opening in Porthleven and Winchester in 2014). Back where it all began, the whitewashed dining room with vast contemporary canvases and focal seafood counter presents an upmarket straightforwardness that matches the food… . There are classic ideas from Europe and Asia – lobster and fennel risotto, or crisp smoked mackerel with Thai-inspired flavours – and the confidence to keep things simple. Singapore chilli crab is a hands-on main course, or go for the comfort of fish and chips.

2017

Is it really 36 years since Rick and Jill Stein's Seafood Restaurant first appeared in the Guide? Rick Stein may not sweat over the stoves these days but his flagship operation remains close to his heart – and is still a place of pilgrimage, benefiting from the press of custom that a strong presence on the telly can provide. It's an inviting, contemporary space with an 'instant and warm welcome', where the seasonal notes of exemplary fresh ingredients form the backbone of a menu with a pronounced global reach… . At a winter meal there was praise for fish and shellfish soup with rouille, excellent mussels with yellow kroeung (Cambodian curry paste), coconut milk and Kaffir lime leaves, and a superb Indonesian seafood curry with monkfish, pollack, squid and prawns. Elsewhere, desserts get positively avant-garde for peanut-butter cheesecake with lime curd and banana ice cream.

2020

Even with the rise of a fresh batch of local chefs with media clout to rival Rick Stein's, this harbourside spot still casts its spell. A long menu (there's a shorter lunchtime set) is rooted in Stein's beloved North Cornwall, and celebrates the region's oceanic bounty in, say, a fruits de mer platter that heaves with mussels, oysters, crab claws and the rest, magnificent lobster, or an exquisite piece of hake with palourde clams that delivers sufficient flavour as to render the fathomless pool of sauce superfluous. The menu jets off on lively culinary adventures, reflecting Stein's own, dropping in on Indonesia for an ever-popular curry that brims with bass, cod and prawns, and Japan for spring-in-your-step sashimi. Non-fish eaters might enjoy a grilled bavette steak or risotto primavera, and you could finish with a crisp-based walnut tart, although you may well be tempted by a waiter's swooning suggestion of the 'volcanic' hot chocolate fondant.

2024 Rick Stein gets a lot of stick for transforming Padstow into Padstein, but no one has done as much to persuade Brits to eat the fish hauled from our native waters rather than exporting it all to mainland Europe.... Long before the TV producers came calling, Stein was a practising seafood cook, who opened this place with his then wife Jill in 1975. These days, the kitchen is overseen by son Jack (whose brothers Charlie and Edward look after wine and interior design respectively), which explains why it still has the feel of a family-run, family-friendly operation, albeit one that must be booked months ahead and saved up for. Some dishes seem inspired by Stein senior's globetrotting TV career: mussels masala with coconut, ginger and green chillies, say, or an Indonesian seafood curry of cod, bass and prawns.... Roast turbot is a signature here, firm white fish encased in a layer of crisp skin and with a delicacy of flavour that makes the citrussy hollandaise redundant; save it instead as a dipping sauce for thin-cut chips. Elsewhere, the menu changes depending on the catch from the boats moored up on the quay opposite. To start, snacks might feature some fresh seafood on ice: a Porthilly oyster with Cabernet Sauvignon vinegar and shallot dressing, say, or a fleshy langoustine tail to dunk into fresh mayo. Flakes of snowy-white crab are paired with intensely savoury brown meat and a saline wakame salad, while another gently Asian starter matches scallops with soy, ginger and spring onion. An 8oz steak is the lone meat option, though vegetarians fare rather better with a dedicated menu showcasing veg sourced from the nearby farm of former Stein chef Ross Geach who, like so many of the suppliers and customers – is a local with a long-standing relationship with the restaurant.

Stocks, Sauces & Salads

Fish stock

Makes 1.2 litres

1kg fish bones, such as lemon sole, brill and plaice
1 onion, chopped
1 fennel bulb, chopped
100g celery, sliced
100g carrot, chopped
25g button mushrooms, sliced
1 thyme sprig

First, make the fish stock. Put the fish bones and 2.4 litres of water into a large pan, bring just to the boil and simmer very gently for 20 minutes. Strain the stock through a muslin-lined sieve into a clean pan, add the vegetables and the thyme and bring back to the boil. Simmer for 35 minutes, or until reduced to about 1.2 litres. Strain once more and use or store as required. It will keep for about 3 days in the fridge or about 6 months in the freezer.

Chicken stock

Makes 1.7 litres

bones from a 1.5kg uncooked chicken or 450g wings
1 large carrot, chopped
2 celery sticks, sliced
2 leeks, sliced
2 fresh or dried bay leaves
2 thyme sprigs

Put all the ingredients into a large pan with 2.4 litres of water and bring the liquid just to the boil, skimming off any scum from the surface as it appears. Reduce the heat and leave to simmer very gently for 2 hours – it is important not to let the liquid boil, as this will force the fat from even the leanest chicken and make the stock cloudy. Strain the stock through a muslin-lined sieve and use as required. If you're not using it immediately, leave it to cool, then chill and refrigerate or freeze for later use. It will keep for up to about 3 days in the fridge or about 6 months in the freezer.

Harissa

Makes about 200g

1 red pepper
1 teaspoon tomato purée
1 teaspoon ground coriander
a pinch of saffron strands
2 medium–hot red Dutch chillies, stalks removed and roughly chopped
¼ teaspoon cayenne pepper
¼ teaspoon salt

Spear the stalk end of the red pepper on a fork and turn the pepper in the flame of a gas burner or blowtorch, until the skin has blistered and blackened. Alternatively, roast the pepper in a hot oven at 220°C/200°C fan for 20–25 minutes, turning once, until the skin is black. Remove the pepper from the heat and leave to cool. Break it in half and remove the stalk, skin and seeds. Put the pepper flesh and all the remaining ingredients into a food processor and blend until smooth. Set aside.

Asian chicken stock

Makes 1.7 litres

bones from a 1.5kg raw chicken or 450g chicken wings
1 bunch of spring onions or 1 onion, sliced
40g garlic cloves, peeled and bruised with the blade of a knife
75g fresh ginger root, peeled, thinly sliced and bruised with the blade of a knife
1 star anise
1 teaspoon black peppercorns

Put the chicken bones or wings into a large pan with 2.4 litres of water. Place the pan over a high heat and bring the water to the boil, skimming off the foam as it rises to the surface. Reduce the heat to a simmer and add the remaining ingredients. Leave to simmer very gently (don't let it boil) for 1½–2 hours, using a spoon to skim off any fat, until the stock is reduced and flavourful. Strain the stock through a muslin-lined sieve and use as required. If you're not using it immediately, leave it to cool, then chill and refrigerate or freeze for later use. It will keep for up to about 3 days in the fridge or about 6 months in the freezer.

Kachumber salad

Serves 4

300g vine-ripened tomatoes, thinly sliced
½ cucumber, peeled and sliced
100g red onions, halved and thinly sliced
1 medium–hot green chilli, seeded and finely chopped
½ teaspoon freshly ground cumin seeds
¼ teaspoon Kashmiri chilli powder
a large handful of fresh coriander leaves, roughly chopped
salt and freshly ground black pepper
1 tablespoon freshly squeezed lime juice

If you're serving your meal with a kachumber salad, bring it together shortly before plating up. Layer the tomatoes, cucumber and onions in a shallow bowl with the chopped chilli, ground cumin, chilli powder, coriander, some black pepper and salt to taste. Sprinkle over the lime juice, check the seasoning, then serve.

Memories

"There are some memories the like of which could never be repeated – cooking with James Knappett and Roy Brett for Ed Stein's wedding was a total privilege."

Paul Harwood (Chef, 1999–2013)

"It's the simple dishes that I love the best. Sashimi to start, followed by the crab linguine."

Trevor East (Guest, 1990s–present)

"When we first visited The Seafood, since the very earliest days, there were ferns hanging from the ceiling and it had an intimate feel about it. Rick would come out of the kitchen to check everything was alright. I loved the cosy atmosphere."

Lady Susan Wolfson (Guest, 1975–present)

"Some of my earliest memories are of Rick coming into my family's greengrocer in Padstow to buy produce for The Seafood Restaurant. At 24, I was Head Chef at Stein's Café. Now, I'm the seventh generation of my family to work the land at Trerethern Farm. We still supply The Seafood with fruit and veg from just a mile away."

Ross Geach (Owner, Padstow Kitchen Garden)

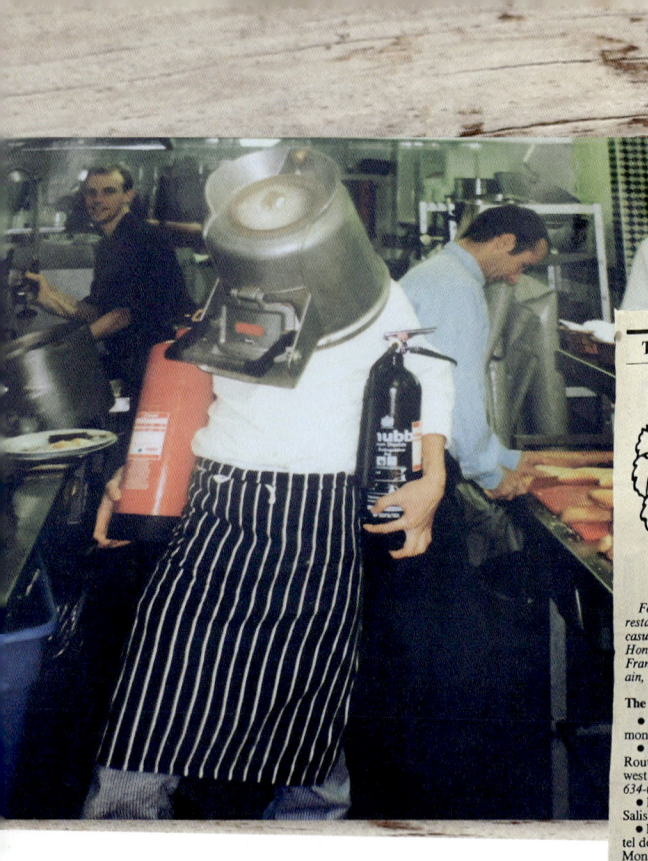

"When my wife and I come to eat at The Seafood, we love the table for two that is tucked away in the right-hand corner, although we'll always hope for the round table near the bay if we're with friends."

Peter Cunningham (Guest, 1986–present)

THE TOP 10

Following is the IHT's list of the 10 best restaurants in the world, and the 10 best casual tables. The list includes reviews on Hong Kong, Tokyo, the United States, France, the Benelux countries, Spain, Britain, Switzerland, Germany and Italy.

The Top Tables

- No. 1: **Joël Robuchon**, 59 Avenue Raymond-Poincaré, Paris 16, tel: 47-27-12-27.
- No. 2: **Restaurant Fredy Girardet**, 1 Route d'Yverdon, Crissier (6 kilometers west of Lausanne), Switzerland, tel: (21) 634-0505.
- No. 3: **Lai Ching Heen**, The Regent, Salisbury Road, Hong Kong, tel: 721-1211.
- No. 4: **Le Louis XV-Alain Ducasse**, Hôtel de Paris, Place du Casino, Monte Carlo, Monaco, tel: 92-16-30-01.
- No. 5: **Osteria da Fiore**, San Polo-calle del Scaleter, Venice, tel: (41) 721-308.
- No. 6: **Jiro**, Chuo-ku, Ginza 4-2-15, Tsukamoto Sozan Building (B1, basement), Tokyo, tel: 3535-3600.
- No. 7: **Guy Savoy**, 18 Rue Troyon, Paris 17, tel: 43-80-40-61.
- No. 8: **Taillevent**, 15 Rue Lamennais, Paris 8, tel: 45-63-96-01 and 45-61-12-90.
- No. 9: **Restaurant Daniel**, 20 East 76th Street, New York, tel: (212) 288-0033.
- No. 10: **Da Cesare**, 12 Via Umberto, Albaretto della Torre (45 kilometers south of Asti), Italy, tel: (173) 520-141.

Casual Dining

- No. 1: **Al Forno**, 577 South Main Street, Providence, Rhode Island, tel: (401) 273-9767.
- No. 2: **La Tupina**, 6 Porte de la Monnaie, Bordeaux, tel: 56-91-56-37.
- No. 3: **Frontera Grill**, 445 North Clark Street, Chicago, tel: (312) 661-1434.
- No. 4: **City Chiu Chow Restaurant**, East Ocean Centre, 98 Granville Road, Tsim Sha Tsui East, Kowloon, Hong Kong, tel: 723-6226.
- No. 5: **Ca l'Isidre**, Les Flors 12, Barcelona; tel: 441-1139.
- No. 6: **The Seafood Restaurant**, Riverside, Padstow, Cornwall PL28 8BY, England, tel: (841) 532-485.
- No. 7: **Checchino dal 1887**, 30 Via Monte Testaccio, Rome, tel: (6) 574-6318.
- No. 8: **Cibrèo**, 8r Via del Verrocchio, Florence, tel: (55) 234-1100.
- No. 9: **Viridiana**, Juan de Mena 14, Madrid, tel: 523-4478.
- No. 10: **Le Caméléon**, 6 Rue de Chevreuse, Paris 6, tel: 43-20-63-43.

"Sitting outside the restaurant on the steps as we all watched the eclipse is a favourite memory. And discovering the two greatest loves of my life – my wife, Rachel, who also worked at The Seafood; and seafood cookery. The rest is history."

Nathan Outlaw (Junior Sous Chef, 1998–1999)

"Andrew Ridgeley of 1980s pop-group Wham! was probably my favourite guest – he would pop his head around the back door to say hello."

David Wong (Junior Sous Chef, 1992–1994)

"I loved that we could walk out of the restaurant, get a catch from the local fishermen and bring it back to create something new for the menu. I was very lucky to be surrounded by great produce. And by great people. It made going to work so easy. Twenty-five years later, and the people I worked with at The Seafood Restaurant are still among my best friends."

James Knappett (Chef de Partie, 1999–2001)

"Rick and Jill used to put on some amazing staff barbecues on the beach, which Rick would cook. We had to have a re-think once other people on the beach began to join the party."

Shaaron Nicholas (Front of House, 1980s)

"On some shifts, we used to attempt the extremely haphazard task of collecting seawater in Rick's old van, which, frankly, never ended well."

Dave Miney (Chef, 1989–1994)

If there wer the Stei

Rick and Jill Stein run T Seafood Restaurant in Padstow. For nine months of the year, th serve superbly cooked dishes to a host of eager gourmets, attracted the restaurant's glowing mention in all the good food guides. At t height of the season, they cater for 100 discerning diners each nig

It was when the laundry b started creeping up on the cost of the lobsters that the Steins worried. It was costing them £7! a month to keep the front of house in a manner that matched the cuisine. So they called in Mi and set up their own laundry facilities, with a washing mach

tumble dryer and, a rotary iron Problem solved, and the laun bills fell back into proportion.

Then, in June 1986, they d sified and started letting the eig rooms above the restaurant. C

a Good Laundry Guide, would be in that, too.

and vacuum cleaners, too. All of them designed to give trouble-free service for many years to come, no matter what you throw at them; and built to a standard to ensure that they do. Whether you cater for the seafood lover or serve steaks by the hundred, you'll find the model you want in the Miele range.

night, the load on the laundry facilities was almost doubled, with sheets, towels and pillowcases. But the Miele machines simply absorbed this extra work without a hitch, coping with everything this successful business threw at them, even the kitchen staff's traditional chef's uniforms.

Miele make a whole range of commercial, industrial and catering washing machines, tumble dryers and irons. They make dishwashers

Ring us on Abingdon (0235) 28585 or fill in the coupon below for full details of the Miele range.

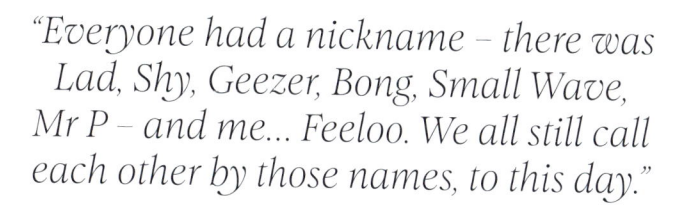

Miele

> "Everyone had a nickname – there was Lad, Shy, Geezer, Bong, Small Wave, Mr P – and me... Feeloo. We all still call each other by those names, to this day."
>
> Fiona Haley (Chef, 1990–1994)

> When I turned 70, I had an incredible treat. Head Chef at the time, Stephane Delourme, created a six-course tasting menu filled with dishes of my choosing. He also asked me if might like to bring any of my favourite wines from my own collection to drink alongside – and I did! They made me a special menu card and we had a dedicated member of waiting staff. Then, towards the end of the evening, Rick Stein himself came and sat down at the table to wish me a happy birthday – what more could I ask?"
>
> Ian Kemplay (Guest, 1975–present)

The Seafood Restaurant
AT PADSTOW HARBOUR

There's nothing like fresh seafood

There's only one place to eat it

A whelks throw from the quayside, opposite the large quayside car park.

Your meal cooked personally by chef/patron Richard Stein.

À la carte specialities include:
- Seafood Thermidor
- Lobster grilled fresh from our tanks
- Oysters from our own beds
- Le plat de fruits de mer
- Roast Sea Bass

PADSTOW 532485
Open Lunchtime and Evening

Recommended by Egon Ronay, Michelin, A.A., English Tourist Board, Taste of England, Touring Club de Belgique

---

SET PRICE MENU

Seafood Pancakes
Gravad Makrel
Summer Vegetable Soup

Grilled Lemon Sole
with lobster butter

Chargrilled Scotch Rump Steak

A selection of home made sweets
including a fresh cream ice cream with hot fudge

"One day, a customer accused Rick of serving up frozen oysters – twice – only to find himself removed from the restaurant with the whole place erupting in applause and cheers as he was escorted out."

Pauline Tune (Waitress, 1995)

"I have learnt everything I know about running restaurants from Rick and Jill. I wouldn't be doing what I am now if it weren't for the time I spent with them."

Sam Harrison (General Manager, 1997–2000)

General Index

Page numbers in *italic* refer to the illustrations

AA Food Guide 74
AA Food Service Award 243
AA Seafood Restaurant of the Year 176
Absolute Press 54
Agen 201
Allen, Myrtle 195
Arnold, Roni *38*, 42, *43*, 96, 97
Australia 24, 27, 28, 33, 87, 88, 92, 96, 140, 141, 147, 162, 258

Baker, Bill 42, 96, 97, 166
Bali 214
Ballymaloe House, County Cork 195
Bangkok 87, 92, 140
Barber, Richard *52*, 54
Barnes, London 83, 241
BBC *52*, *53*, 54, 140, 174
Beaudoin, René *100*
beer 45
Blanc, Raymond 250
The Blue Lobster, Padstow *15*, *35*, 112
Blumenthal, Heston 74, 89
books 54, *54–5*
Bordeaux 97, 98, 201
The Boscastle Belle (boat) *101*, 128
Brett, Roy 37, 203, *272*
Brittany 87
Bromley, Frances 68, *68–9*
Bryn Cottage, Padstow 205
Burgundy 97

Camel estuary *52*, 138, 172
César Award 72, 174
Chalky (dog) 45, *45*, 87
Charente, France 193
cheese 20
China Town, Sydney 258
Chinese restaurants 125
Choo, Jimmy 68
cocktails 98
CODE, Top 100 Most Influential Women in Hospitality 243
Cooking with the Stars (TV programme) 90
Corbet, Miles *34*
The Cornish Arms, St Merryn 80, 204, 242
Cornish Cider Company 138
Corte Sconta, Venice 166
Covid-19 pandemic 98, 101, 242
crab 30
Croatia 253
Croft, Jon 54
Cunningham, Peter 274

David, Elizabeth 232
Decanter magazine 72, 141
Delicious magazine *81*
Delourme, Stephane *34*, 42, *43*, 88, 277
The Design Show, London 68
Driver, Christopher 210

East, Trevor 273
Egon Ronay Guide 71–2, 175
English Seafood Cookery (book) 19, 54, *54–5*, 140, 141

Far East 28–31
Far Eastern Odyssey (TV programme) 214
The Fat Duck, Bray, Berkshire 74, 89
Fistral, Newquay 83, 240
Fleurie, France 144
Floyd, Keith 37, *52*, *53*, 54, 56, 140, 154
Floyd on Fish (TV programme) *52*, *53*, 140
Food & Travel Timeless Classic Award 74
Food Magazine 74, 243
Fortnum & Mason 74, 243
France 28, 62, 87, 97, 116, 144, 245
French Odyssey (TV programme) 201

Geach, Ross 254
Gilbey, Tom 97
Glenfiddich award 140, 173
Goa, India 27, 30–31, 56, 92, 160, 210
Golden Century, Sydney 258
The Good Food Guide 56, 71, 105, 138–9, 172–3, 202–3, 210, 238–9, 268–9
The Good Hotel Guide 72, 174
Great Western Nightclub, Padstow *10*, *12*, *13*, *15*, 76, 104–5

Haley, Fiona *38*, 39, 276
Harrison, Sam 279
Harwood, Paul *34*, *272*
Holzen, Heinz von 214
Hopkinson, Simon 173
The Horn of Plenty, Gulworthy, Devon 120, 172
Hotel & Restaurant Magazine 175

India 27, 30–31, 56, 92, 160, 210
Indonesia 214, 269
Inshaw, David *57*
Irish Sea 172
Italy 80

Japan 224, 246, 269
Jill Stein Interiors 64–9, 83, 89, 205

Kelly, Phil *48–9*, *73*
Kemplay, Ian 277
Kew, Katinka 54, *54–5*
King, Sue 52
Knappett, James 37, *37*, *272*, 275

Little, Alastair 173
lobsters 39
Loch Fyne 172
Loire Valley 87
Lyon 144

mackerel 31
Marlborough, Wiltshire 83, 241
Marseille 184, 201

Martindale, Penrose, Cornwall 207
media 51–2
menus *14*
Michelin stars 120, 267
Miney, Dave 39, 276
Murt, Johnnie 101, 128
Murt, Pete 260
Murt family 128

New England 158
Newquay, Cornwall 240
Newstead, Jack (Jill's father) 44, *44*
Nicholas, Shaaron 19, 276
Normandy 87
Novelli, Jean-Christophe 37, 41

Observer Food Monthly 74
Origin Coffee 242
Outlaw, Nathan 6–7, 37, 79, 274
Outlaw, Rachel 274
Owsley-Brown, Matthew 39

Paris 108, 181
Pate, Stuart 176, 234
Penguin Books 54
Peru 250
Poole Harbour, Dorset 241
Porth Navas, Cornwall 172
Porthleven, Cornwall 268
Prichard, David 52, 140
Prospect House, Padstow 205
Prosser, Sally 15
Provence 116, 154, 184, 221
Puckey, Mark *34*
The Purple Tiger 11, 104, 177, 205, 240

Rabey, Penny 19, 35
RAC/*Sunday Times* Taste of Britain 70, 71, 107
Rance, Patrick 20
Rick Stein App 242
Rick Stein Barnes, London 83, 241
Rick Stein Champagne *100*
Rick Stein Meal Kits 242
Rick Stein's Café 142, 175, 203
Rick Stein's Seafood Bar and Fishmongers, Padstow 240
Ridgeley, Andrew 275
Ronay, Egon *70*, 71–2
Ruby's Bar, Padstow 240
Rui (hotel manager in Goa) 27, 30–31

St Austell Brewery 204
St Decamon's, Padstow 174
St Edmund's House, Padstow 176
St Merryn, Cornwall 80
St Petroc's, Padstow 143, 174, 203, 205
Saint Tropez 154
San Sebastian, Spain 101
Sandbanks, Dorset 83, 241
Sanderson fabrics 66
Scabetti 68, *68–9*
Scotland 232
The Seafood Restaurant *61*
    awards and honours *70*, 71–4, 107, 174–6, 242, 243
    conservatory 63, 106
    fiftieth anniversary *100*, 243

280

interior decor 64–9, *64–5*
kitchen 62–3, 174
opening 11–16, *17*, 104
in Marlborough 241
refurbishment 60–8, 83, 205, 239
rooms 60–2, 107
staff *34*, 35–47, *37*, *38*, *40*, *46*, 51
website 242
in Winchester 207, 268
Seamills 139
Sellars, Paul 36, 37, 51
Sharland, David *34*
Sharp's Brewery 45
"Shoal" (light sculpture) 68, *68–9*
Singapore 27, 30, 56, 87, 92, 141, 147
Sobey, Tom 242
Soho, London 125
Stein, Charlie 27, 42, *75*, 76, *77*, *82*, 84, 89, 90, 92–8, *93–5*, *99*, 101, 204, 241, 242
Stein, Ed *26*, 27, 33, *75*, 76, *77*, *78*, 79–83, *81*, *82*, *94–5*, 101, 204, 242, *272*
Stein, Jack *25*, *26*, 27, 33, *43*, 74, *75*, 76, *77*, *82*, 84–90, *85–6*, *91*, *94–5*, 101, 177, 204, 243
Stein, Jill *12*, *16*, *20*, *29*, *38*, *67*, *70*, *77*, 101
  awards and honours 74, *75*, 206, 243
  barbecues *276*
  café 142, 175
  deli 106
  as Front of House 21
  holiday properties 206, 207, 242
  hotel 143
  interiors 64–9, 83, 89, 205
  opens The Seafood Restaurant 11–16, 104
  winter escapes 24–7, 28
Stein, Kate 66, *67*, 79, 80, 83, 240, 242
Stein, Rick *12*, *16*, *29*, *34*, *43*, *50*, *70*, *77*, *81*, *94–5*, 101
  awards and honours *70*, 71–4, 107, 174–6, 240, 243
  barbecues *276*
  café 142, 175
  cookery school 175
  deli 106
  hotel 143
  and the media 51–2
  opens The Seafood Restaurant 11–16, 104–5
  overseas influences 28–31
  philosophy of simple food 33
  television programmes 52, *53*, 54, 56, 96
  winter escapes 24–7, 28
Stein, Sarah (Sas) 33, 89
Stein Group 74, 88, 98, 204, 242
Steins at Home meal kits 242
Stein's Coffee Shop, Padstow 242
Stein's Deli, Padstow 106, 203, 204
Stein's Fish & Chips, Padstow 177
Stein's Fisheries 206
Stein's Patisserie, Padstow 176, 234, 242
Stevenson, Sonia 120
Street Brown, Nick *37*
The Sunday Times 70, 71–2, 107
Sydney 250, 254, 258

Taste of the Sea (TV programme) 56, 174
Taylor, Luke *34*
Thailand 27, 56, 209, 210
Top 100 Best Large Company 242
Trerethern Farm, Cornwall 254
Trevone, Cornwall 96, 206
Trevose Head, Cornwall 111
Tune, Pauline 39, 278
Tyrrell, Martin *37*

Under a Mackerel Sky (book) 207

Venice 166
Vernon, Mary 44
Vintner, London 97, 241

Wadebridge, Cornwall 64
Waite, Camilla 256
Waitrose Best Restaurant award 74
Walnut Tree Inn, Llanddewi Skirrid 172
Walter, Johnny 11–12, *12*, 15, 24, 54, 60, 104–5
Walter, Teri 11, *12*, 15, 24, 54, 60, 104
Walton, John *37*
Wham! 275
The Whitehouse Club, Padstow 104
Wilson, Harold 268
Winchester 83, 207, 268
Wine, Dine and Stein (TV programme) 90, 241
wines 96–8, *100*
Wolfson, Lady Susan 21, 45, 273
Woman's Realm 52, 139
Wong, David 39, 275
World on a Plate (book) 90, 240

Zuma, London 66

Cookery Index

aïoli 154–5, 221–2
Armagnac, prune tart with 200–201
Asian chicken stock 271
asparagus: ragout of sautéed turbot 254–5

bacon: mushroom and bacon garnish 144–6
bass *see* sea bass
beans: grilled cod with aïoli and butter beans 221–2
   mussels with black beans, garlic and ginger 182
beurre blanc, oysters with 150–51
black beans: mussels with black beans, garlic and ginger 182
black butter 108
black risotto 253
bouillabaisse 184–5
bourride of red mullet, gurnard and fresh salted cod 154–5
bread: croûtons 116–19, 144–6, 154–5, 184–5
   rouille 116–19, 184–5
   summer pudding 266–7
   treacle tart 134–6
bream: steamed bream with garlic, ginger and spring onions 124–5
butter: beurre blanc 150–51
   black butter 108
   clarified butter 198
   Hollandaise sauce 190–91
   persillade butter 264–5
   toasted hazelnut and coriander butter 162–3
   vanilla butter vinaigrette 180–81
butter beans: grilled cod with aïoli and butter beans 221–2
capers: ray wings with black butter 108
   tartare sauce 188–9
caramel: caramel sauce 234–6
   crème brûlée ice cream 170–71
casserole of hake with shallots and wild mushrooms 230–31
chicken: Asian chicken stock 271
   chicken stock 270
chillies: dressing 209, 217
   harissa 270
   hot shellfish with garlic and lemon juice 166–7
   Indonesian seafood curry 214–17
   monkfish vindaloo 210–11
   Singapore chilli crab 147–9
chips 188–9
chocolate fondant 234–6
chorizo sausage: oysters Charentais 192–3
chowder, cod and mussel 158–9
clams: clams with XO sauce, spring onions and coriander 258
   cleaning 165
   hot shellfish with garlic and lemon juice 166–7
   razor clams with persillade butter 264–5

clotted cream ice cream 134–6
cockles: hot shellfish with garlic and lemon juice 166–7
coconut: green bean and coconut salad 214–17
coconut milk: Indonesian seafood curry 214–17
cod: cod and mussel chowder 158–9
   fish pie 178–9
   grilled cod with aïoli and butter beans 221–2
   see also salt cod
conger eel: bouillabaisse 184–5
coriander: clams with XO sauce, spring onions and coriander 258
   marinated tuna with passion-fruit, lime and coriander 250–51
   squid, mint and coriander salad 208–9
   toasted hazelnut and coriander butter 162–3
court-bouillon 108
crab: crab with wakame salad 246–7
   freshly boiled and dressed crab 128–9
   removing meat 248–9
   seared scallop succotash 256–7
   Singapore chilli crab 147–9
cream: clotted cream ice cream 134–6
crème brûlée ice cream 170–71
croûtons 116–19, 144–6, 154–5, 184–5
cucumber: cucumber, dill and potato salad 260–61
   kachumber salad 271
curry: Indonesian seafood curry 214–17
   mackerel recheado 160–61
   monkfish vindaloo 210–11
cuttlefish: black risotto 253

dill oil 260–61
Dover sole à la meunière 131–2
dressings 209, 217
   Pernod and olive oil dressing 232–3
   wakame dressing 246–7
Dublin Bay prawns: grilled Dublin Bay prawns with a Pernod and olive oil dressing 232–3
   hot shellfish with garlic and lemon juice 166–7

eel: bouillabaisse 184–5

fennel: cucumber, dill and potato salad 260–61
   grilled cod with aïoli and butter beans 221–2
   grilled whole sea bass with Pernod and fennel 226–7
   pan-fried fillet of monkfish with new-season garlic and fennel 152–3
fish: fish and chips with tartare sauce 188–9
   fish and shellfish soup 116–19
   fish pie 178–9

fish stock 270
Indonesian seafood curry 214–17
skinning a whole flat fish 133
see also individual types of fish
flat fish, skinning 133
fritto misto of scallops, prawns and squid 219–20

garlic: aïoli 154–5, 221–2
   pan-fried fillet of monkfish with new-season garlic and fennel 152–3
garnish, mushroom and bacon 144–6
gherkins: tartare sauce 188–9
ginger: mussels with black beans, garlic and ginger 182
   steamed bream with garlic, ginger and spring onions 124–5
golden syrup: treacle tart 134–6
green bean and coconut salad 214–17
grey bream: steamed bream with garlic, ginger and spring onions 124–5
gurnard: bouillabaisse 184–5
   bourride of red mullet, gurnard and fresh salted cod 154–5

haddock: fish and chips with tartare sauce 188–9
   see also smoked haddock
hake: baked hake with lemon, bay leaf, onion and garlic 120–21
   casserole of hake with shallots and wild mushrooms 230–31
ham: casserole of hake with shallots and wild mushrooms 230–31
   ragout of sautéed turbot 254–5
harissa 270
   croûtons 154–5
   rouille 184–5
hazelnuts: toasted hazelnut and coriander butter 162–3
Hollandaise sauce 190–91

ice cream: clotted cream ice cream 134–6
   crème brûlée ice cream 170–71
Indonesian seafood curry 214–17

John Dory: bouillabaisse 184–5

kachumber salad 271

langoustines: grilled Dublin Bay prawns with a Pernod and olive oil dressing 232–3
lemon sole: meurette of lemon sole with Beaujolais 144–6
   seafood thermidor 112–14
lobster: bouillabaisse 184–5
   grilled lobster with fines herbes 126–7
   lobster stock 244
   poached lobster risotto 244–5

mackerel recheado 160–1
masala paste 160
mayonnaise: aïoli 154–5, 221–2
   fennel mayonnaise 226–7
   mustard mayonnaise 128–9, 260–61
   wasabi mayonnaise 246–7

meurette of lemon sole with Beaujolais 144–6
mint: squid, mint and coriander salad 208–9
monkfish: bouillabaisse 184–5
   monkfish vindaloo 210–11
   pan-fried fillet of monkfish with new-season garlic and fennel 152–3
   seafood thermidor 112–14
   warm salad of seared monkfish and tiger prawns 198–9
mullet *see* red mullet
mushrooms: casserole of hake with shallots and wild mushrooms 230–31
   mushroom and bacon garnish 144–6
   seafood thermidor 112–14
mussels: bourride of red mullet, gurnard and fresh salted cod 154–5
   cod and mussel chowder 158–9
   hot shellfish with garlic and lemon juice 166–7
   mussels with black beans, garlic and ginger 182
   seared scallop succotash 256–7
mustard mayonnaise 128–9, 260–61
Myrtle's turbot 195–7

olives: tartare sauce 188–9
onions *see* shallots; spring onions
oysters: hot shellfish with garlic and lemon juice 166–7
   opening 194
   oysters with beurre blanc and spinach 150–51
   oysters Charentais 192–3

parsley: persillade 144–6
   persillade butter 264–5
passion-fruit: marinated tuna with passion-fruit, lime and coriander 250–51
pastry: prune tart 200–201
   treacle tart 134–6
peppers: fish and shellfish soup 116–19
   harissa 270
Pernod: grilled whole sea bass with Pernod and fennel 226–7
   Pernod and olive oil dressing 232–3
persillade 144–6
persillade butter 264–5
pickled shallots 264–5
pilau rice 211
pork: oysters Charentais 192–3
potatoes: cod and mussel chowder 158–9
   cucumber, dill and potato salad 260–61
   fish and chips 188–9
   fish pie 178–9
   grilled potatoes 132
prawns: fish and shellfish soup 116–19
   fritto misto of scallops, prawns and squid 219–20
   grilled Dublin Bay prawns with a Pernod and olive oil dressing 232–3
   hot shellfish with garlic and lemon juice 166–7
   Indonesian seafood curry 214–17
   peeling 218

seafood thermidor 112–14
warm salad of seared monkfish and tiger prawns 198–9
prune tart with Armagnac 200–201

ragout of sautéed turbot 254–5
raspberries: summer pudding 266–7
ray wings with black butter 108
razor clams with persillade butter 264–5
red currants: summer pudding 266–7
red mullet: bourride of red mullet, gurnard and fresh salted cod 154–5
rice: black risotto 253
   poached lobster risotto 244–5
   Rick's everyday pilau rice 211
risotto: black risotto 253
   poached lobster risotto 244–5
rouille 184–5
   fish and shellfish soup 116–19

salads: crab with wakame salad 246–7
   cucumber, dill and potato salad 260–61
   green bean and coconut salad 214–17
   kachumber salad 271
   squid, mint and coriander salad 208–9
   warm salad of seared monkfish and tiger prawns 198–9
salmon: escalopes of salmon with a sorrel sauce 108
   sashimi of salmon, tuna, sea bass and scallops 224
salt cod 157
   bourride of red mullet, gurnard and fresh salted cod 154–5
   sashimi of salmon, tuna, sea bass and scallops 224
sauces: caramel sauce 234–6
   Hollandaise sauce 190–91
   tartare sauce 188–9
   velouté 112–14
sausages: oysters Charentais 192–3
scallops 164
   fritto misto of scallops, prawns and squid 219–20
   grilled scallops in the shell 162–3
   sashimi of salmon, tuna, sea bass and scallops 22
   seafood thermidor 112–14
   seared scallop succotash 256–7
sea bass: fillets of sea bass with vanilla butter vinaigrette 180–81
   grilled whole sea bass with Pernod and fennel 226–7
   sashimi of salmon, tuna, sea bass and scallops 22
   seafood thermidor 112–14
shallots: casserole of hake with shallots and wild mushrooms 230–31
   pickled shallots 264–5
Singapore chilli crab 147–9
skinning a whole flat fish 133
smoked haddock: fish pie 178–9
sole: Dover sole à la meunière 131–2
   meurette of lemon sole with Beaujolais 144–6
   seafood thermidor 112–14
sorrel sauce, escalopes of salmon with 108

soups: bouillabaisse 184–5
   cod and mussel chowder 158–9
   fish and shellfish soup 116–19
   ragout of sautéed turbot 254–5
spinach: oysters with beurre blanc and spinach 150–51
spring onions: clams with XO sauce, spring onions and coriander 258
   steamed bream with garlic, ginger and spring onions 124–5
squid: fritto misto of scallops, prawns and squid 219–20
   squid, mint and coriander salad 208–9
stews: bourride of red mullet, gurnard and fresh salted cod 154–5
   casserole of hake with shallots and wild mushrooms 230–31
stock: Asian chicken stock 271
   chicken stock 270
   fish stock 270
   lobster stock 244
   red wine stock 144–6
succotash, seared scallop 256–7
summer pudding 266–7
sweetcorn: seared scallop succotash 256–7
tartare sauce 188–9
tarts: prune tart with Armagnac 200–201
   treacle tart 134–6
tiger prawns: warm salad of seared monkfish and tiger prawns 198–9
tomatoes: fish and shellfish soup 116–19
   kachumber salad 271
   lobster stock 244
treacle tart 134–6
trout: pan-fried trout with cucumber, dill and potato salad 260–61
tuna: marinated tuna with passion-fruit, lime and coriander 250–51
   sashimi of salmon, tuna, sea bass and scallops 22
turbot: Myrtle's turbot 195–7
   ragout of sautéed turbot 254–5
   roast tronçon of turbot with Hollandaise sauce 190–91

vanilla: clotted cream ice cream 134–6
   vanilla butter vinaigrette 180–81
velouté 112–14
vinaigrette, vanilla butter 180–81
vindaloo curry paste 210–11

wakame salad, crab with 246–7
wasabi mayonnaise 246–7
whelks: hot shellfish with garlic and lemon juice 166–7
wine: court-bouillon 108
   meurette of lemon sole with Beaujolais 144–6
   red wine stock 144–6
winkles: hot shellfish with garlic and lemon juice 166–7

XO sauce: clams with XO sauce, spring onions and coriander 258

Credits

RESTAURANT REVIEW CREDITS

The Good Food Guide logo, symbols and extracts on pages 138–9, 172–3, 202–3, 238–9 and 268–9 © *The Good Food Guide*, with kind permission. Please visit www.thegoodfoodguide.co.uk

PHOTO CREDITS

Every effort has been made to trace copyright holders. Rick Stein Ltd and Jon Croft Editions apologise for any errors or omissions, and will, if informed, make corrections in any future editions of this book.

All food photography, landscape and incidental photography © Rick Stein Ltd/Sam A Harris, except: pages 10, 12, 13, 14, 16, 17, 20, 25, 26, 29, 38 (top and bottom), 44, 45, 50–51, 64, 68, 70, 75, 100 and unless otherwise listed herein pages 272–279 © Jill Stein/Rick Stein Ltd; pages 18, 55, 139, 173, 239 © The Estate of Katinka Kew; page 34 © Rick Stein Ltd/Rebecca Bernstein; pages 37, 275 (centre, right) © James Knappett; page 40 © Rick Stein Ltd/Craig Easton; pages 43 (top), 274 (top, left) © Stephane Delourme; pages 43 (bottom), 275 (top, right), 279 (bottom, right) © David Wong; pages 48–9, 73 © Rick Stein Ltd/Phil Kelly; page 53 © BBC Photo Archive; page 57 © Rick Stein Ltd/David Inshaw; page 273 (top, left) © Lady Susan Wolfson and (bottom, right) © Ross Geach; page 274 (bottom left and right) © Paul Harwood

The photograph on page 81 © *Delicious*/Andrew Montgomery, reproduced with kind permission: www.deliciousmagazine.co.uk

ARTWORK CREDITS

The artworks used on pages 100–101, 133, 157, 164–5, 194, 218 and 248–9 © Kate Stein Design, adapted from Kate Stein's personal fabric range, with kind permission. Kate.stein.homewares@instagram.com

RECIPE CREDITS

The recipes on the following pages have been revised, updated and rewritten with new introductions by Rick Stein and original recipe and wine notes by Jack Stein and Charlie Stein.

By Rick Stein (all BBC Books, unless otherwise listed) – pages 108 and 184: *French Odyssey* (2005); pages 111, 120, 132, 151, 152, 154, 160, 166, 190, 193 and 226: *Taste of the Sea* (1995, 2017); pages 112, 158 and 230: *Fresh from the Sea* (Penguin, 1996); pages 116, 126, 146, 162, 210, 214, 232, 246, 254, 258: *Fish & Shellfish* (2014); pages 125 and 144: *Seafood* (2001); pages 128, 178, 188 and 195: *Seafood Lover's Guide* (2002); pages 134, 171, 221, 224 and 250: *Coast to Coast* (2008); pages 181, 182, 201 and 220: *Fruits of the Sea* (1997); pages 198 and 209: *Seafood Odyssey* (1999); page 245: *Secret France* (2019); page 253: *Venice to Istanbul* (2015); and page 267: *Food Heroes* (2002)

By Jack Stein – pages 256 and 264: *World on a Plate* (Absolute Press, 2018)

Acknowledgements

AUTHORS' ACKNOWLEDGEMENTS

Our thanks to Jon Croft and Meg Boas – you have embraced our vision for a 50th Anniversary book and made it happen, and to Jon, a special thank you for your dedication to getting to know us individually and bringing together our words to tell the story of The Seafood; Jude Barratt, our meticulous Project Editor, your attention to detail and commitment to excellence have been invaluable; Peter Moffat, brilliantly assisted by Jack Coles – you have created a book that stunningly captures our passion for elegant design; and Sam Harris, you are a master at taking gorgeous photographs of both our food and our restaurant home. Thank you.

PUBLISHER'S ACKNOWLEDGEMENTS

Thanks to The Seafood Restaurant's staff and guests, past and present, who have contributed memories and photographs for this book.

Visit Us

The success of The Seafood Restaurant lies not only in the stories of Rick, Jill, Ed, Jack and Charlie, but also in the loyalty of the guests, past and present, who have come to eat there. Whether you are a regular or you are new to us, we are always happy to welcome you. This is where you can find us – in Padstow and beyond. We hope to see you very soon.

www.rickstein.com

For reservations for any of our locations, please call our central reservations number: 01841 532700 Or, email: reservations@rickstein.com

In Cornwall

RESTAURANTS WITH ROOMS

The Seafood Restaurant
Riverside
Padstow PL28 8BY

St Petroc's Hotel and Bistro
4 New Street
Padstow PL28 8EA

Rick Stein's Café
10 Middle Street
Padstow PL28 8AP

RESTAURANTS

Stein's Fish and Chips
South Quay
Padstow PL28 8BL

The Cornish Arms
St Merryn
PL28 8ND

Rick Stein Fistral
Headland Road
Newquay
Cornwall TR7 1HY

ACCOMMODATION

Prospect House
Mill Road
Padstow PL28 8BT

St Edmunds House
5 St Edmunds Lane
Padstow PL28 8BZ

BAR

Ruby's Bar
4 New Street
Padstow PL28 8EA

SHOPS

Stein's Deli
South Quay
Padstow PL28 8BL

Stein's Coffee Shop
1 Lanadwell Street
Padstow PL28 8AN

Stein's Gift Shop
8 Middle Street
Padstow PL28 8AP

Stein's Seafood Bar
& Fishmongers
South Quay
Padstow PL28 8BL

COOKERY SCHOOL

Rick Stein's Cookery School
South Quay
Padstow PL28 8BL

Beyond Cornwall

RESTAURANTS

Rick Stein Sandbanks
10–14 Banks Road
Sandbanks
Poole BH13 7QB

Rick Stein Barnes
Tideway Yard
125 Mortlake High Street
Barnes SW14 8SN

Rick Stein Marlborough
Lloran House
42a High Street
Marlborough SN18 1HQ

Rick Stein Winchester
7-8 High Street
Winchester SO23 9JX

Key Suppliers

We have had so many important suppliers over our fifty-year history, it would be impossible to mention (and thank) them all. These, though, are some of our closest wine suppliers and some of the local family businesses who make such a difference to what we do.

WINE

Camel Valley Wines
(Bob & Sam Lindo)
Nanstallon
Bodmin
PL30 5LG

01208 77959
info@camelvalley.com
www.camelvalley.com

Château Bauduc
(Gavin Quinney & Family)
31 Rue Bauduc
33670 Créon
France

0800 316 3676
gavin@bauduc.com
www.bauduc.com

Château René Beaudouin
(René & Vanessa Beaudouin)
112 Rue de Langeais
51420 Nogent Labbesse
France

+33 (0)6 79 70 07 73
www.champagne-rene-beaudouin.com

Domaine des Deux Roches
(Julien Collovray & Romain Bourgeois)
Lieu-dit «En Cuette»
181 Route de Mâcon
71960 Davayé
France

+33 (0)3 85 35 86 51
info@collovrayterrier.com
www.deuxroches.com

Quinta de la Rosa
(Sophia Bergqvist & Family)
5085-241, Pinhão
Portugal

+351 254732254
sophia@quintadelarosa.com
www.quintadelarosa.com

PRODUCE

Murt's Shellfish (Johnny Murt)
80 Boyd Avenue
Padstow
PL28 8HD

07889 031447
johnny@murtsshellfish.co.uk

Matthew Stevens & Son
(Fish & Seafood)
Penbeagle Industrial Estate
St Ives
TR26 2JH

01736 795 135
tradeinfo@mstevensandson.co.uk

Phillip Warren & Son Butchers
(Meat)
1 Dunheved Court
Pennygillam Way
Launceston
PL15 7ED

01566 772244
info@philipwarrenbutchers.co.uk

Padstow Kitchen Garden
(Ross Geach)
Trerethern Farm
Padstow
PL28 8LE

hello@padstowkitchengarden.co.uk
www.padstowkitchengarden.co.uk

The Seafood Restaurant Cookbook

First published in 2025 in Great Britain by
Jon Croft Editions
29 James Street West, Bath BA1 2BT
info@joncrofteditions.com
www.joncrofteditions.com
In association with The Seafood Restaurant Ltd
Riverside, Padstow, Cornwall, England, PL28 8BY

This edition © Jon Croft Editions 2025
Text copyright © Rick Stein Ltd 2025
Commissioned recipe photography copyright © Rick Stein Ltd/Sam A Harris 2025

For copyright of all other photographs and illustrations, see page 284, which is to be regarded as an extension of this copyright page.

Rick Stein Ltd has asserted its moral right under the Copyright, Designs and Patents Act, 1988, to be identified as Author of this work.

All rights reserved. No part of this publication may be reproduced or transmitted in any form or by any means, electronic or mechanical, including photocopying, recording, or any information storage or retrieval system, without prior permission in writing from Jon Croft Editions and Rick Stein Ltd.

Jon Croft Editions and Rick Stein Ltd do not have any control over, nor responsibility for any third-party websites referred to in this book. All Internet addresses and other contact details are correct at the time of going to press. The author and publisher regret any inconvenience caused as a result of any changes to postal addresses, emails, telephone numbers or websites, but can accept no responsibility for them.

A catalogue record for this book is available from the British Library.

ISBN 978-0-9933540-8-3
10 9 8 7 6 5 4 3 2 1

Publisher: Jon Croft
Associate Publisher: Meg Boas
Project Editor: Judy Barratt
Art Direction and Design: Peter Moffat
Design Assistant: Jack Coles
Photographer: Sam A Harris
Proofreader: Sarah Epton
Indexer: Hilary Bird

Printed and bound in Slovenia by Latitude Press.